2/9/19

To the Miller

From: the Pletan Family

Hope to see you soon!

with love.

Hurfreesboro, TN.

STANDING
FIRM

A ONE-YEAR DAILY DEVOTIONAL

STANDING FIRM

FINDING COURAGE IN THE WORD OF GOD

ALLEN JACKSON

A Message from Pastor Allen Jackson

It's impossible to avoid the shaking that life brings. It's only by anchoring ourselves in the immovable things of God that we can be truly stable—able to stand when the storms come. This book is a tool for you, giving you a moment each day with Scripture and prayer. Use it alongside your Bible-reading time, or look up the daily Scripture in your Bible to find the full story. Resolve to intentionally know God through His Word better today than you did yesterday. He will be a firm foundation for you in every season.

May this devotional be a blessing to you and your family. I pray that each day would bring you new strength, new hope, and new opportunities to say *yes* to the Lord.

Allen Jackson
Pastor, World Outreach Church

INVOLVED WITH JESUS

"Just as it was in the days of Noah, so also will it be in the days of the Son of Man. People were eating, drinking, marrying and being given in marriage up to the day Noah entered the ark. Then the flood came and destroyed them all."

LUKE 17:26-27

Noah preached the whole time he was building an ark and accumulating a zoo, but he didn't get one convert. Jesus said the people continued eating, drinking, and marrying—all very normal activities—but they were oblivious to God's purposes unfolding in such an obvious way around them. Jesus says people will be just as unaware on the day He is revealed. Even for Jesus-followers, no matter how many signs He provides or invitations He gives to be involved in His plans, it's easy to think, "This message is not for me!" I suggest that you begin your day with a simple prayer: "Lord, is there anything You would like to show me today? Is there anything I can do for You—at work, in my family, with my neighbors?" Be willing to invite God into all the activities of your day— and when you feel Him giving you an opportunity to be involved in His purposes, take it.

• THINK ABOUT IT •

Do you look for the Lord at work around you and invite God into the activities of your day? Reflect on ways you can intentionally cultivate the habit of doing those things.

Prayer

Heavenly Father, You are the Creator and the author of my story. There is nothing in my life that has escaped Your sight. You not only know my past, but You are also aware of what lies ahead. Help me to honor You and follow You with a yielded heart and a joyful spirit. Living alongside You is the only way for me to be satisfied. In Jesus' name, amen.

THE PRIORITY OF HIS WILL

"This, then, is how you should pray: 'Our Father in heaven, hallowed be your name, your kingdom come, your will be done on earth as it is in heaven.'"

MATTHEW 6:9-10

As Jesus instructs His followers how to pray, He says that after honoring our Heavenly Father, we should ask for God's will to be done on earth. When we pray that, I think we're usually imagining that someone else will get it together and begin to do God's will. But I think Jesus meant for us to pray that for ourselves too, because truthfully, most of us don't want to do God's will; we want God to do our will. When we think and pray that way we miss the privilege of participating in God's purposes for us. Wherever God has placed you right now—even in frustrating, challenging circumstances—there is no higher calling than saying, "God, I want to do Your will. I want to honor You in this place." I am not suggesting it will always be easy; but it will change your perspective on life, and you'll be amazed at the plans God has for you.

• THINK ABOUT IT •

Are there dreams, hopes, and plans you've held onto so tightly that they've minimized the space where God might work in your life? What would be required of you to lay them down before God and give Him first place in your priorities?

Prayer

Heavenly Father, I choose Jesus as Lord of my life. Grant me the will to obey and serve You without reservation, choosing Your truth with the commitment to guard my heart against competitors. Thank You for Your love and faithfulness in my life. Your Kingdom come and Your will be done on earth as it is in Heaven. In Jesus' name, amen.

DAY 3

THE PATH TOWARD FREEDOM

"When he comes, he will convict the world of guilt in regard to sin and righteousness and judgment. . . ."

JOHN 16:8

Jesus did not gain the authority for the Holy Spirit to be at work in our lives so that we could show off by doing miracles. He wanted us to have the Holy Spirit so that we ourselves could be transformed. Without the Spirit's help our sinful nature will choose godlessness because we think it will make us happier than godliness. When we try one ungodly path and it doesn't work out so well, we will try another ungodly path. That will go on until we allow the Spirit of God to show us the sinful attitudes of our heart and lead us on a pathway that will bring freedom and contentment and spiritual maturity to our lives. God's Spirit will help us find freedom from the things that leave us frustrated and perhaps even tormented. If you can honestly say, "I have done my best to make myself happy, and I am not," allow the Spirit of God to help you. He is waiting to be asked!

• THINK ABOUT IT •

The Holy Spirit will lead us toward the satisfaction that is only found when we are being transformed into the likeness of Christ. Are you intentionally inviting Him to work in your life?

Prayer

Heavenly Father, I commit myself into Your care, wisdom, and strength. My desire is to please and honor You all of my days. Give me the boldness and humility to follow You with joy and a steady, constant faith. Thank You for Your great deliverance and the compassion for others You are cultivating in me. In Jesus' name, amen.

RESPONSIBILITY COMES WITH PRIVILEGE

For since the creation of the world God's invisible qualities—his eternal power and divine nature—have been clearly seen, being understood from what has been made, so that men are without excuse.

ROMANS 1:20

I have often been asked how God can hold people in the far reaches of the world accountable for responding to a gospel they have never heard. People say, "What about the people who don't have a Bible, or never get to attend a church, or live where Christianity is illegal?" This verse says that from the beginning of creation, God has given every human being a personal revelation of Himself and an opportunity to respond to Him. We will be judged according to that response, but that judgment is going to take into account our opportunities. We are in a nation where we have the freedom to worship how we choose and to learn from Christian resources of all kinds. That is a tremendous privilege, and it comes with tremendous responsibility to all the people who haven't believed yet. So the focus of our lives shouldn't be fear for those in places where the opportunities seem less, it should be intentionality about maximizing the opportunities presented to us.

• THINK ABOUT IT •

The Bible says that to whom much is given, much is required. How are you responding to the invitations God has placed before you?

Prayer

Heavenly Father, I humble myself before You today to acknowledge You as the Creator of Heaven and earth. Please help me recognize and welcome Your invitations and opportunities. Grant me the wisdom I need to care for and maintain all that You have entrusted to me. May Your name be exalted and glorified in all my life. In Jesus' name, amen.

DAY 5

WALK THE TALK

We will tell the next generation the praiseworthy deeds of the LORD, his power, and the wonders he has done.

PSALM 78:4

God expects us to help our children and grandchildren gain momentum in their faith. It's not really a hard thing to do because kids are clever, and they know what matters to us. We teach a powerful lesson when we express gratitude for what we have seen God do and share our anticipation for what He will do in the future. However, if we say to our children, "God should be the most important thing in your life," but they see us spending most of our time talking about sports or hobbies, they are clever enough to see the discrepancy in that. Those other things are not evil, but our children should be able to easily see that they are secondary to the enthusiasm that we cultivate for the things of God.

· THINK ABOUT IT ·

How do the young people in your life see you spending your time and resources? What do you talk about when you are with them? What lessons are they learning about your priorities?

Prayer

Heavenly Father, thank You for the blessing of freedom to exalt Your name in my home and in the public arena. I commit my time and resources to advance Your Kingdom. Direct my steps that my life would honor You alone. May the words of my mouth and the meditation of my heart be pleasing to You. In Jesus' name, amen.

A PASS/FAIL EXAMINATION

For he has rescued us from the dominion of darkness and brought us into the kingdom of the Son he loves, in whom we have redemption, the forgiveness of sins.

COLOSSIANS 1:13-14

Making outwardly righteous people understand that they were sinners in need of forgiveness was one of the greatest challenges Jesus faced during His days in the earth. People today are no different; it's still difficult for most of us to understand that without Jesus we are living in "the dominion of darkness." We tend to think of our sins in pretty small terms: "Everyone in my family does that." "I'm not perfect, but I don't do anything really bad." We need to understand that entrance into the Kingdom of God is a pass/fail exam, and God's standard is absolute holiness—no exceptions, no compromise. But because of Jesus' sacrificial death on the cross, God has brought all who believe in Him as Savior "into the kingdom of the Son he loves." Even though we don't deserve it and can do nothing to earn it, we are freely given a right standing before God—and that is the greatest gift any of us will ever receive.

· THINK ABOUT IT ·

Are there sinful thoughts or behaviors in your life that you tend to minimize? Confess them to the Lord, and think about how you can change your attitudes and actions going forward.

Prayer

Heavenly Father, I turn from self-righteous pride and ask forgiveness for all my sins, especially those I have excused. I choose to forgive all who have harmed, wronged, or rejected me. I set them free today. Thank You for Jesus' sacrifice that allows me confident access to You, Almighty God, where I know You will hear and deliver. In Jesus' name, amen.

PART OF OUR ASSIGNMENT

"Righteous Father, though the world does not know you, I know you, and they know that you have sent me. I have made you known to them, and will continue to make you known in order that the love you have for me may be in them and that I myself may be in them."

JOHN 17:25-26

One of the ways we show love for other people is by caring about what they care about. The same is true for our relationship with God: Because we love Him, we will care about what He cares about. A great deal of what Jesus revealed to us about God is how much He cares for people. The people around us matter to Him, so they should matter to us too. When you share your Jesus-story with the people around you, it's because you care enough to warn them about the devastation that ungodliness will bring and you want them to know God's blessing and fulfillment. Let's live with the awareness that we are people of God, living to carry out His purposes in a specific place and time, and the people He has placed around us are a part of our God-assignment.

• THINK ABOUT IT •

Do the people in your various spheres of influence know that you care about them because God cares about them? Consider ways you might share the love of Christ with the people in your life.

Prayer

Heavenly Father, through Jesus' sacrifice, I have experienced forgiveness, freedom, and deliverance. I offer myself to You without reservation, yielding myself to Your agenda. Enable me to be a person of compassion, forgiveness, and humility. I accept Your invitation to use my influence to glorify and uplift Your name. In Jesus' name, I pray. Amen.

OUR SOLE FOCUS

"It is written: 'Worship the Lord your God and serve him only.'"

LUKE 4:8

When God gave the Ten Commandments, He first reminded Moses that "I am the LORD your God," then issued the first commandment: "You shall have no other gods before me" (Exodus 20:1-2). In the ancient world, various people groups worshipped a whole host of gods, places, objects, animals, and even natural events. The Egyptian sorcerers called forth their pagan gods during the Exodus account only to see them humiliated before the God of Abraham, Isaac, and Jacob. The Romans of the New Testament had no objection if the Christian God wanted to be one more of their pantheon of gods. Their objection was to claiming He was the only God, because Caesar proclaimed himself to be a god. The first commandment led to the execution of many early Christians, because they refused to acknowledge any other gods before God Almighty, including Caesar. This a fundamental notion to the unfolding story of God's work in the earth, from the earliest chapters right through the New Testament and into the twenty-first century: God alone should be the focus of our worship.

• THINK ABOUT IT •

Consider how you spend your time and resources, and what occupies your thoughts. Is there anyone or anything other than God that contends for first place in your life?

Prayer

Heavenly Father, You are the Creator and sustainer of all things—the one and only true God—full of grace, mercy, and power. I choose to honor You with all of my days. Help me throw off anything that hinders or leads me away from You. I choose this day to make You the primary focus of my life, the only One I long to please. In Jesus' name, amen.

DAY 9

GREST INVITATIONS

May the God of peace . . . equip you with everything good for doing his will, and may he work in us what is pleasing to him, through Jesus Christ, to whom be glory for ever and ever.

HEBREWS 13:20-21

God wants to respond to you supernaturally when you respond to Him. That's true with our profession of faith, it's true with our baptism in water, and it's also true with whatever invitation Almighty God has before you right now. It may be an invitation to realign some habits in your life. It may be an invitation to forgive someone for whom you have carried anger for a long season. It may be an invitation to serve in a new way or to give with greater generosity. There are many ways that God presents invitations to us. Don't resent them; celebrate them. If you recognize Almighty God has put something before you, know with certainty His supernatural power is waiting to meet you when you cooperate with Him. What a privilege that is!

• THINK ABOUT IT •

Can you remember a time when you said yes to an invitation He placed before you and were enabled to carry it out by His supernatural power?

Prayer

Heavenly Father, grant me an understanding heart to know You through a revelation of Jesus, more real than the challenges of my life. Help me be a willing servant who is prepared for Your invitations. I reject fear and choose to walk in Your light. Thank You for Your great mercy and power that helps me when I cooperate with You. In Jesus' name, amen.

DAY 10

ACCEPTED AND LOVED

He was despised and rejected by men, a man of sorrows, and familiar with suffering. Like one from whom men hide their faces he was despised, and we esteemed him not.

ISAIAH 53:3

Isaiah was a prophet in Jerusalem, a court prophet at home in the palace. Hundreds of years before the birth of Jesus, he prophesied about the coming Messiah. You would think that the Messiah the people had been waiting for so eagerly would be welcomed, not "despised and rejected." But Jesus—the sinless, obedient Son of God—endured a great deal of rejection, even though He was doing exactly what God wanted Him to do. It's highly probable that you and I will face rejection along life's journey, but we can take comfort in the fact that God loves us and accepts us—not because we are good enough or because we have done something to earn it, but because of the redemptive work of Jesus on our behalf.

• THINK ABOUT IT •

Have you, like Jesus, felt despised and rejected or known suffering and pain? Give your circumstances to the Lord, then rejoice in His great love for you.

Prayer

Heavenly Father, I confidently come to You through the cross where Your sinless Son endured rejection, abandonment, shame, and guilt so that I could be free. I choose to forgive those who have rejected or harmed me. Today, I will rejoice in Your great love and the victory Jesus of Nazareth won for me through His death and resurrection. In Jesus' name, amen.

DAY 11

THIRD PERSON PRESENT

May the grace of the Lord Jesus Christ, and the love of God, and the fellowship of the Holy Spirit be with you all.

2 CORINTHIANS 13:14

There is no story of Christianity without the redemptive work of Jesus of Nazareth. It's equally true that there is no story of Christianity without the influence, direction, and power of the Holy Spirit. Sometimes we act as if the entire story of our faith is centered in the person of Jesus and the Holy Spirit is not very important. We'd rather leave Him on the sidelines with the fanatical, fringe elements. However, we have no Jesus-story without the presence of the Spirit of God. He is at work in Scripture from Genesis to Revelation, and to the degree that we will allow it He is at work in and through you and me—empowering us, guiding us, and directing us to a better way to live.

• THINK ABOUT IT •

Consider how the Holy Spirit has worked and is working in your life. Are there areas where you can give Him greater access?

Prayer

Heavenly Father, thank You for sending Your Holy Spirit—I ask You to fill me with His presence. Give me an obedient and cooperative heart that I might clear away all ungodliness. Help me to have the discernment to know and embrace Your ways. Please guide me toward a more abundant life in You. In Jesus' name, amen.

HIS SPECIAL CARE

Jesus went into Galilee, proclaiming the good news of God. "The time has come," he said. "The kingdom of God is near. Repent and believe the good news!"

MARK 1:14-15

The "good news" Jesus brought was that the Kingdom of God was near. Every kingdom has its own authorities and boundaries and rules. If you are going to thrive as a citizen in that place, you need to recognize and cooperate with those things. Being a Christ-follower does not mean that we join a church and get a new morality and a new dress code for the weekends. Being a Christ-follower means that we are citizens of the Kingdom of God, where we acknowledge the authority of our King and the boundaries He wants us to live within and the rules He wants us to abide by. As Jesus-followers it is frustrating and fruitless to expend energy trying to get God to recognize our interpretation of those things. When we acknowledge and accept His authority and make a conscious decision to joyfully yield to it, we will be happier and more productive citizens of His Kingdom.

• THINK ABOUT IT •

How is God's Kingdom like an earthly kingdom? How is it different from an earthly kingdom?

Prayer

Heavenly Father, You are the author and perfecter of all things—the Creator and sustainer of life. Through Jesus, I am a citizen of Heaven and in Your special care. I humble myself and acknowledge Your all-powerful authority. Today, I joyfully yield to You to become an even more productive participant in Your Kingdom. In Jesus' name, amen.

DAY 13

A HEART EXAM

When the disciples heard this, they were greatly astonished and asked, "Who then can be saved?"

MATTHEW 19:25

One of the saddest accounts in the New Testament is of the man known as the Rich Young Ruler. He had a one-on-one conversation with Jesus that ended in disappointment when he could not bring himself to let go of his possessions and follow the Messiah. I can see the disciples' faces; they had been so excited that he was going to join the group. He had connections and resources, and they thought about the tremendous asset he would be to the team. I can imagine the discouragement that swept over them when he walked away. Stunned, they must have said to each other, "If he can't make it, nobody can." The disciples were learning the same lesson the Lord had shown Samuel during his search for a king of His choosing: "Man looks at the outward appearance, but the LORD looks at the heart" (1 Samuel 16:7).

• THINK ABOUT IT •

Most of us fight the temptation to judge others by their outward appearance. Consider your own tendency to do this, then ask the Lord for the ability to see people with His eyes.

Prayer

Heavenly Father, forgive me for times when my desire for earthly treasure has influenced my perspective. Help me not lean into my own understanding but realize every blessing comes from Your hand. Thank You that You bless me generously so I might live abundantly, ready to accept Your invitations and live for Your glory. In Jesus' name, amen.

A GLOBAL COMMUNITY

"With your blood you purchased men for God from every tribe and language and people and nation."

REVELATION 5:9

The Kingdom of God is not composed of people from any single nationality or race. Scripture says that one day before the throne of God, people from every nation, race, tribe, and language will gather to declare that Jesus Christ is Lord. What an incredible experience that will be! We hear lots of dialogue about the right of all the people of the world to experience freedom and liberty and opportunity and equality. Those are worthy goals, but the reality is that they emerge from a worldview that is guided by honoring God. You and I, as ambassadors for His Kingdom, have the opportunity and privilege of praying for the nations of the world, that Jesus Christ would be revealed and lifted up among the people, for He alone is the source of good things.

• THINK ABOUT IT •

What is your response when you hear news reports of the challenges faced by the people of the world? Do you think that's just the way it is in that country? Or do you ask your Heavenly Father to reveal Jesus Christ to the people of that nation?

Prayer

Heavenly Father, I bow my knee to You today, as one day all peoples will bow before Your throne and proclaim Jesus as Lord. Give me a heart to intercede for the Church You are building throughout the earth. Please deliver me from anything that wastes the time You have given me here on earth. May my life honor You alone. In Jesus' name, amen.

A SIMPLE OBJECTIVE

"O Nebuchadnezzar, we do not need to defend ourselves before you in this matter. If we are thrown into the blazing furnace, the God we serve is able to deliver us from it, and he will rescue us from your hand, O king. But even if he does not, we want you to know, O king, that we will not serve your gods or worship the image of gold you have set up."

DANIEL 3:16-18

Daniel's friends had infuriated the king by refusing to bow to the golden image of his god, and the king was going to take his revenge by throwing them into a blazing furnace. The young men understood that the objective of this conversation wasn't their freedom; it was to honor God. Freedom and opportunity were right in front of them, but they put their trust in God and refused to bow to the world's idol. We're a long way removed from bowing to golden idols of political leaders, but we're not removed from idols—they have names like success, popularity, wealth, power, pleasure, and comfort. The goal of each of our conversations and decisions is really pretty simple: to honor God.

• THINK ABOUT IT •

Do success, popularity, wealth, power, pleasure, or comfort fight with honoring God for supremacy in your heart and mind? Consider what you might do differently in order to make honoring God your first priority.

Prayer

Heavenly Father, thank You for the examples of faith and courage You have given to me in Scripture. Like these men of faith, make me a person of character, courage, and boldness for Your Kingdom. I put my trust in You, knowing that there is no fear in Your perfect love. I choose to honor You all of my days. In Jesus' name, amen.

A DOUBLE BLESSING

Then Peter came to Jesus and asked, "Lord, how many times shall I forgive my brother when he sins against me? Up to seven times?" Jesus answered, "I tell you, not seven times, but seventy-seven times."

MATTHEW 18:21-22

It is sometimes hard to forgive, isn't it? A mental picture helps me when I am struggling with forgiveness. I envision taking that offense, stuffing it in a trash bag, tying it up, then dropping it on a conveyor belt, and watching it move away. If it's a real problem, it probably will return a few seconds after I watch it disappear. I may have to do that a hundred times that first day because I have been living with it so long, thinking about it, and stoking the fire that fuels it. I have to keep stuffing that trash bag and sending it away. But two weeks later it will only show up occasionally. Two months later remembering that offense may not elicit any response at all. Forgiveness is not a once-in-a-lifetime event; it is a tool we will need with us all through life. Forgiveness is a double blessing: It not only cancels the debt we feel someone owes us and sets them free, but it also sets us free.

• THINK ABOUT IT •

Are there people you are harboring resentment toward for any reason? Mentally bundle up your feelings and surrender them to the Lord. Canceling the debt will set you both free.

Prayer

Heavenly Father, thank You for forgiving me while I was yet still a sinner and in rebellion toward You. I choose to forgive anyone for any and all offenses against me. I ask You to have mercy on my adversaries, blessing them by revealing Your love and drawing them close to You. Today I rejoice that Your mercy endures forever. In Jesus' name, amen.

DAY 17

BLOOMS IN THE DESERT

I ask then: Did God reject his people? By no means!

ROMANS 11:1

Israel is a tiny little nation, tucked away at the end of the Mediterranean, yet it garners a disproportionate amount of international interest and even hatred. I visited Israel for the first time in 1970, when it was still a developing nation. The roads were two-lane, and many of them were unpaved. Today Israel is surrounded by nations that would like to destroy it, yet it has become one of the most modern nations of the world. The only way to explain the success of Israel, other than the sacrifices of the people who live there, is the sovereign intervention of Almighty God. Like the nation of Israel, with God's help we too can flourish in difficult places. So often we imagine that life can only be fulfilling and meaningful if all of our circumstances are perfect and everyone around us approves and applauds. Even though life is seldom like that, you can rest in the knowledge that you are loved and accepted by Almighty God. So don't let difficulties and challenges rob you of the notion that God is watching over your life, because He is, and He wants good things for you.

• THINK ABOUT IT •

Reflect over your life and think of a time you have faced rejection since you decided to follow Jesus. How did He lead you and provide for you during that time?

Prayer

Heavenly Father, thank You for opening my heart and mind to the truth of Your Word. I pray for Your Church—awaken us to Your purposes. Help us humbly turn to You in repentance. Forgive this nation for our rebellion; we ask for Your mercy instead of judgment. We pray for the peace of Jerusalem. In Jesus' name, amen.

GOD IN US

Do you not know that your body is a temple of the Holy Spirit, who is in you, whom you have received from God? You are not your own; you were bought at a price. Therefore honor God with your body.

1 CORINTHIANS 6:19-20

The image of our bodies as temples of the Holy Spirit is a little hard for us to grasp. But to a first-century audience, particularly one of Jewish orientation, it would have been very significant because the Temple was at the center of their lives. One of the radical aspects of Paul's teaching was he took away the focus on the Jerusalem Temple. He said, "God is living in you, so now your body is the temple." This realization helps us make daily decisions that honor the Lord. For example, don't take the temple any place you wouldn't take the Lord. If you wouldn't say it in the temple, it probably doesn't need to be said. If you wouldn't show it on a big screen in the temple, you probably don't need to see it. This simple change in perspective will help us grow in spiritual maturity and learn to cooperate with God's purposes for our lives.

• THINK ABOUT IT •

God gave us a free will, but He also says there are some things that are not good for us. How can thinking of your body as a dwelling place for the Holy Spirit help you make life-decisions?

Prayer

Heavenly Father, thank You for Your Holy Spirit, who opens my eyes to see and receive Your truth. I rejoice that my body is His temple and thank You that Satan has no place in me and no power over me, through the blood of Jesus. You are my hope and Redeemer—help me to honor You in body and soul. In Jesus' name, amen.

DAY 19

TOP OF THE LIST

You are a chosen people, a royal priesthood, a holy nation, a people belonging to God, that you may declare the praises of him who called you out of darkness into his wonderful light. Once you were not a people, but now you are the people of God; once you had not received mercy, but now you have received mercy.

1 PETER 2:9-10

To be a Christ-follower makes us a part of God's covenant people in the earth, and we will never have a designation that will exceed that. Most of us attach labels to ourselves, and how we relate to our world filters through those categories. We may see ourselves first through our gender or our nationality or our race or our marital status. Peter is suggesting that at the top of our self-awareness is the knowledge that we are the people of God, Christ-followers. This doesn't change those other classifications, but they all come after our most important identity: We belong to Jesus of Nazareth.

• THINK ABOUT IT •

What labels do you apply to yourself? Think about how you would put them in order—is Christ-follower at the top of your list?

Prayer

Heavenly Father, I choose to identify above all as a follower of the Lord Jesus Christ. Thank You for choosing me to declare Your praises, calling me out of darkness into Your wonderful light. May reverence of You flourish within me and Your wisdom guide, restore, and renew me. May my life bring You honor and glory forever. In Jesus' name, amen.

LIFTED ABOVE

Though I walk in the midst of trouble, you preserve my life; you stretch out your hand against the anger of my foes, with your right hand you save me. The LORD will fulfill his purpose for me; your love, O LORD, endures forever— do not abandon the works of your hands.

PSALM 138:7-8

I've come to the conclusion that the circumstances that beset our lives from season to season do not intimidate God. It would be easy to think, "God, this situation will destroy all that You could do through me!" But God looks at our circumstances from His viewpoint. "What's bothering you, Moses? The Egyptian army has you backed up against the sea? I'll take care of it. You need water for a couple million people? Try the rock." "What's the problem, David? An angry giant? I can handle this. Do you have your slingshot?" Whatever the situation, His desire is to lead us through and lift us above our circumstances, not to abandon the work He has started in us. The Lord has promised to fulfill His purposes in us, and I choose to believe Him.

• THINK ABOUT IT •

Have there been times when you have been overwhelmed by your circumstances but God lifted you above them? Be quick to give Him glory for His deliverance and provision in your life.

Prayer

Heavenly Father, Your name is above all names, Your ways higher than my ways—I choose to open my heart to cooperate with You more fully. I rejoice in Your faithfulness and trust You for protection from the snare of my enemies. I choose to diligently serve You and seek Your purposes and Your love, which endures forever. In Jesus' name, amen.

DAY 21

ON ASSIGNMENT IN THE FIELD

We are therefore Christ's ambassadors, as though God were making his appeal through us. . . .

2 CORINTHIANS 5:20

We are Christ's ambassadors, representatives on His behalf. We have been deployed to be advocates for Him, helping people understand His perspective and His purposes. In whatever spheres of influence God has given you—your family, your workplace, your classroom, your friends, your neighborhood—you are an ambassador. That means every time you hear someone say, "Why would God . . .?" or "I don't understand Christians," God is inviting you to stand up for Him. We often think it would be good if our community and our nation were more Christ-centered, and we pray that God would raise up someone to make an appeal on His behalf. The truth is that He already has—and it is us.

• THINK ABOUT IT •

Do you willingly accept your role as Christ's ambassador? It can be an intimidating assignment, but the Holy Spirit has promised to empower you with everything you need to represent Him well.

Prayer

Heavenly Father, prepare me to respond to Your invitations with the certainty that You are making Your appeal to others through my life. May those who are watching recognize that I am Your representative, transformed to be more Christ-centered that I might serve them more effectively. In Jesus' name, amen.

IN SPITE OF OUR DIFFERENCES

"A new command I give you: Love one another. As I have loved you, so you must love one another. By this all men will know that you are my disciples, if you love one another."

JOHN 13:34-35

Christ-followers have a directive from Jesus to love one another, saying we are to do it "as I have loved you." It is not a suggestion; it is a command, because our love for one another identifies us as His disciples. That means you and I need to learn to subjugate differences and personal preferences to Jesus' authority so that we can accept and feel genuine affection for one another. My carnal nature elevates those differences and preferences, convincing me that the only people worthy of my affection are those just like me. The only way to overcome that sinful thinking is to focus on Jesus' sacrificial love and our responsibility as His followers to demonstrate His love to others. When we learn to love others despite our differences, it brings great freedom and joy, exponentially increasing our gospel witness.

• THINK ABOUT IT •

Jesus' obedience to go to the cross for our sin is a living demonstration of what it means to love God and one another. Paul prayed the Ephesians would be able "to grasp how wide and long and high and deep is the love of Christ" (Ephesians 3:18). Does your love for others honor Jesus by accurately reflecting His love for you?

Prayer

Heavenly Father, thank You for displaying Your love by giving us Jesus. My heart is overwhelmed with the greatness of Your commands and the difference they make in my life. Help me to walk in obedience that I might demonstrate what it means to be Your disciple. May my love not grow cold; may I never grow weary of doing good. In Jesus' name. Amen.

DAY 23

STEADFAST IN THE STORMS

Blessed is the man who perseveres under trial, because when he has stood the test, he will receive the crown of life that God has promised to those who love him.

JAMES 1:12

The stories we teach children are the stories we pray never happen to them. We tell them about Jonah and the whale and pray they are never swallowed by a large sea creature. We tell them about Daniel in the lions' den and pray they never climb into the big cat enclosure at the zoo. We tell them about David and Goliath and pray they are never challenged by a nine-foot bully. We know from our own experience that trials will come, so we cultivate in them the kind of faith in the living God that will sustain them through life's challenges. In an age-appropriate way, let's teach our children that in situations that are less than ideal, God will be with us and bless us for trusting Him and staying strong.

• THINK ABOUT IT •

Have you faced challenging times when you stood strong with the Lord, and He blessed you for it? If you have not told the young people in your life about the Lord's faithfulness to you, find an opportunity to do so.

Prayer

Heavenly Father, prepare me to persevere through life's trials that I might receive the crown of life promised to those who stand faithful to Your Word. Give me the strength of character like that of those in Scripture. Let Your Holy Spirit bring me the necessary understanding to be faithful when the unexpected happens. In Jesus' name, amen.

CULTIVATING GROWTH

"Produce fruit in keeping with repentance."

MATTHEW 3:8

In this verse producing fruit means making changes, specifically the life changes that flow from a repentant heart. One of the characteristics of maturing Christ-followers is our willingness to change—to let His character be formed in us. It is not just a trait of those who are new to the faith; it should also be true of those of us who have been following Jesus for a lengthy season. To be a Christ-follower is to recognize that one day every one of us, as Scripture teaches, will stand before the Judge of all the earth. We'll be given an open-book test, and we've been told how to prepare so that we need not fear it. We should be able to show up at that appointment thrilled about the reward that is awaiting us. The process begins with believing that Jesus is Lord, then confessing it with your mouth, publicly acknowledging it, and continually producing the "fruit in keeping with repentance."

• THINK ABOUT IT •

As you think about your faith journey, there probably have been seasons when you have experienced more spiritual growth and change than others. This is likely true of all of us, but let's pray that the Holy Spirit would give us fewer slow seasons and more forward progress. Then we can seek His help to move ahead.

Prayer

Heavenly Father, hear my prayer and cleanse me from all sin. I desire Your character above my own ways. Thank You that Jesus, Your Son, died on the cross for my sin. Let this season bring forth good fruit in my life and a willingness to seek You and Your ways every day. Your presence is a gift, and I desire to be pleasing to You. In Jesus' name, amen.

DAY 25

A PECULIAR PEOPLE

"I am God, and there is no other; I am God, and there is none like me. I make known the end from the beginning, from ancient times, what is still to come. I say: My purpose will stand, and I will do all that I please."

ISAIAH 46:9-10

The sovereignty of God means that God can do what He wants, when He wants, the way He wants, and He needs no one's approval. From New Testament times until today, the value of the Church of Jesus Christ in the earth is to be a peculiar people—a people who recognize the sovereignty of God and fear the Lord, a people who yield to the principles of Scripture so that the purposes of God can come forth in our lives. In our humanity we struggle with the desire to do things our way and to worship and serve God on our terms. But only when we acknowledge His sovereignty and yield to Him and His purposes will we experience the fullness of His power at work on our behalf.

• THINK ABOUT IT •

Each of us wrestles with a tendency to think that our plan is better than God's plan. If you are struggling with this, rest in the sure knowledge that He knows "the end from the beginning" and wants the best for you—always.

Prayer

Heavenly Father, help me to shine as a light in a dark world, submitted to Your authority. Teach me to trust You in everything I do. Thank You for Your Word and the strength it gives as it reveals what is in our hearts. Let Your Word dwell in my heart and transform my thinking, making me more like You. In Jesus' name, amen.

PERSECUTED FOR HIM

For it has been granted to you on behalf of Christ not only to believe on him, but also to suffer for him....

PHILIPPIANS 1:29

Compared to believers around the world, American Christians have had it pretty easy. When I have had opportunities to sit with believers from Iran or Rwanda or China or Sudan, I have discovered that their trust in God is far greater than what most of us have been required to develop. I've come to the conclusion that God is asking us to grow up the Church in our culture. He has uniquely resourced the Church in our nation so that we can be generous to the Body of Christ in the earth, but we should not imagine God's blessings have come to us because of some unique characteristic that makes us special. Let's be diligent in praying for our brothers and sisters around the world who are being persecuted for their faith. Let's pray for the American Church, that we would become mature and bold believers who are ready to stand for Christ in any situation.

• THINK ABOUT IT •

Information about persecuted Christians and the organizations that work to defend them is widely available on the Internet. Consider adding one of these organizations and the believers they represent to your prayer list.

Prayer

Heavenly Father, protect all those who serve You. Hear the cry of those who suffer, and reveal Your love to them through Jesus. Forgive me for taking my freedom for granted. Help me intercede effectively for Your persecuted Church, and receive my praise and worship from a grateful heart that is strengthened by knowing You. In Jesus' name, amen.

DAY 27

THE HIGHEST PURPOSE

It was he who gave some to be apostles, some to be prophets, some to be evangelists, and some to be pastors and teachers, to prepare God's people for works of service, so that the body of Christ may be built up. . . .

EPHESIANS 4:11-12

There is no greater investment of a human life than serving God. I hear parents hoping that their children will have careers that pay well, but I do not hear many parents expressing a desire that their children will grow up to serve the Lord. There have been times in the history of the Church in this nation when parents aspired that their children would spend their lives and their strength in the service of the Lord. Certainly not everyone is called to full-time Christian ministry. But our highest purpose, whether we are a butcher, a baker, or a candlestick maker, is to serve the Lord with our lives in the midst of those callings.

• THINK ABOUT IT •

Our attitudes about ministry are easily conveyed to those around us, even children. Do your words and actions convey positive messages about being called as a prophet, evangelist, pastor, or teacher?

Prayer

Heavenly Father, whatever I do and wherever I go, I choose to give You first place. May I always seek Your agenda above my own. I ask for Your Holy Spirit's help to serve You in my home, at my job, in my community, and among my friends and family. Help me live my life investing in Your purposes and caring for Your people. In Jesus' name, amen.

AN UNRELENTING QUEST

The Lord stood at my side and gave me strength, so that through me the message might be fully proclaimed. . . . And I was delivered from the lion's mouth. The Lord will rescue me from every evil attack and will bring me safely to his heavenly kingdom. To him be glory for ever and ever.

2 TIMOTHY 4:17-18

Paul imprisoned in Rome, is writing encouragement to Timothy, his young protégé. There was no moaning or complaining, only triumph and expectation. In the New Testament the people of the world are divided into two categories: the Jewish people and everyone else—referred to in Scripture as the Gentiles. Though his circumstances were at best unpleasant, Paul was still focused on his assignment to take the good news of Jesus to the Gentiles. Beyond that, he was looking forward to a heavenly kingdom void of prisons and chains. From the vantage point of history, we can read what Paul wrote to Timothy and see that he was right. Even from a prison cell, Paul had a greater impact on the non-Jewish world than any other person ever has. God has a plan for our lives, too. His promises to keep us and use us for His Kingdom purposes are just as true and trustworthy as His promises to Paul.

• THINK ABOUT IT •

Paul's life as a believer was marked by an unrelenting quest to know God more fully and glorify Him among the Gentiles. What are your goals as a believer?

Prayer

Heavenly Father, may my life attract friends and acquaintances toward a relationship with You. Paul suffered without complaint. He was tested and did not become bitter. He sacrificed and still found joy in serving. Help me walk in joy, knowing Your promises bring life. I am only passing through this life; my treasure is knowing You. In Jesus' name, amen.

DAY 29

A CREATIVE INVITATION

Then an angel of the Lord appeared to him, standing at the right side of the altar of incense. When Zechariah saw him, he was startled and was gripped with fear. But the angel said to him, "Do not be afraid, Zechariah; your prayer has been heard. Your wife Elizabeth will bear you a son, and you are to give him the name John."

LUKE 1:11-13

Zechariah, a Temple priest, was serving at his appointed time. While standing next to the altar of incense, he saw an angel. His response was fairly predictable: fear. The angel then said, "Zechariah, I'm here because of your prayer." Zechariah and Elizabeth were an older couple with no children. Their prayers opened the doors for God to move, and the result was the birth of John the Baptist and all that his life entailed. We will never know what the outcome would have been if Zechariah and Elizabeth hadn't prayed but instead contented themselves with grumbling resentment. But they did pray, and because of their persistence they had a divine appointment and a baby on the way. Prayer is not a last resort. Prayer is a creative invitation to Almighty God to unleash His power in our lives.

• THINK ABOUT IT •

Have there been times when God honored your persistent prayers, even when the results seemed unlikely? Thank Him for His faithfulness, and find an opportunity to tell someone else what the Lord has done for you.

Prayer

Heavenly Father, teach me to believe, praying with faith and submitting to Your purposes. All things are possible with You. I humbly bring You issues that are beyond change without Your intervention. Help me persevere until You reveal Your answers. Give me wisdom to ask for the right things and trust Your timing. In Jesus' name, amen.

WHEN THE WATER RISES

Every living thing on the face of the earth was wiped out; men and animals and the creatures that move along the ground and the birds of the air were wiped from the earth. Only Noah was left, and those with him in the ark.

GENESIS 7:23

It's impossible for us to imagine the ridicule Noah must have faced as he built the ark. He no doubt endured constant harassment from his contemporaries, who would've mocked his explanation that he was doing what God had asked him to do. But I suspect there was a time, once he and his family were inside and the rain began to fall and the water began to rise, that Noah was very, very grateful he had said yes to God's invitation to build that ark. I suspect that as he walked the decks of that massive ship, Noah was not grumbling about how much work it had been. I suspect he gratefully recognized that God had made supernatural provisions for him and his family. Our stories may not be as dramatic as Noah's, but when we say yes to God's invitations, He is able to do things for us that we cannot do for ourselves.

• THINK ABOUT IT •

Has there been a time when God asked you to do something that didn't make sense at the time but you said yes anyway? What resulted from your willingness to accept His invitation?

Prayer

Heavenly Father, I believe all good things originate from You. When life feels out of control, I choose to yield to You and trust that You are working out Your purposes. I will not fear rejection from others. Instead of worrying, I will keep walking in obedience to Your Word, doing the best I know to do and trusting in Your Holy Spirit. In Jesus' name, amen.

A BIGGER PLAN

Since ancient times no one has heard, no ear has perceived, no eye has seen any God besides you, who acts on behalf of those who wait for him.

ISAIAH 64:4

God has always been faithful to me, but I'll admit that I've questioned Him about His timing, especially when it seemed that He was allowing a challenging situation to continue rather than change it. I have to remind myself that God's perspective is infinitely bigger than mine as He looks across the span of the ages to see people and circumstances and events that I cannot see. If you're unhappy with God right now because of His sense of timing, I would encourage you to trust Him. God has a plan for your life and mine, and He will do what needs to be done—when it needs to be done—to accomplish His plan and purposes for those of us who wait for Him.

· THINK ABOUT IT ·

Are you having trouble waiting on God to act in some area or circumstance of your life? How can you change your thinking in order to rest in the knowledge that He will act in His time?

Prayer

Heavenly Father, I admit that I have at times been impatient and have doubted that You were listening to my prayers. I know I ought to trust You now as I have in the past. You have never failed me or let me down. Your love has been poured out in my life many times. Help me, Lord, to be still and wait on Your answer. In Jesus' name, amen.

THE DEFINING POINT

If you confess with your mouth, "Jesus is Lord," and believe in your heart that God raised him from the dead, you will be saved.

ROMANS 10:9

I believe in Jesus Christ, God's only Son, our Lord. That last phrase is somewhat different. It's not about Jesus' position in the Trinity. It's not about His title. It's about the relationship we have with Him. There will be all sorts of beings in hell who believe that Jesus is the Son of God. Even the Devil and the demons believe that, but they chose not to confess Him as Lord. One of the mistakes we make is thinking that sitting in church or embracing a set of rules makes us a Jesus-follower. The real defining point with regard to the Kingdom of God is our decision about our relationship with Jesus of Nazareth and whether we choose to yield to Him as Lord of our lives.

• THINK ABOUT IT •

Is Jesus truly Lord of your life—your whole life? Lord of your relationships? Your resources? Lord of your hopes and dreams?

Prayer

Heavenly Father, I believe You sent Your Son to die on the cross for my sin and be raised again from death that I might have abundant life in Him. Forgive me for thinking I could save myself or that my effort could gain Your acceptance. I yield my life to You—my relationships, resources, and dreams—knowing Your plan is perfect. In Jesus' name, amen.

DAY 33

A LIFE RESPONSE

As a prisoner for the Lord, then, I urge you to live a life worthy of the calling you have received.

EPHESIANS 4:1

Paul, imprisoned for his devotion to the Lord, was reminding the Ephesians that our entire lives are a response to God. Not just the time we block out for worship, personal devotions, or a small group meeting—the normal, everyday activities of our lives should be "worthy of the calling you have received." It's easy to be deceived into thinking we can be godly for a few moments here and there and the rest of the time is ours to do as we please. It is our time to use as we choose. But those choices are responses to God, and He takes notice of them. How we select a movie to watch is a response to God. How we react when our child fouls out of the game is a response to God. How we conduct business and how we interact with our families are responses to God. Life—it's all a response to God, and "worthy of the calling" is a good standard to keep in mind as we go about our daily routines.

• THINK ABOUT IT •

How would you feel if Jesus were sitting beside you as you watched your usual television shows? Would He approve of your conversations with your coworkers? Would He be pleased to see your normal interactions with your family members?

Prayer

Heavenly Father, with my whole heart I will seek You. Heighten my awareness of Your presence wherever I am. Help me not wander from Your protective boundaries. I will fix my eyes on Your precepts and meditate on Your ways. Thank You for Your mercy and grace. I choose to live my life to bring glory to You. In Jesus' name, amen.

RESISTANCE

By faith Moses, when he had grown up, refused to be known as the son of Pharaoh's daughter. He chose to be mistreated along with the people of God rather than to enjoy the pleasures of sin for a short time.

HEBREWS 11:24-25

This passage about Moses reveals something about the nature of sin: It is tempting because it promises something pleasant—an experience, a feeling, an objective—that is satisfying for the moment. If it weren't pleasant, it wouldn't be tempting. I'm not tempted by thoughts of overpaying my taxes or overindulging on broccoli, and I don't imagine you are either. One of the falsehoods we tell ourselves is that sin is not tempting. We need to be honest and admit that it is. Sinful thoughts are a struggle, but the passage also says that the decision to act on those thoughts is a choice. Moses chose to give up the life of a royal prince because he knew he could not enjoy that pagan lifestyle and still please God. We might not have to make such a dramatic choice, but we do make choices throughout the routine activities of our days to either enjoy the fleeting pleasures of sin, or, like Moses, align ourselves with God.

• THINK ABOUT IT •

As Jesus-followers we have access to the power of the Holy Spirit to help us resist temptation. Do you intentionally invite Him into the areas of your life where you are most tempted?

Prayer

Heavenly Father, thank You for Your wonderful promises that bring hope to my life every day. Search me and know my heart; try me and know my thoughts. If You see any wicked way in me, lead me in the way everlasting and cleanse me from every sin (Psalm 139:23-24). Thank You for choosing me and redeeming me. In Jesus' name, amen.

DAY 35

HIS GREAT POWER

Then Asa called to the LORD his God and said, "LORD, there is no one like you to help the powerless against the mighty. Help us, O LORD our God, for we rely on you, and in your name we have come against this vast army. O LORD, you are our God; do not let man prevail against you."

2 CHRONICLES 14:11

An army was threatening his nation, and King Asa made a declaration of faith that speaks to us through the centuries. If you're not in the habit of praying the Scriptures, I commend it to you. It's a marvelous one-verse prayer for when you face challenges that you feel powerless to overcome. They come to all of us—in the form of a medical diagnosis, a relational challenge, a financial need—they come in many, many ways. Life is more difficult than I would wish, not just for wicked people but for good people doing the best they know. In the challenges of life, however, there is no one like Almighty God to help us when we feel powerless.

· THINK ABOUT IT ·

Consider a time when you felt powerless. How did God give you strength during that season?

Prayer

Heavenly Father, just as you helped King Asa when he declared, "There is no one like You," You rescue me when I am powerless against a mighty enemy. Help me, Lord, for I rely on You, and in Your name I have come against a vast army. Lord, You are my God; do not let man prevail against You. Great is Your name in all the earth! In Jesus' name, amen.

AMBITIOUS FOR GOD

Do nothing out of selfish ambition or vain conceit, but in humility consider others better than yourselves.

PHILIPPIANS 2:3

There's nothing wrong with ambition; God created us with the desire and determination to succeed. But selfish ambition is different; it is destructive because it lacks humility and is all about "me"—my material possessions, my advancement, my recognition. Sometimes we couch it in far more acceptable language: "I'm not ambitious for myself; I'm just ambitious for my family. I want them to have every possible advantage." How about cultivating ambition for the Kingdom of God? Teach your children to be ambitious for the things of God, to weep when God's Kingdom is diminished and to celebrate when it's extended. Teach them to be ambitious for Jesus, not embarrassed by Him. Teach them to humbly consider others before themselves. These attitudes will bring untold blessings to your life and the lives of your children.

· THINK ABOUT IT ·

Have there been times in your life when you harbored an attitude of selfish ambition? Have there been times when you have humbly considered others before yourself? What was the outcome of those attitudes? How was your relationship with God during those times?

Prayer

Heavenly Father, You are my heart's desire. I confess, sometimes I am far from You because of selfish ambition. Please forgive me. Help me to see others prosper; teach me to weep with those who weep. Give me opportunities to serve Your people that they might know You more fully and Your Kingdom be extended. In Jesus' name, amen.

SIGNIFICANT PLANS

For we are God's workmanship, created in Christ Jesus to do good works, which God prepared in advance for us to do.

EPHESIANS 2:10

It is incredible to realize that God not only created us and gifted us individually, but that He also has prepared tasks for each of us to do in order to advance His purposes. I think most of us, when we imagine what God prepared for us, tend to think He must have planned something pretty remarkable. I think, "God, when you thought of me you surely planned for massive stadiums filled with desperately wicked people waiting to hear me preach so they can sprint down the aisles, burst into tears, and repent." I doubt any of us think God created us to scrub the bathroom tile or help a coworker finish a project or take a neighbor to a doctor's appointment. While these acts of service might seem rather mundane in the eyes of the world, they are significant acts of ministry when we offer them in Jesus' name and commit them to His plan and purposes.

· THINK ABOUT IT ·

If you haven't already done so, take an inventory of your spiritual gifts to help discern how God has created you to serve others and expand His Kingdom.

Prayer

Heavenly Father, You are the Creator and designer of my life, holy and righteous in all things. Your plans and purposes are perfect. I believe that I am Your workmanship, created in Christ Jesus to do good works, which You prepared in advance for me to do. I submit my life, my talents, and my relationships to You to use as You desire. In Jesus' name, amen.

DAY 38

RIGHTEOUS RIGHT HAND

"Do not fear, for I am with you; do not be dismayed, for I am your God. I will strengthen you and help you; I will uphold you with my righteous right hand."

ISAIAH 41:10

What are you afraid of? Some of us have trouble admitting our fear, but fear is a part of life. If you are not afraid of anything, you are not paying attention! What you are afraid of, though, makes a difference. You've probably seen lists of phobias, like papyrophobia, the fear of paper, and cometophobia, the fear of being hit by a falling comet. They are funny if they are not your phobias. You are more likely to be afraid of losing your job or facing rejection or being diagnosed with a serious disease. God has given us an antidote for fear, and it is trust—not trust in ourselves and our abilities, but trust in Him. He has promised to strengthen us, help us, and uphold us; and I can think of no more powerful protection than His "righteous right hand."

• THINK ABOUT IT •

What are the things that frighten you? Are you able to trust God with your fears? Has trust become more than a theory? Has it moved from your head into your heart?

Prayer

Heavenly Father, my life is open before You; I desire to hide nothing. I confess there are times when fear overtakes my heart and worry fills my mind and controls my emotions. Forgive me for not trusting You. Lord, instead, help me cry out to You to strengthen me and to uphold me with Your righteous right hand when I am afraid. In Jesus' name, amen.

A TRANSFORMING ALMIGHTY

"We give thanks to you, Lord God Almighty, the One who is and who was. . . ."

REVELATION 11:17

The title "Almighty" is about power, and in this verse it is proclaimed by the elders surrounding God on their thrones in Heaven. That God is "almighty" is quite a claim today because in a world of political correctness it is very politically incorrect. There is enormous pressure to say that all belief systems are the same, that it is completely inappropriate to suggest that one belief system is in any way superior to another. To do so, we're told, makes us narrow-minded and bigoted and judgmental. I disagree. To believe in absolute truth is not a bigoted position—it is a liberating position. Christianity is not intended to demean or belittle other people. It is intended to give us a love and compassion for all persons, because apart from the Person of Jesus Christ and our belief in Him, there is no distinction between us and anyone else. What we have chosen to believe—that God is indeed Almighty and that Jesus of Nazareth is His Son and the Savior of the world—has made transformation possible for any person who will believe. What a wonderful gift!

• THINK ABOUT IT •

That God is "almighty" means that His power is unlimited. How does this impact the way you pray to Him and worship Him?

Prayer

Heavenly Father, You are God Almighty, the One who is and was and is to come. You are holy and all-knowing. I choose to believe, humbly submitting myself to You that I might learn Your ways. My ways have led me toward destruction, yet I know Your promises bring life. I give all praise and honor to You, my Lord. In Jesus' name, amen.

WHATEVER THE COST

As Jesus was walking beside the Sea of Galilee, he saw two brothers, Simon called Peter and his brother Andrew. They were casting a net into the lake, for they were fishermen. "Come, follow me," Jesus said, "and I will make you fishers of men." At once they left their nets and followed him.

MATTHEW 4:18-20

As Jesus invited men to follow Him and become His disciples, they were faced with the choice to leave everything they knew to travel with Him around the land of Israel. The story is so familiar to us that we tend to overlook the disruption it must have meant to their lives. Do you think their friends questioned their sanity? Do you think their families were concerned? Do you think these brothers might have had to change their plans to buy another boat and expand their business? We may not be called to leave everything behind to follow Jesus, but we are called to make His priorities our priorities and to embrace His perspectives— even when it might cause change and disruption in our lives.

• THINK ABOUT IT •

Did your decision to follow Jesus require you to leave anything behind? Has your embrace of His priorities and perspectives caused tension in any of your relationships? How has He rewarded your faithfulness to Him?

Prayer

Heavenly Father, Your plans and purposes are high above all human thought. Thank You for inviting me to follow You. I choose today to know You above all else—Your perspectives and Your priorities. I release every concern that has taken a higher priority than Yours. Help me walk in a manner that I will bring honor to Your name. In Jesus' name, amen.

PROMISED RESTORATION

"I will repay you for the years the locusts have eaten. . . . You will have plenty to eat, until you are full, and you will praise the name of the LORD your God, who has worked wonders for you. . . ."

JOEL 2:25-26

One of the persistent promises of Scripture is that God is a God of restoration. But when you're in a season when locusts seem to be devouring everything in sight, it can be difficult to remember that He has promised to repay what has been lost—and frankly, why do we have to deal with locusts anyway? Maybe one day I will know that answer in full, but during the times I am swatting at locusts I must make a conscious decision to trust Him—to keep His promises and praise Him for what He will do in the future. When we go through those seasons we have a choice of whether to let doubt and resentment or faith and hope become the dominant thoughts that influence our lives. Let's trust Him to restore what has been lost and wait patiently to see the ways He will provide for us.

• THINK ABOUT IT •

Have you ever experienced seasons "the locusts have eaten"? How did God restore what was lost? Did you grow in spiritual maturity during that time?

Prayer

Heavenly Father, You are my provider. I will trust in You, and my confidence will not be shaken by the situations in my life. Whenever I experience pain or loss, help me to trust in Your character more than in my circumstances. I will praise Your name and remember all the wonders You have worked for me. In Jesus' name, amen.

LIKE A DOVE

As soon as Jesus was baptized, he went up out of the water. At that moment heaven was opened, and he saw the Spirit of God descending like a dove and alighting on him.

MATTHEW 3:16

This is a beautiful image isn't it, the Holy Spirit descending like a dove onto the newly baptized Jesus? We too need the help of the Holy Spirit, so we want to become people who allow Him to move and work in our lives. When we meet Jesus in John's Gospel, His image is of "the Lamb of God" (John 1:29). If you want to know where the Holy Spirit resides, He comes upon individuals who reflect the characteristics of the Lamb with meekness, purity, gentleness, and humility. If we will cultivate those things, we will foster the involvement of the Holy Spirit. We will overcome our anxiety and uncertainties about Him and gain a comfort and familiarity with His presence. The results will be a force for good in our lives that can only come from God.

• THINK ABOUT IT •

The Holy Spirit has a place in our lives that nothing else can fill—not personal Bible study, not small group interaction, not the best preaching. Is the Holy Spirit truly welcome in your life?

Prayer

Heavenly Father, establish Your Word with power and authority. Thank You for sending Your Holy Spirit to be our Helper, speaking to us on Your behalf and honoring Jesus. May He pour over Your Church and bring repentance, cleansing, and a harvest of righteousness. I thank You for Your Holy Spirit and welcome Him into my life. In Jesus' name, amen.

DAY 43

MYSTERIOUS AND MIRACULOUS

"How will this be," Mary asked the angel, "since I am a virgin?" The angel answered, "The Holy Spirit will come upon you, and the power of the Most High will overshadow you. So the holy one to be born will be called the Son of God."

LUKE 1:34-35

The virgin birth is a stumbling block for some people. It's one of those things that can't be fully understood with the information we have. But I don't feel it diminishes my intellect one iota to say I believe that it happened. There are many things I can observe but not fully explain. I cannot describe the physical process through which energy is radiated from the sun, absorbed by a green plant with chlorophyll on the surface of the earth, which is ingested by a brown cow that produces white milk from which we get yellow butter and strawberry ice cream. But I can enjoy the benefits of that process without feeling intellectually violated. I benefit from a vast number of things that I lack the ability to fully process, and I'm at peace with that.

• THINK ABOUT IT •

The virgin birth is just one of God's actions that cannot be scientifically explained. Have you made peace with the fact that God is not bound by the principles we use to explain our world? Are you prepared to explain your belief to people who do not share it?

Prayer

Heavenly Father, You sent Your Son, Jesus Christ, into the world to redeem Your human creation. How You chose to do this was a miraculous display of love. Open my heart to Your majesty and limitless power that the name of Jesus might be lifted up in my life. May Your truth be extended and Your will be done on earth as it is in Heaven. In Jesus' name, amen.

A CHOICE FOR FREEDOM

Bear with each other and forgive whatever grievances you may have against one another. Forgive as the Lord forgave you.

COLOSSIANS 3:13

One aspect of forgiveness is releasing the person from the debt we think is owed. When we refuse to forgive, we are refusing to cancel the debt. We hold onto it and look at it, enjoying the agitation it produces. Some of us have refused to forgive for so long that our resentment defines us. We wear our unforgiveness like a badge. We don't understand that it has put us in bondage as well. But when we decide to "forgive as the Lord forgave," we say to ourselves, "They don't owe me an apology. I am not going to withhold approval or respect or anything else until they meet whatever my requirement is. I am going to set them free." When you cancel that debt, the other person is not getting away with something; you are releasing the situation to Him who judges justly—you will be free as well.

• THINK ABOUT IT •

Are there people you have held in bondage with your unforgiveness? How has that affected them . . . and you? Release the situation to God, who judges justly.

Prayer

Heavenly Father, I believe Jesus is Your only begotten Son who died for my sin and rose victoriously from the grave, now seated at Your right hand. You counsel that to receive forgiveness, I must forgive. I choose to forgive everyone of anything, specifically _____ for _____ . I cancel all debts; they owe me nothing. In Jesus' name, amen.

DAY 45

AGELESS

The word of the LORD came to me, saying, "Before I formed you in the womb I knew you, before you were born I set you apart; I appointed you as a prophet to the nations."

JEREMIAH 1:4-5

We know Jeremiah as the famous prophet. But when God called him to be His messenger to the people, Jeremiah told God that he was too young and inexperienced for such an important role. God assured Jeremiah that He had known him and set him apart for this very purpose before he was born. God has a purpose and a plan, a direction, a call, an intent, for every human being. That is only one side of the equation, however. The other is how we respond to God. Jeremiah chose to cooperate with God, and he became one of the most remarkable prophets in all of Israelite history. What will your choice be when God calls you to follow His direction?

• THINK ABOUT IT •

Jeremiah was a young man when God called him, but God calls people of all ages. Some of God's calls are lifelong, while others are just for a season. What is God calling you to at this stage of your life? How are you responding?

Prayer

Heavenly Father, I rejoice that I am known by You and that Your purposes can be fulfilled in my life. Help me to recognize and embrace Your plan for this season of my life. Grant me the strength and wisdom to complete the course that You have set before me. Give me fresh boldness to follow and the willingness to proclaim Jesus as Lord. In Jesus' name, amen.

NO GUILT, NO SHAME

That is what some of you were. But you were washed, you were sanctified, you were justified in the name of the Lord Jesus Christ and by the Spirit of our God.

1 CORINTHIANS 6:11

I encounter many people who are living with the burden of unrelenting shame. It is an awful, enslaving thing. It says, "You didn't just make a mistake—you are a mistake. You are wrong, and you will always be wrong. You are a failure, and that will never change." First Corinthians 6 reminds us to think back to what we were when God called us and realize the changes He has brought to our lives. Yes, "that is what some of you were," but He has washed you, sanctified you, justified you, and delivered you from any guilt and the shame that resulted from it. God is more than able to deliver us from the shame of our stories, so let's trust Him to do that. Let's live in the freedom that Jesus purchased for us on the cross.

• THINK ABOUT IT •

God did not choose us in ignorance. He chose us in full knowledge of our history. If there is anything in your past that is weighing you down with shame, release it to the Lord and live in the freedom He provides.

Prayer

Heavenly Father, thank You for the sacrificial blood of Jesus Christ that has washed away my sin, setting me apart for Your purposes. May this freedom break into my awareness and the Word of God come alive in me as never before. Let Your power be made evident in my life. My hope is in You, my God and Redeemer. In Jesus' name, amen.

DAY 47

AN EXTRAORDINARY MOMENT

The angel said to the women, "Do not be afraid, for I know that you are looking for Jesus, who was crucified. He is not here; he has risen, just as he said. Come and see the place where he lay. Then go quickly and tell his disciples: 'He has risen from the dead and is going ahead of you into Galilee. There you will see him.' Now I have told you."

MATTHEW 28:5-7

The Bible tells us everything we need to know for life and godliness, but it doesn't tell us everything we'd like to know. We're given little information about what happened in Heaven when Jesus died on the cross. What was the emotional level in Heaven when Jesus was placed in the tomb, sealed with a slice of stone? What happened when God announced He needed an angel to roll that stone back, or when that wheel began to rock? Can you imagine the anticipation on the angel's face as he sat in the empty tomb, just waiting for someone to come looking for Jesus? "He's not here! He was here, but He's gone! Just like He told you He would be!"

• THINK ABOUT IT •

What is your attitude when you think about the resurrection of Jesus? Does it still amaze and excite you? Do you smile when you think about it? Let's not let the event that sealed our relationship with God ever become ordinary in our thinking.

Prayer

Heavenly Father, thank You for the unique ways You have spoken to Your people. Thank You for showing me the reality of Your love through the amazing work of Jesus' resurrection. I choose to reflect on the power displayed on my behalf at the cross and through my risen Lord. Help me to love and obey Your Word, every day! In Jesus' name, amen.

AN INVITATION FOR FAITH

*Trust in the LORD with all your heart and lean not on your own understanding;
in all your ways acknowledge him, and he will make your paths straight.*

PROVERBS 3:5-6

For a long season of my life, I was terrified to really say yes to the Lord. I assumed that if I did, He would dismiss every dream I had and send me down the Amazon River in a dugout canoe. As years have passed I have discovered how wrong that notion was. He has used my gifts and talents in ways that I had never dreamed. Saying yes to the Lord is the most rewarding, adventuresome, challenging invitation that's available to any human being. That has been my personal experience, and I've also observed it in the lives of others. You may be thinking, "If only I had more information!" I've never made a God-choice yet where I felt like I had all the information I would like to have. But if I had, that would have eliminated the need for any faith at all. Cooperate with God's invitations. It will make an eternal difference in your life.

• THINK ABOUT IT •

What invitation is before you today? Are you pondering a relationship, or a financial choice, or a career change? If you recognize that the invitation is from God, confidently choose to follow His leading.

Prayer

Heavenly Father, my life is uncertain at times, and I struggle with saying yes to Your invitations. Today I yield to You. I choose to trust You and Your plans for me. I believe that You know what is best, and that You will make my path straight. In Jesus' name, amen.

DAY 49

THE ONLY PATH

May the God of hope fill you with all joy and peace as you trust in him, so that you may overflow with hope by the power of the Holy Spirit.

ROMANS 15:13

Whom or what do you trust? Where do you look for hope? The people and things you trust in are the ones you hope to depend on. Some of us trust in our physical strength. Some of us trust in our intellectual capacity or education. Some of us trust in our willingness to work hard and persevere when the going gets tough. Some of us trust in our family or financial assets. Religious people often trust in our belief that we're more right than everybody else. Your eternal destiny is determined by what you trust in, so it's more than a rhetorical question. It is not enough to say, "I go to church there, so I just believe what they believe. That's where I place my hope." The only path to salvation and a relationship with God is confessing that Jesus of Nazareth is Lord of your life and putting your trust in Him. Other things may bring a measure of ease and comfort to your days in the earth, but there is no comparison to the joy and peace and hope God will give you when you trust in Him.

• THINK ABOUT IT •

What do you believe in? Whom do you trust? Where do you look for hope?

Prayer

Heavenly Father, thank You for Your Word. It is a light unto my path. I know there is only one way to God, through Jesus Christ alone. I believe You for salvation and yield my life to You. The world is shaking, and everything in it is unstable. Help me, through Your Holy Spirit, to seek Your joy and peace and hope when I have doubt. In Jesus' name, amen.

DAY 50

HE KNOWS ME WELL

On the evening of that first day of the week, when the disciples were together, with the doors locked for fear of the Jews, Jesus came and stood among them and said, "Peace be with you!"

JOHN 20:19

The disciples were in hiding three days after they had witnessed the crucifixion of the most remarkable man they'd ever met. Having seen Jesus walk on water and raise the dead, they thought He was invincible, but then the unthinkable happened. They knew they were probably next, so they hid. Jesus had told them He would be crucified but resurrected again three days later. What would you expect the disciples to be doing on day three? I hope I'd be tailgating outside the tomb! Their fear at that point, however, was more real than anything Jesus had told them. When His words were fulfilled and He was raised back to life, where did He go? Looking for His friends! He could have been mad at them. They had abandoned and denied Him, after all. He could have walked into that room and sent them packing, starting over with twelve others. But Jesus went where they were and said, "Peace be with you!" He knew their fears and weaknesses, but He also loved them and understood their needs.

• THINK ABOUT IT •

God knows what we need, even better than we know it ourselves. Is that settled in your heart? Does your life reflect that reality?

Prayer

Heavenly Father, You know me better than I know myself. You know what will cause me to be fearful before I even know it is coming. Thank You for the cross of Jesus and a Savior who has provided for my weakest moments ahead of time. When trials come, help me to turn to Him with confidence to forgive, heal, and restore me. In Jesus' name, amen.

ALWAYS SOVEREIGN

Then the LORD answered Job out of the storm. He said: "Who is this that darkens my counsel with words without knowledge? Brace yourself like a man; I will question you, and you shall answer me. Where were you when I laid the earth's foundation? Tell me, if you understand. Who marked off its dimensions? Surely you know! Who stretched a measuring line across it? On what were its footings set, or who laid its cornerstone. . . ?"

JOB 38:1-7

Have you ever desired an opportunity to ask God some hard questions? That's where Job arrived—questioning God—when God began to ask His own questions, reminding him of His qualifications to rule over Job's world and life. God has been and will always be sovereign over the earth. He is prepared for every eventuality this world will ever see. He is not intimidated by evil or frightened by wickedness. He is never caught off guard by the needs or disappointments of our lives. We may not understand how and when He chooses to intervene; but there is nothing under the sun for which God is not prepared, and He acts for our good. This is an amazing principle to hold in our hearts.

• THINK ABOUT IT •

Do you ever question God's intentions toward you and think that your way surely must be better than His? Remind yourself of God's sovereignty and meditate on the ways He has been faithful to you in the past.

Prayer

Heavenly Father, let the fear of God flourish in my heart. You, Lord, are the author of true wisdom and knowledge. I rejoice that You created me and are watching over me. You are my Redeemer and hope. I know the angels of the Lord encamp around those who fear You, and You deliver them. Blessed is the man who takes refuge in You. In Jesus' name, amen.

AWKWARD PLACES

The birth of Jesus Christ was as follows: when His mother Mary had been betrothed to Joseph, before they came together she was found to be with child by the Holy Spirit. And Joseph . . . being a righteous man and not wanting to disgrace her, planned to send her away secretly. But . . . an angel of the Lord appeared to him in a dream, saying, "Joseph, son of David, do not be afraid to take Mary as your wife . . . ." Joseph awoke from his sleep and did as the angel of the Lord commanded him. . . .

MATTHEW 1:18-20, 24 • NASB®

It's easy to miss the shock value of this familiar story. Your godly fiancée announces she's pregnant. As a godly man, to avoid mutual humiliation, you break your engagement. Then an angel appears in a dream: "Don't worry. This is a God-thing." Most would beseech God and counsel with trusted people. But Joseph "awoke . . . and took Mary as his wife." Does your imagination of cooperating with God include shattered dreams? This event completely upended Mary and Joseph's dreams. Our stories may not be as dramatic, but let's be prepared if God asks us to stand in awkward places that His purposes might be fulfilled.

• THINK ABOUT IT •

God has a plan. He needs people willing to cooperate with Him, even when it requires standing in awkward places. Have you ever stood in an awkward place for Him? What was the outcome?

Prayer

Heavenly Father, You are the Creator and the Author of my story. Nothing in my life has escaped Your sight—past, present, or future. Help me honor You and follow You with a yielded heart and joyful spirit. Living alongside You is the only way for me to be satisfied. Protect me from the temptation to walk in my own strength. In Jesus' name, amen.

THE STUMBLING BLOCK

"Let all the house of Israel know for certain that God has made Him both Lord and Christ—this Jesus whom you crucified."

ACTS 2:36 • NASB®

Christ is not a name attached to Jesus of Nazareth; it is a title. I believe that Jesus of Nazareth is the Christ—the Anointed One, the Messiah. I believe He is the Son of God. This understanding is at the center of the Christian faith and the reason a great deal of the pushback on the Christian faith focuses on Jesus. You can say He was a teacher, a miracle worker, a healer, and a wise man who impacted human history and get almost universal agreement. But He becomes a stumbling block when you assert that He is God's Son, the Anointed One, the Messiah who died on the cross for you and me. Yes, "the message of the cross is foolishness to those who are perishing, but to us who are being saved it is the power of God" (1 Corinthians 1:18).

• THINK ABOUT IT •

How do the descriptions "Anointed One," "Messiah," and "Son of God" help you understand the life and work of Jesus? How does the message of the cross bring to you the power of God?

Prayer

Heavenly Father, thank You for sending Jesus. I acknowledge my need of a Savior; forgive me of my sins. Jesus, be Lord of my life. I want to live for Your glory and Your honor. I yield my will to You. Let the name of Jesus be lifted up. Let the name of Jesus be exalted. Let the name of Jesus be honored in this generation. In Jesus' name, amen.

ORDER FROM CHAOS

In the beginning God created the heavens and the earth.

GENESIS 1:1

The Bible does not give us the complete story of the Earth's origins. We're simply told that God is the initiator. It does say the Spirit of God hovered over the face of the deep, that it was a chaotic place, and that God spoke and order began to emerge out of the chaos. The Bible is the story of God's interaction with humanity, but there are many things we're not told. It says on this side of eternity we will not see everything clearly, but a time is coming when we will. For now we know that God is the God of creation, but He will make all things new. He is the God of floods, but He is also the God of arks. He is the God who asked Abraham to sacrifice his son, but He is also the God who provided the ram. He is the God who put Goliath in the path of a young shepherd, but He is also the God who provided a sling with five smooth stones. God is almighty, the ruler over all things, and we can trust Him with our lives.

• THINK ABOUT IT •

Have there been times in your life when God created order out of a chaotic situation? Perhaps you could begin recording those instances in a journal to refer to when you are facing trials in the future.

Prayer

Heavenly Father, thank You for Your Word and the truth it reveals to me about Your character. Give me a longing desire to read my Bible to simply know You better. Thank You for Your Holy Spirit, given to me to teach me, convict me of sin, and to comfort me during times of suffering. Thank You that Your Word is full of wisdom for me. In Jesus' name, amen.

DAY 55

A DISCIPLINED SPIRIT

Get rid of all bitterness, rage and anger, brawling and slander, along with every form of malice.

EPHESIANS 4:31

We live in a world that seems to be overwhelmed with anger. We see on the news reports from every community and country that people are becoming enraged and even violent over insignificant things. Parents punish their children in unspeakable ways over normal childhood behavior. Road rage is responsible for serious accidents and even fatalities. Domestic violence exists behind the closed doors of many relationships. Teenagers are shot dead over athletic shoes. God has given us the ability to feel anger, but our lives should not be controlled or dominated by it, whether it's ours or someone else's. There is a context in which it's appropriate and ways of expressing it that are helpful, and there also are contexts in which it is not appropriate and ways of expressing it that are destructive. We've been given the responsibility of making those decisions in a mature and godly way.

• THINK ABOUT IT •

Do you sometimes erupt with anger over things that other people seem to handle calmly? Ask the Lord for a disciplined spirit to help you channel your emotions in a way that is not damaging to others. He will give you a freedom from anger that you did not know was possible.

Prayer

Heavenly Father, I am thankful You have provided a way for me to live a disciplined life controlled by Your Holy Spirit. Help me cultivate the fruit of the Spirit in my life. Let love, joy, peace, patience, kindness, goodness, faithfulness, gentleness, and self-control grow daily in my heart. In Jesus' name, amen.

DAY 56

THE LION

His head and hair were white like wool, as white as snow, and his eyes were like blazing fire. His feet were like bronze glowing in a furnace, and his voice was like the sound of rushing waters. In his right hand he held seven stars, and out of his mouth came a sharp double-edged sword. His face was like the sun shining in all its brilliance.

REVELATION 1:14-16

When we say we believe Jesus Christ ascended into Heaven, it's a declaration of His position. He picked up the glory and honor and majesty that He laid aside when He came to the earth. I imagine that the limits of human language don't allow John to fully describe Jesus' magnificence, but he still gives us a marvelous presentation of the victorious Lord. This is the Jesus who is coming back to the earth. He's not coming back as a Suffering Servant or a Lamb silent before His shearers. When He comes back to the earth, He's coming as the Lion of the Tribe of Judah—the triumphant King and Judge of all humanity. Come, Lord Jesus!

• THINK ABOUT IT •

This image of Jesus is probably not the first one that comes to mind when you think about Him. But this is the same Jesus who died on the cross so that you could enter God's Kingdom—and this is the Jesus who will conquer Satan and banish him from our lives forever.

Prayer

Heavenly Father, I love You, and I want to please You in all I do, in all I am, and all I will ever be. I look at who You are and feel so unworthy. Today I choose You. I choose to turn from the spirit of the world and embrace Your purposes. Embolden me to be a powerful advocate for the Kingdom of God. Come quickly, Lord Jesus! Amen.

DAY 57

ALL REVEALED

You will be blessed in the city and blessed in the country.

DEUTERONOMY 28:3

In Deuteronomy 28 we read the blessings God will bestow on those who are obedient, and they are more than just rhetoric. When it says God will bless you in the city and in the country, it doesn't mean God will bless the urbanites and the rural folk. It means God is watching over our lives; He knows where we are, and His blessings are associated with the way we choose to live. We see people who lead deceptive, manipulative lives. They imagine that God can be mocked, that they have outsmarted Him. But the God we worship, the omniscient and omnipotent God of the universe, knows everything we think and do. Every one of us will have an appointment with Him someday. All will be revealed, and justice is coming. Let's honor the Lord with our lives so that we will be ready to meet Him with joyful anticipation.

• THINK ABOUT IT •

Do you live as if God is aware of your every thought and action?

Prayer

Heavenly Father, take my life for the purposes of Your Kingdom's work. Let courage arise within me to share Your love with the lost. Lord, go before me and prepare a path. May those who oppose Your purposes fail. Send a spirit of repentance for a new awakening in our nation and around the world. In Jesus' name, amen.

SOMETHING BETTER

A faithful man will be richly blessed. . . .

PROVERBS 28:20

God has a plan for our good. I don't know why, but I find that many of us have a perpetual struggle to believe this. We have this nagging sense that if we say yes to God without reservation we will forfeit something good—pleasure or freedom or opportunity or resources. We believe that we will be rewarded in eternity, but for now we worry that we will be denied something. This is not a biblical idea. In fact, the consistent message of Scripture is that God rewards our faithfulness and our trust in Him. This has certainly proven true in my life. When I've been willing to cooperate with God—even when I feel like I've sacrificed something to do it—He's always given me something better in return.

• THINK ABOUT IT •

Can you remember a time when you sacrificed something that seemed very important in order to cooperate with God? What were the results?

Prayer

Heavenly Father, Your faithfulness is promised to Your people through all generations. I recognize my hesitancy to believe that and quickly cooperate with You. Help me believe Your Word and accept Your invitations. I choose to become an encourager to those pursuing You. I want to honor You with my life and my resources. In Jesus' name, amen.

A SEASON OF PREPARATION

Endure hardship as discipline; God is treating you as sons. For what son is not disciplined by his father? . . . we have all had human fathers who disciplined us and we respected them for it.

HEBREWS 12:7, 9

My father believed in discipline. When I was in the midst of some disciplinary process, I never remember telling him, "This feels so just and appropriate. I want you to know how much I respect what you're doing." I respected it as I looked back on it later in my life, but I didn't respect it at the time. Discipline is never fun, whether we are children learning how to behave or adults learning how to relate to God. But we'll either be disciplined by God or we will forfeit the opportunities that are ahead of us, because we will need to be spiritually mature to thrive in the season to come, both as individuals and as the Church.

• THINK ABOUT IT •

Are you in a season where God is inviting you to greater maturity through discipline? Remember that He loves you as one of His children. Trust that He is preparing you for your future good.

Prayer

Heavenly Father, help me see that when You discipline me it is because I am Your child. Teach me to be still and know that You are God. I confess I often lose sight of You and become defensive. Instead, I long to let Your Holy Spirit turn my focus back to You as my Father. You care about me— You make all things work together for my good. In Jesus' name, amen.

IMAGE OF THE FATHER

"This, then, is how you should pray: 'Our Father in heaven, hallowed be your name. . . .'"

MATTHEW 6:9

The tone of our relationship with God is set very specifically with a word—He is our Father! When the disciples asked Jesus to teach them to pray, He taught them a prayer that has endured through the ages. He said to address God as "Our Father in heaven." It's a very significant understanding because God identifies with humanity in a very unique way. God is the template—the pattern—and we are created in His image. There's a spiritual genetic code that connects us to God and separates us from the rest of the created beings on the planet. He is our Father, and He doesn't relate to us as creatures; He relates to us as His children.

• THINK ABOUT IT •

We are not simply the highest rung on the evolutionary ladder; God created us in His image. What does it mean to you to be created in the image of God?

Prayer

Heavenly Father, even my earthly father taught me what was right and wrong in his eyes. You are my Heavenly Father who created all things and people for Your purposes. You created me in Your image. Deliver me from the plans of the evil one who would try to distort Your image, and be glorified in all my life. In Jesus' name, amen.

THE CHOICE IS YOURS

This day I call heaven and earth as witnesses against you that I have set before you life and death, blessings and curses. Now choose life, so that you and your children may live and that you may love the LORD your God, listen to his voice, and hold fast to him.

DEUTERONOMY 30:19-20

Moses is calling the people of Israel to account for their choices. Reminding them of God's provision in their lives, he is now asking them to consider what their personal response to God will be. This is extraordinarily important. Your responses to God's invitations cannot be pushed aside because of other people. They are not group choices; they are personal—yours alone. When your appointment with Almighty God arrives, it will not help to say, "I would have chosen You more fully, but my wife had a bad church experience growing up and she can't get over it." Or, "I would have been a more godly person, but my husband wasn't into the church thing and wouldn't go with me." Or, "I would have been a better Christ-follower, but my pastor was a lousy preacher." We find a myriad of reasons to exempt ourselves, but the reality is He has given us the privilege of freedom. Blessings or curses: The choice is ours.

• THINK ABOUT IT •

Have you overcome external reasons in order to choose God in your life? How has that influenced your relationship with the Lord?

Prayer

Heavenly Father, I have seen Your love and experienced Your faithfulness. I am guilty of being a rebel in much of my life. I choose to obey You rather than find my own way down the path before me. Forgive me for not seeking You with my whole heart. Your ways are greater than mine, and I choose You. Help me listen to Your voice. In Jesus' name, amen.

LIFE INTERRUPTED

Saul was still breathing out murderous threats against the Lord's disciples. He went to the high priest and asked him for letters to the synagogues in Damascus, so that if he found any there who belonged to the Way. . . he might take them as prisoners to Jerusalem. As he neared Damascus. . . suddenly a light from heaven flashed around him. He fell to the ground and heard a voice say to him, "Saul, Saul, why do you persecute me?" "Who are you, Lord?" Saul asked. "I am Jesus, whom you are persecuting," he replied.

ACTS 9:1-5

Saul, an educated Jewish Pharisee, had earned favor with the Jerusalem leaders and was fast-tracking his career. He was so successfully persecuting Jesus-followers that they commissioned him to Damascus. Then Saul met Jesus in a defining, abrupt, and uninvited moment—a complete redirection. When God invites you into His plans, changes may come, relationships may be realigned. There may be a sense that your time and energy have been wasted. Your life may bear different fruit than what you thought it would. I'm thankful that God is still interrupting us, still giving assignments, and still inviting us to make sacrifices for His Kingdom purposes. However disruptive those invitations may seem, we will be blessed if we say yes to them.

• THINK ABOUT IT •

Have you given God permission to interrupt your plans? Do you have an imagination of how He might use you for His purposes if you did?

Prayer

Heavenly Father, give me wisdom to follow You only. Thank You for the truth of Your Word. May Your Holy Spirit help me align my perspective to Yours and see Your invitations as opportunities that will bear good fruit, even when they bring change to my life. Remove the fear of change from my heart, and help me to trust You completely. In Jesus' name, amen.

TRANSFORMATIONAL READING

For everything that was written in the past was written to teach us, so that through endurance and the encouragement of the Scriptures we might have hope.

ROMANS 15:4

People think of the Bible in many ways. Some of us simply think of the Bible as a place to record our family's births and deaths and marriages. Others of us actually do respect the Bible as an important theological work that's worth reading, but consider it mainly a reference book from which we can glean historical information or construct a doctrinal viewpoint. That understanding is not wrong; it's just incomplete. It would be like a starving man reading a cookbook: it's not completely pointless, but it certainly won't nourish him. The point of reading the Bible is transformation. It teaches us endurance and gives us encouragement so that we can have hope for the future. The Bible was written long ago, but it is completely relevant for you and me. If we will open our hearts to it, it will bring significant change to our lives.

• THINK ABOUT IT •

How do you think of the Bible? How have you allowed it to impact your life?

Prayer

Heavenly Father, I thank You for Your Word. Thank You for the writers who were inspired by the Holy Spirit to record it so that every generation could better know You and follow You. My Bible is "a lamp unto my feet and a light unto my path." Help me to be an ambassador for the Kingdom of God by putting Your words into my heart. In Jesus' name, amen.

THE BATTLE IS HIS

"This is what the LORD says to you: 'Do not be afraid or discouraged because of this vast army. For the battle is not yours, but God's.'"

2 CHRONICLES 20:15

This verse is part of a marvelous account of God's deliverance. When King Jehoshaphat found his nation surrounded by enemies intent on war, he called for prayer and fasting. The Spirit of God gave this proclamation to one of the priests, and the people were moved to worship. They gave the battle to God, and the result was an astounding victory that could only be attributed to His intervention. In recent years the Church in our nation has been a bit intimidated. We have seen the vast army standing in opposition to God's purposes, and we have been reluctant to rise up and speak the truth. It is time for the Church to seek God's help, for the battle is His, and then engage our culture with the love of Christ.

• THINK ABOUT IT •

Most of us do not have a national platform to influence the culture—we do it one conversation at a time. What opportunities do you have to influence our culture for Christ?

Prayer

Heavenly Father, just as Your servant, Jehoshaphat, found himself surrounded by enemies, I often find myself surrounded with threats of failure and condemnation. No matter what I face, I choose to believe what Your Word says, "Do not be afraid or discouraged because of this vast army. For the battle is not yours, but God's." In Jesus' name, amen.

DAY 65

A REAL CONVERSATION

"Those whom I love I rebuke and discipline. So be earnest, and repent. Here I am! I stand at the door and knock. If anyone hears my voice and opens the door, I will come in and eat with him, and he with me."

REVELATION 3:19-20

My grandparents had a painting of Jesus standing at a door knocking. I always understood it to be evangelistic—open the door and let Him in and become a Christ-follower. But that is not the context. The scripture is written to the Laodicean church about God disciplining lukewarm faith. He wants to have a close, personal relationship and be a welcomed friend at our meal table for real conversation about our triumphs and troubles. What are you going to do with that? We have repented, believed, and accepted Jesus as Lord of our lives. But many of us have put that experience in a trophy case on the mantle with the homerun ball we hit in high school. We walk past it, recollecting: "It was November 12th of my junior year. Yep, that was the day I repented." The truth is that repentance is an important tool for a Christ-follower's journey, and we need to keep it close at hand. God loves us enough to correct us, and our appropriate response is repentance.

• THINK ABOUT IT •

Have there been times when you have experienced God's discipline? Were you quick or reluctant to repent? How did it change you?

Prayer

Heavenly Father, I desire to be Your child and You to be my Father, which requires trusting You. When You correct me, I will listen, agree with You, and change course. Give me ears to hear, eyes to see, and Your Holy Spirit to reveal my harmful ways that I might walk in obedience. May my choices always bring glory to Jesus. In Jesus' name, amen.

PREVIEW OF COMING EVENTS

By faith Noah, being warned by God about things not yet seen, in reverence prepared an ark for the salvation of his household....

HEBREWS 11:7 • NASB®

God, in His mercy and grace, gives us previews into what is coming. Why did Noah build a boat? It wasn't because he saw a storm system on the radar or because his boys liked to ski. He built a boat because God told him there was a flood coming. But he didn't build his ark out by the dock—he built it in the middle of a field. God gave Noah insight so that he could make choices to keep his family safe. God still does that. Proverbs tells us the outcome of life choices so we can decide what to do. Revelation gives a vivid picture of what the future holds for those who choose Jesus and those who don't. We don't have to wander through life aimlessly, wondering what the outcome will be. God gives us previews—if we will choose to pay attention.

• THINK ABOUT IT •

How have God's previews influenced your life choices? Have you ever ignored His messages and suffered the consequences?

Prayer

Heavenly Father, I am so thankful for Your loving care through the warnings You give Your people. I put my trust in You alone. You have given me Your Word and Your Holy Spirit to teach and guide me. I am equipped for everything I need for the coming days. I submit myself to Your purposes, and thank You for Your protection. In Jesus' name, amen.

DAY 67

SHORT SHELF LIFE

"In your anger do not sin": Do not let the sun go down while you are still angry, and do not give the devil a foothold.

EPHESIANS 4:26-27

It is clear from this verse that it is possible to recognize anger and use the opportunity to minimize Satan's influence in our lives. God created us with the capacity for anger, and some things should make us angry. Sometimes we become angry over matters that don't merit such a strong response, and we should learn to ask the Holy Spirit for an extra measure of self-control in those instances. But in all instances of anger, the counsel is, don't sin. The great news about anger is that it has a short shelf life. Since you are to "not let the sun go down while you are angry," if you time it just right you can get almost twenty-four hours out of it, but that's the most. If you hold onto it longer than that, you give Satan an entry point into your life.

• THINK ABOUT IT •

Are you slow to anger? Or are you known for your quick temper or your ability to hold a grudge? Ask the Lord to show you when and how to express your anger appropriately.

Prayer

Heavenly Father, forgive me for the times I have given place to Your enemy through undisciplined emotion or unresolved anger. Help me cultivate the gentleness and self-control that comes from Your Spirit. Thank You for Your forgiveness, and remind me to forgive others daily when I have been hurt. In Jesus' name, amen.

INTENTIONAL PRAISE

Praise the LORD, O my soul; all my inmost being, praise his holy name. Praise the LORD, O my soul, and forget not all his benefits—who forgives all your sins and heals all your diseases, who redeems your life from the pit and crowns you with love and compassion, who satisfies your desires with good things so that your youth is renewed like the eagle's.

PSALM 103:1-5

Humans tend to blame God for not paying attention when we are going through something difficult. But when things are going well we'll take the credit for our brilliance and hard work. We need to be reminded that we lead our lives under the authority and blessing of Almighty God, because it doesn't take much to cause us to forget. Let's be intentional about thanking God for His involvement in our lives. Let's make an effort to remember the specific times and ways He has acted on our behalf, because we are prone to let our God-experiences slip into the hazy past of our memories. Let's not forget the many benefits of being the children of Almighty God.

• THINK ABOUT IT •

Are you intentional about remembering the ways God has provided for you and thanking Him for them? Do you tell others about the ways He is at work in your life?

Prayer

Heavenly Father, I acknowledge all Your benefits. Through the cross I have complete forgiveness for my sins and healing from all disease. You have redeemed my life from destruction. You have crowned me with love and compassion, and You satisfy my life with good things. Thank You for all the ways You have enriched my days. In Jesus' name, amen.

DAY 69

FREEDOM FROM SHAME

I thank Christ Jesus our Lord, who has given me strength, that he considered me faithful, appointing me to his service. Even though I was once a blasphemer and a persecutor and a violent man, I was shown mercy. . . .

1 TIMOTHY 1:12-13

Paul wrote two letters to Timothy, his young protégé, and both include a good deal of emotion. Paul was an unwavering evangelist whose influence continues until today. But prior to that he had been Saul of Tarsus, fully invested in defending the religious establishment. He had been there when Stephen was murdered because of his advocacy for Jesus. He was so energized by that event that he began to systematically destroy the Church in Jerusalem. Then, on the road to Damascus, he met Jesus. Now years later, he's writing from a prison cell and says, "Timothy, you know the truth. I was a blasphemer, a persecutor, and a violent man." Don't you imagine that Paul went through a period of soul-searching and regret? But God allowed him to find freedom from shame, and he went on to have a great impact in the Kingdom of God.

• THINK ABOUT IT •

All of us have done things we are ashamed of, but God does not want us to live in bondage to shame. Have you repented of those deeds and given your past to God?

Prayer

Heavenly Father, I need a Savior. My heart is rebellious by nature. Thank You for paying the price for my rebelliousness on the cross. Grant me a submissive, repentant heart like Paul displayed when he met Jesus on the Damascus Road. You are my refuge and fortress—the One who delivers me from all shame and guilt. In Jesus' name, amen.

DETOURS AND U-TURNS

God wanted to make the unchanging nature of his purpose very clear to the heirs of what was promised. . . .

HEBREWS 6:17

Do you know God has a purpose for your life and mine? The Bible says that even before we were born, God ordered our days. His purpose for us does not change, even when we get off the road and take a detour. That's a polite way of saying it, isn't it? You may be thinking, "I had more than a detour. I got lost in the desert for a while." But the remarkable thing about the grace and love and power of God is that He can restore and redeem and renew no matter how far we have strayed. One of the things that transforms our relationship with the Lord is having the confidence to come to God when we need Him. We need Him the most when we have walked away from Him. When you think you have done all the wrong things, even when you feel very far away from Him, say, "God, I need Your help. I want to come back to You. I want to fulfill Your purpose for me." He'll be there waiting for you.

• THINK ABOUT IT •

Have you ever taken a detour away from God and His purpose for your life? What caused you to seek Him and return to Him? What was the result?

Prayer

Heavenly Father, I am deeply grateful for Your grace and love—thank You for revealing Your purposes for my life. I need Your help and forgiveness today. All my confidence is in You. Whenever I stray, You are faithful to turn me back and give me true restoration. May my life be used to serve You and Your people. In Jesus' name, amen.

DAY 71

QUARRY STONES

"Listen to me, you who pursue righteousness and who seek the LORD: Look to the rock from which you were cut and to the quarry from which you were hewn; look to Abraham, your father, and to Sarah, who gave you birth. When I called him he was but one, and I blessed him and made him many."

ISAIAH 51:1-2

A rock quarry is an interesting thing. The earth's surface is stripped away to reveal different kinds of stone in different parts of the world. Pink limestone from Tennessee was used in the construction of the U.S. Capitol. Michelangelo used marble from Carrera, Italy, to create his statue of David. Stone from those regions is still used to make beautiful things today. But no matter where the stone ends up, it retains its heritage; it is always from the quarry where it was cut. God's people are like those stones. The Israelites needed to be reminded of their lineage through the faithfulness of Abraham and Sarah. We need to be reminded that God has taken the rough stones of our sinful nature and molded each of us into a beautiful creation that reflects His glory.

• THINK ABOUT IT •

Do you struggle with believing your identity as a child of God? Remember what you were . . . and who you are today.

Prayer

Heavenly Father, all glory, honor, and praise are Yours. You called me from a life of sin to be Your own child. You have set me in a place of service and helped me prosper spiritually. Help me continually remember who I am in You through the cross. Awaken me to all I have, and use my life to serve You and encourage others. In Jesus' name, amen.

TRUTH, LOVE, AND CONSEQUENCES

God "will give to each person according to what he has done." To those who by persistence in doing good seek glory, honor and immortality, he will give eternal life. But for those who are self-seeking and who reject the truth and follow evil, there will be wrath and anger.

ROMANS 2:6-8

Scripture clearly teaches God gives us choices—choices with consequences. The most important one we will ever make is to choose Jesus and live, or reject Him and face death. That is not a popular notion in contemporary Christendom. It's not uncommon to hear people say, "Christianity is just love. Jesus said to love everybody." There is truth in that, but not the whole truth. God is a God of love, and Jesus did say we should love one another. But loving doesn't mean you affirm all behavior and action. Jesus did not do that. He often disagreed forcefully with religious leaders. So it's not the whole truth to say the message of the New Testament is "Whatever you want to do is fine as long as you love people." We should search hard for the truth, because our choices have consequences. God, who judges rightly, "will give to each person according to what he has done."

• THINK ABOUT IT •

Do you have friends or family who misconstrue the truth that "God is love"? How do you respond to them?

Prayer

Heavenly Father, You reveal Your truth through Your Word and Holy Spirit. I want to know Your character and become persistent in pleasing and honoring You. Help me recognize Your discipline redirects me toward a more abundant and fully yielded life. May I display Your character to others that they also might trust in You. In Jesus' name, amen.

DAY 73

RESCUED

For he has rescued us from the dominion of darkness and brought us into the kingdom of the Son he loves, in whom we have redemption, the forgiveness of sins.

COLOSSIANS 1:13-14

A serious fisherman friend of mine was far into the Gulf of Mexico when he saw something odd—a man in the water. His boat had capsized and his companion drowned. He had been in the water for hours and given up hope of rescue. When my friend pulled him out of the water, the man was emotionally undone at his rescue! When Scripture says God rescues us, that image holds. When God pulled you out of the kingdom of darkness, you were hopelessly "lost at sea." You could do nothing to pull yourself out of that predicament. The assets we typically depend on will not always deliver us; that's what makes salvation remarkable. There is a power at work on our behalf that does something for us we could never do for ourselves. That is the grace of God.

· THINK ABOUT IT ·

The Bible says salvation is only found through Jesus of Nazareth: We believe He is the Christ, accept Him as Lord, and serve Him as King. The Bible says believing that in your heart and confessing it with your mouth brings salvation. If you have not made that confession, consider doing it now. If you have, rejoice in the fullness of your salvation.

Prayer

Heavenly Father, thank You for Your faithfulness to every generation. I believe in the power and strength You revealed through the cross of Jesus. If there is any doubt in me, I ask You to forgive me and help transform my doubt into trust-filled belief. I trust Your Word is true, and I trust You to provide all I need to endure. In Jesus' name, amen.

IN FOR ROUTINE SERVICE

Humility and the fear of the LORD bring wealth and honor and life.

PROVERBS 22:4

Humility is hard-won for many people, but here are some behaviors that can encourage it to emerge in even the most prideful among us. Serve someone. I don't mean casual, random, and occasional service; I mean making routine commitments to serve other people. Share power in places where you have influence and authority; invite other people into the decision-making process, and respect their right to be there. Be quietly generous. God will show you when and how. Share credit. Acknowledge and celebrate the contributions of other people. Find opportunities to praise people for the hard work they do. These are just a few ways to foster a humble spirit, and they will require some intentionality. But if you can achieve true humility and fear the Lord, the rewards are worth your efforts: wealth and honor and life.

· THINK ABOUT IT ·

If you struggle with a prideful spirit, consider how you might incorporate one of these behaviors into your normal routine.

Prayer

Heavenly Father, genuine humility does not easily come. I choose to purposefully humble myself before You that I might hear Your voice more clearly in this season. Help me submit to Your Word and cultivate a true reverence for You. I love You, Lord, and I need Your Holy Spirit to help me understand my place in Your purposes. In Jesus' name, amen.

DAY 75

DAILY ROUTINES – AMAZING OPPORTUNITIES

"'In the last days, God says, I will pour out my Spirit on all people.'"

ACTS 2:17

Prior to the redemptive work of Jesus, the Spirit of God was visited upon individuals temporarily at various places and times. For example, Scripture says that the Spirit of God would come on Samson and he would have tremendous strength. But here Peter, speaking on the Day of Pentecost, said, "What you're watching today in Jerusalem is evidence of what the prophet Joel said a hundred years ago: God will pour out His Spirit on all flesh in the last days." Here's my suggestion: Learn to recognize and respond to the promptings of the Holy Spirit. Determine in your heart to be fully yielded to His work in your life. Don't draw boundaries and say, "I'm not going to be one of those people!" Cooperate with the Spirit of God. His is the greatest power available for the transformation of a human life.

• THINK ABOUT IT •

Do you prefer to keep the Holy Spirit contained, or is He allowed to work freely in your life? How might you make Him more welcome?

Prayer

Heavenly Father, thank You for caring for me—Your faithfulness encourages me to trust Your promises. Thank You for Your Holy Spirit and that in seeking You, I find Him helping me daily. I want to fully embrace Him, allowing Him to teach me Your ways. May daily routines become amazing opportunities as I yield to His guidance. In Jesus' name, amen.

IT TAKES A COMMUNITY

Until we all reach unity in the faith and in the knowledge of the Son of God and become mature, attaining to the whole measure of the fullness of Christ.

EPHESIANS 4:13

I frequently hear, "I don't have to sit in church to be a Christian." I agree. The decision to follow Christ is an intensely personal choice. Location is not important; you can become a Christ-follower in the grocery store parking lot or at forty thousand feet. But the notion in Scripture is that we need each other to grow up as believers. Needing other people makes many of us uneasy, because we are proud and independent people. Americans were saying "I'll do it my way" before Frank Sinatra sang it. But one of the signs that we are maturing as Christ-followers is when we are willing to invest ourselves in being a part of a faith community. It's often trying and frequently disappointing. But in the process of learning to live in unity as the Body of Christ, the Spirit of God enables us to grow up.

• THINK ABOUT IT •

If you are invested in a community of faith, how has that helped you grow toward spiritual maturity? How have others been able to invest in you? How have you been able to invest in others?

Prayer

Heavenly Father, I want to please You and love Your people as You do. Increase my faith so that Your perspective becomes my first priority. May my investment in You and Your people be so obvious that all who know me will understand pleasing You is my greatest aim. Thank You for Your Church and all of the ministries it provides. In Jesus' name, amen.

ABOVE THE CIRCUMSTANCES

Then the king ordered Ashpenaz. . . to bring in some of the Israelites from the royal family and the nobility—young men without any physical defect, handsome, showing aptitude for every kind of learning, well informed, quick to understand, and qualified to serve in the king's palace. . . . They were to be trained for three years, and after that they were to enter the king's service. Among these were some from Judah: Daniel, Hananiah, Mishael and Azariah.

DANIEL 1:3-6

God used Daniel in extraordinary ways, but he was a slave most of his life. Even though taken captive as a young man, Daniel rose to great power in a foreign king's court. Six centuries before the birth of Jesus, God gave Daniel revelations we still read today to understand the seasons ahead. Daniel could have spent his life filled with resentment, but instead he chose to honor the Lord where he was. Injustice will come to our lives too. It will leave a mark, but it does not have the power to rob us of God's purposes. Say to the Lord, "I will honor You in this place," and He will bring you opportunities, even in the midst of difficult circumstances.

• THINK ABOUT IT •

Has the sting of injustice touched your life? How did the Lord change you and use you through that situation?

Prayer

Heavenly Father, I am so thankful You saved me out of a life of self-centeredness and into a life as Your child—from a past of godless pursuits to a future in eternity with You. Your Word says that I am not my own but I have been "purchased with a price"—the blood of Jesus. I want to honor You with my body and my life. In Jesus' name, amen.

SEEKING FAVOR

When Pilate saw that he was getting nowhere, but that instead an uproar was starting, he took water and washed his hands in front of the crowd. "I am innocent of this man's blood," he said. "It is your responsibility!"

MATTHEW 27:24

Pilate was Roman governor of Judea. Jerusalem's Jewish religious leaders were jealous of Jesus and His evident spiritual authority. So they falsified charges against Him and had Him arrested, hoping for His execution. Pilate knew Jesus was innocent of the charges. But to successfully govern the city, he needed the people's allegiance, so he did the politically expedient thing—condemning an innocent man. Think about the opportunity that Pilate was given. God's Son was standing before him, telling him the truth about His Kingdom. Pilate could have fallen to his knees and said, "I want to be a part of that." Instead he chose the approval of man and the status quo. We each have to make our own decisions about Jesus. Do we seek the favor of a mocking crowd, or do we acknowledge the truth we know about Him? I hope you'll choose to honor Jesus.

• THINK ABOUT IT •

Imagine what will occur when the roles are reversed and Pilate stands before Almighty God to be judged. Have you made any of Pilate's arguments to yourself, or do you consistently honor Jesus publicly?

Prayer

Heavenly Father, forgive me for when I have chosen man's approval over Yours. Please give me courage to stand before all—dignitaries and kings or neighbors and relatives—to proclaim Your work in my life. Help me set priorities that reflect the relationship I say I have with You. Protect my mind and my heart from any deception. In Jesus' name, amen.

LIKE THE WIND

"The wind blows wherever it pleases. You hear its sound, but you cannot tell where it comes from or where it is going. So it is with everyone born of the Spirit."

JOHN 3:8

A Jewish ruler, Nicodemus, had secretly come to ask Jesus questions about the Kingdom of God. He was a Pharisee, and his life revolved around observing every detail of the Law. That, in addition to his Jewish heritage, should have secured his place in God's Kingdom, he thought. But he knew something was different about Jesus and the authority He demonstrated. Jesus told him that His Kingdom is invisible, like the wind, and reaches beyond any boundary or set of rules man can devise. But that invisible Kingdom has a very visible impact on our lives. Like the wind, we cannot see it but we can feel it and see how it is transforming our thoughts, desires, and habits. When we cooperate with the Spirit of God, He brings a liberty and freedom to us that can come no other way. Those who stand outside God's Kingdom cannot see it, and they may be suspicious of you. That's okay. Keep inviting them in. Everyone is welcome.

• THINK ABOUT IT •

No one will be excluded from the Kingdom of God except by their own decision. If you were asked by an unbelieving friend to describe the Kingdom of God, how would you do that?

Prayer

Heavenly Father, today is the day the Lord has made, and I choose to be thankful in it. My joy comes from You dwelling inside me through the cross. I know the Kingdom of God is in me, and I am a child of the King. When I face trials and challenges, may I turn my eyes toward the promises extended to those who belong to You. In Jesus' name, amen.

LIFEBOAT OR FOUNDATION

This is what the Sovereign LORD says: "See, I lay a stone in Zion, a tested stone, a precious cornerstone for a sure foundation; the one who trusts will never be dismayed."

ISAIAH 28:16

Do you think of Jesus as your lifeboat or your foundation? Do you live by the saying, "When all else fails, pray"? Or is He your first priority— the One you seek to please with your words and actions? If you don't know how to answer these questions, look at your spending and your calendar—they will give you away. Let me recommend to you that you look to Him as your foundation. A lifeboat will sink if it is overloaded or if it encounters something unseen in the water. You are far more likely to withstand the hardships and storms of life when you build on Jesus, "a tested stone, a precious cornerstone for a sure foundation."

• THINK ABOUT IT •

Do your spending and your calendar reflect Jesus as your lifeboat or your foundation? What can you do to make sure your life is built on the bedrock of a relationship with Him?

Prayer

Heavenly Father, I am thankful You allow me to call upon You, and You hear and answer my prayers. I believe my life-storms must submit to You. I believe You can heal bodies. I believe You can restore marriages and families. Your power and possibilities are beyond imagination—help me to seek Your will and purposes in all things. In Jesus' name, amen.

WHEN DISCIPLINE SHOWS UP

"My son, do not make light of the Lord's discipline, and do not lose heart when he rebukes you, because the Lord disciplines those he loves, and he punishes everyone he accepts as a son."

HEBREWS 12:5-6

I have discovered that God's discipline in my life is not typically administered by unseen things or circumstances. His discipline shows up in my life with skin on it. God uses people in my life who are not even aware that they're being used for His purposes. They are coworkers or family members or other people I interact with in some way. Something happens that exposes an aspect of my character or my behavior, and it's obvious that God is asking me to change. When this happens my first reactions are usually frustration and resentment, sometimes followed by anger. But God is saying to me, "Hold on, Allen. That's Me working on you. I'm doing it because I love you."

• THINK ABOUT IT •

What is your reaction when God's discipline in your life shows up with skin on? Do you become discouraged and resentful? Or do you ask God to show you how He wants you to change?

Prayer

Heavenly Father, I want to be obedient, but sometimes do a poor job of submitting. Forgive me for when I have been lazy and taken Your grace for granted. I know that, because of Your love for me, You will discipline me. You are God, and I trust Your judgment about when I need Your correction. Thank You for never giving up on me. In Jesus' name, amen.

INSIDE OUT

The fruit of the Spirit is love, joy, peace, patience, kindness, goodness, faithfulness, gentleness and self-control. Against such things there is no law. Those who belong to Christ Jesus have crucified the sinful nature with its passions and desires. Since we live by the Spirit, let us keep in step with the Spirit.

GALATIANS 5:22-25

When God's Spirit is given residence in our lives, these characteristics will begin to emerge. We can't get these things by taking a pill. Wouldn't you like to get a pill of patience? Or jump out of bed in the morning and take a joy capsule? "I'm feeling a little blue. I think I'll take two." We can't medicate our way to peace, though many people try—with pharmaceuticals, with spending, with chasing after pleasure. These qualities come from within us when we participate in the eternal Kingdom of our God. They do not come easily or automatically, because we must crucify our sinful nature. It is not just swept away from us; we have to continually tell it, "You are not welcome here!" Jesus taught this over and over again when He was here. He kept saying, "A godly life starts on the inside."

• THINK ABOUT IT •

Do you think of spiritual transformation as an outside-in process or an inside-out process? How do you crucify your own sinful nature?

Prayer

Heavenly Father, I desire to please You above all else, but my mind gets in the way, and my body rebels. I want to be a person increasingly yielded to Your Holy Spirit, allowing Him to change me inside. I confess my words often reveal the darkness in my heart. Teach me to let the Word of God grow the fruit of the Spirit in me. In Jesus' name, amen.

DAY 83

A VITAL OUTCOME

I have chosen the way of truth; I have set my heart on your laws. I hold fast to your statutes, O LORD; do not let me be put to shame. I run in the path of your commands, for you have set my heart free.

PSALM 119:30-32

It is improbable that you will be very successful at running life's race unless you intend for that to happen. Olympic runners do not tell reporters, "I've always thought this event looked like fun, so a couple of weeks ago I decided to try it." They say, "I've invested years of my life in preparing for this event." The outcome is too important for them to leave anything to chance, so they make great personal sacrifices to do what is necessary to compete at that level. Let's be just as intentional about running our race toward spiritual maturity. Let's make daily choices to be faithful. Let's set our hearts on His commands and hold fast to what we know is the right way to live, even when it feels like we are sacrificing something that might bring us momentary pleasure. When we seek the guidance of the Holy Spirit, He will help us run our race in a manner that honors the Lord.

• THINK ABOUT IT •

Are you intentionally seeking and running on a path that will honor the Lord? What can you do to be more purposeful in your quest toward spiritual maturity?

Prayer

Heavenly Father, Your mercies are new each morning, helping me experience Your love and forgiveness as I read Your Word. It washes and renews my mind, bringing transformation. Help me seek You with greater intentionality. I trust You to lead me toward maturity in Jesus Christ as I practice a daily relationship with You. In Jesus' name, amen.

SPECIFIC PLACES, SPECIFIC THINGS, SPECIFIC PURPOSES

"Last night an angel of the God whose I am and whom I serve stood beside me and said, 'Do not be afraid, Paul. You must stand trial before Caesar; and God has graciously given you the lives of all who sail with you.' So keep up your courage, men, for I have faith in God that it will happen just as he told me."

ACTS 27:23-25

Paul is sailing to Rome for trial after arrest in Jerusalem on false charges. En route his ship is caught in a storm, and the sailors fear destruction. But an angel assures Paul the ship will arrive safely, as he must stand trial in Rome. Had I written the story, I would have solved everything in Jerusalem to avoid all the drama. But God needed Paul in Rome and others to learn about Him along the way. Sometimes circumstances overwhelm us, and we opt out of God's plan. But the Bible reveals we are needed in specific places to do specific things to fulfill God's specific purposes. When you are in circumstances that you neither like nor choose, don't give up. Remember God's people make a difference in the world, and He has a plan and purpose for your life.

• THINK ABOUT IT •

Have there been times when God put you in a situation that you did not choose and could not understand? How did God use you in that place?

Prayer

Heavenly Father, I want to please You. Give me increasing faith, Lord, that always puts Your perspective ahead of my own. May my faith in You be obvious, so that all who know me will see that pleasing You is my greatest aim. Use me in my difficulties to honor You. In Jesus' name, amen.

OUTSIDE THE COMFORT ZONE

I have been in danger from rivers, in danger from bandits, in danger from my own countrymen, in danger from Gentiles; in danger in the city, in danger in the country, in danger at sea; and in danger from false brothers.

2 CORINTHIANS 11:26

It's a sobering comparison for anyone, especially a pastor, to put their ministry efforts up against those of Paul, who was arguably the greatest advocate for Christianity the world will ever know. He experienced deprivation and danger at every turn, yet he never stopped telling people about the salvation found only in Jesus of Nazareth. When we are thinking about stepping outside our comfort zone to do something for God, we often wonder, "How will God provide? How exposed will I feel? Will the results be worth it? Maybe I should just stay quiet and stay behind. It seems like a safer option." If you have ever said yes to the Lord and responded to His invitation, you have discovered the truth of the paradox that Paul experienced daily: we experience the greatest security when we dare to step out and follow God. I believe that, and it enables me to overcome my sense of vulnerability and say yes to the Lord.

• THINK ABOUT IT •

Has there been a time when you stepped out of your comfort zone to do something for God? How was your life changed?

Prayer

Heavenly Father, many times my life looks and feels like a crisis in motion. Those are the times when I need You the most. Please forgive me when I fall into worry and my emotions give way to stress. Strengthen me to give You my best, both in and out of my comfort zones. In Jesus' name, amen.

THE STRENGTH OF PATIENCE

Better a patient man than a warrior, a man who controls his temper than one who takes a city.

PROVERBS 16:32

The Bible says there is strength in patience. That is difficult for many of us to understand. We have learned to intimidate and manipulate and use the force of our will to get our way. Some of us have adopted anger as a tool to get things done at work or at home or on the playing field. But this Scripture says that expressing anger is not as effective as showing patience; that we have forfeited a great deal if we have learned to get our way with anger, because there is much that will not come to us that way. There is a strength that will be demonstrated in our lives if we will dare to believe what God has said and choose patience.

· THINK ABOUT IT ·

Does patience come easily to you, or are you tempted to manipulate through anger or the force of your will? How can you show more patience in your interactions each day?

Prayer

Heavenly Father, You have been amazingly patient and longsuffering as You waited on my response to Your invitations. I want to be a person who is lovingly patient with others while they are on this journey with me. When people are unkind or fall short, give me a godly response so that my life will resemble Your character and ways. In Jesus' name, amen.

WOBBLY KNEES

Without faith it is impossible to please God, because anyone who comes to him must believe that he exists and that he rewards those who earnestly seek him.

HEBREWS 11:6

As I reflect back on my life, I can see that I have never made a significant decision about following God with a sense of bold abandon. I have made every one of those God-choices with wobbly knees and a racing heart. The situation has seldom played out like I imagined it would, but in hindsight I can see that God has been more than faithful. He will be faithful to you too when you seek Him earnestly. You can trust Him. He is a God who fulfills His promises, and He will continue to do so. One day you will stand before Him and account for your choices. You will grieve every place you failed to trust Him, and you will celebrate every place you did.

· THINK ABOUT IT ·

What significant decisions have you placed in God's hands, even with wobbly knees and a racing heart? How has He been faithful to your trust in Him?

Prayer

Heavenly Father, You have invited me toward significant opportunities to submit to Your plan and accomplish things that will strengthen Your Kingdom. When I am afraid of these challenges and hold back, help me to trust You with my whole heart and step forward. You always encourage me and increase my potential when I lean on You. In Jesus' name, amen.

WORSHIP RESTORES

And we rejoice in the hope of the glory of God.

ROMANS 5:2

On the days when challenging circumstances are whirling around me, I immediately begin to feel better when I start to worship the Lord. For me, worship includes reflecting on the things He has done for me. No matter what any one of us is going through, there are plenty of things for us to celebrate: The Almighty God of the universe loves us and calls us His children. He has created a beautiful and amazing world for us to live in. He has a plan and purpose for our lives. He has blessed us with family and friends who love us and care about our well-being. He provides for our needs, and He has given us hope for the future, both in time and eternity, where we will experience the glory of God in its fullness. I'm feeling better, aren't you?

• THINK ABOUT IT •

What are you rejoicing in today? Think of the ways God has blessed you and what the future holds for you, then thank Him for His abundant provision in your life.

Prayer

Heavenly Father, thank You for creating safe places to worship You. Expressing adoration for You matures me spiritually—laying down self-interest and picking up rejoicing, praise, and worship. I do worship You, Father God, and adore You, Jesus Christ, my Lord and Savior. All glory and honor be Yours forever and ever. In Jesus' name, amen.

DAY 89

ASSUMING THE RISK, REAPING THE REWARD

In Damascus there was a disciple named Ananias. The Lord called to him in a vision, "Ananias. . . Go to the house of Judas on Straight Street and ask for a man from Tarsus named Saul, for he is praying. In a vision he has seen a man named Ananias come and place his hands on him to restore his sight." "Lord," Ananias answered, "I have heard many reports about this man and all the harm he has done to your saints in Jerusalem. And he has come here with authority from the chief priests to arrest all who call on your name." But the Lord said to Ananias, "Go!" . . . Then Ananias went to the house and entered it.

ACTS 9:10-15, 17

The Lord sent Ananias to find Saul to prepare him for His purposes. Ananias responded with Saul's resume: "Lord, Saul is a really bad man, putting folks like me in prison. Cold calling him to talk about Jesus might not be a good idea right now." Ananias understood following God's instructions put him at risk. That is still true today. If risk means choosing to go where outcomes feel uncertain, I assure you there is a risk in saying yes to the Lord. If I sensed Him calling me, though, I hope I would step up and say a confident yes, because the benefits are far greater than any possible risk.

• THINK ABOUT IT •

Have you ever heard, or felt, God calling you to do a specific task that made you feel uncomfortable? How did you respond? What were the results?

Prayer

Heavenly Father, thank You for the privilege of being Your ambassador in the earth and inviting me to invest my strength and resources to pursue Your agenda. When You call me to an assignment, help me run with joy to accomplish it in the power of Your Holy Spirit. May my life bring glory to Jesus as Messiah and Lord. In Jesus' name, amen.

BOLD LIGHT

"If my people, who are called by my name, will humble themselves and pray and seek my face and turn from their wicked ways, then I will hear from heaven and will forgive their sin and will heal their land.

2 CHRONICLES 7:14

I'm weary of hearing Christians talk about the increase of wickedness and darkness and perversion and immorality and then point their fingers at all the people and institutions who are responsible for those things. The Bible says we are light in a dark world. So if the darkness is increasing, don't shake your fist at it. Say, "God, forgive me for not being a very bright light." "God, I've been too focused on getting other things done." "God, I haven't wanted to be called a fanatic." "God, forgive me for letting my pride stand in the way of Your purposes." "God, I see the outcome of not making Your priorities my priorities, and I am sorry. Forgive me. I repent." I believe with all my heart that if God's people will repent, the darkness around us will diminish. Repentance is a powerful force for good in the world.

• THINK ABOUT IT •

Does your light shine brightly for Jesus, or does your pride stand in the way? Think about ways you can be a bolder voice for Jesus in the world.

Prayer

Heavenly Father, thank You for discernment through Your Holy Spirit. Help me vigilantly guard my mind. Forgive me for grumbling about the season You have placed me in to serve You and Your people. Help me purify my thoughts and behaviors. May the words of my mouth and the meditation of my heart be pleasing to You. In the Jesus' name, amen.

CHOOSE FREEDOM

Pharaoh took his signet ring from his finger and put it on Joseph's finger. He dressed him in robes of fine linen and put a gold chain around his neck. He had him ride in a chariot as his second-in-command, and men shouted before him, "Make way!" Thus he put him in charge of the whole land of Egypt.

GENESIS 41:42-43

Teenage Joseph in Genesis 37 was his father's favorite son, and his jealous brothers sold him into slavery. When Genesis closes, he's the wealthy, powerful prime minister of Egypt, second to Pharaoh in influence and "in charge of the whole land." His is an improbable story. He survived traumatic life-events, yet God eventually elevated him to a position of power. Joseph could have chosen to take revenge on his family and let them starve during a devastating famine. Instead, he chose to forgive them, testifying that God had used their cruelty to result in many lives being saved years later (Genesis 50:20). When we choose to forgive we free ourselves and others from the burden of anger and resentment, and we allow God to work through us in ways we probably could not imagine.

• THINK ABOUT IT •

Have you ever had the opportunity to forgive someone for an act that seemed unforgiveable? How did that impact you and them? How did that impact the situation?

Prayer

Heavenly Father, I choose Jesus to be my Lord and humbly repent of ungodliness. I choose to forgive any one who has wronged me, rejoicing that through Jesus' blood all my sins are forgiven. Through Jesus' blood, I am redeemed out of the hand of the devil, sanctified, set apart to God. I rejoice in my Lord and Redeemer. In Jesus' name, amen.

LESS TALK, MORE ACTION

All Scripture is God-breathed and is useful for teaching, rebuking, correcting and training in righteousness, so that the man of God may be thoroughly equipped for every good work.

2 TIMOTHY 3:16-17

In reviewing some typical church calendars, you could conclude churches exist to study. We have studies for different age groups, studies for women and men, studies on a variety of topics. Then someone studies to determine if the studies were effective. I'm a committed advocate for learning, but some of us are like "professional students" preferring to stay in school indefinitely than go out in the world and put all that study into practice. The often-quoted first part of this passage, that "all Scripture is God-breathed and is useful for teaching, rebuking, correcting and training in righteousness," has a punchline that we don't hear quite as often: "so that the man of God may be thoroughly equipped for every good work." It requires a much higher level of commitment to put the teachings of Scripture into action than to sit in a group and talk about them, but that is exactly what we're called to do.

• THINK ABOUT IT •

How does the amount of time you spend studying Scripture compare to the amount of time you spend practicing the principles you learn there?

Prayer

Heavenly Father, thank You for providing all I need for life and godliness. Grant me a revelation of Jesus that I may walk more fully in Your light. Teach me Your ways, helping me to not only read Your Word but obey Your instruction. I desire Your truth in my heart. Grant me the strength to complete all You created me for. In Jesus' name, amen.

DAY 93

TELL YOUR JESUS STORY

"All authority in heaven and on earth has been given to me. Therefore go and make disciples of all nations, baptizing them in the name of the Father and of the Son and of the Holy Spirit, and teaching them to obey everything I have commanded you. And surely I am with you always, to the very end of the age."

MATTHEW 28:18-20

When Jesus said, "Go and make disciples," He didn't necessarily mean crossing an ocean to start a theological school. But He does want you to go into the world with the influence that God has given you and be an advocate for Him. Sometimes we think if our neighbors, friends, and coworkers are kind and good, we needn't intrude with our Jesus-stories. But kindness and goodness are not the objectives. Holiness and righteousness are the objectives, and Jesus of Nazareth is the difference-maker. That's why we choose Him as Lord, and when we care about other people—their days in the earth and their home for eternity—we will want to tell them about the difference He has made in our lives. When we are willing, God will give us the courage and make a way for us to tell people about Jesus.

· THINK ABOUT IT ·

Do you find it easy or difficult to tell people what Jesus has done in your life? What are some obstacles you face? What can you do to overcome them?

Prayer

Heavenly Father, thank You for Your grace, enabling me to cooperate with You to live a holy, righteous life. I submit to Your call to help others embrace Your redemptive work. Please give me Your boldness and compassion, helping me see their great need for You. Thank You for removing obstacles hindering Your call for my life. In Jesus' name, amen.

DAY 94

FOR SUCH A TIME AS THIS

"If you remain silent at this time, relief and deliverance for the Jews will arise from another place, but you and your father's family will perish. And who knows but that you have come to royal position for such a time as this?"

ESTHER 4:14

Esther was chosen queen of Persia, but kept her Jewish ethnicity secret. When the king issued an edict for every Jewish person in the empire to be killed on a certain day, he didn't know he'd signed a death warrant for his own queen. Esther's cousin, Mordecai, implored her to plead with the king on behalf of her people. She was reluctant; even the queen was not allowed to approach the king without invitation. But Mordecai was insistent, and she agreed. She successfully interceded for her people, and the king asked Mordecai to write a new decree that would save the Jewish people. God had elevated her to the position of queen "for such a time as this." She could not separate her actions from her decision to be God's servant. Like Esther, our lives are defined by our responses to God's invitations. Every blessing, opportunity, and experience prepares you to respond to an invitation God will extend to you in His time.

• THINK ABOUT IT •

God continually prepares you for the purposes and plans He has for you. Can you identify any "for such a time as this" moments in your life?

Prayer

Heavenly Father, thank You for the time and place in which You have set me to fulfill Your purposes. Please pour out Your Spirit upon me as I more fully yield to You. I want to know You in the power of Your truth. I choose the truth for my life, turning away from all deception. May I respond to every invitation You extend. In Jesus' name, amen.

THE PRIVILEGE OF SERVICE

A dispute arose among them as to which of them was considered to be greatest. Jesus said to them, ". . .For who is greater, the one who is at the table or the one who serves? Is it not the one who is at the table? But I am among you as one who serves."

LUKE 22:24-25, 27

Jesus knows He is about to be betrayed, and He is having a last supper with His followers. The disciples have seen Jesus walk on water, open blind eyes, and raise the dead. They are convinced He is the most remarkable man they've ever known, and they have reoriented their whole lives around Him. Yet their egos are still getting the better of them, and they argue, quite unbelievably to our ears, about which of them is the greatest. Amazingly, Jesus doesn't get angry. He simply reminds them—again—that He came to serve, and those who follow Him are to serve as well. This principle has not changed since that conversation in the Upper Room. The greatest honor of our lives is being a follower and a servant of the Most High God. We should seek to serve Him, and we should seek to serve others in His name.

• THINK ABOUT IT •

Are you prone to expect that others will serve you? Or do you serve others in Jesus' name and with gratitude for the privilege of doing so?

Prayer

Heavenly Father, You are my strength and Redeemer. I look to You in my weakness, trusting Your provision and direction. I rejoice in the privilege of serving You. I choose to rejoice in this season, knowing the joy that is ahead. You are a faithful God, and I ask You to enable me to have a submissive spirit and servant's heart. In Jesus' name, amen.

BONDAGE DEFEATED

But one thing I do: Forgetting what is behind and straining toward what is ahead. . . .

PHILIPPIANS 3:13

So often we allow our lives to be defined by things that happened in the past: the way someone treated us, opportunities that got away, family circumstances that were less than ideal. Life is sometimes painful, and if we've lived long enough we have experienced hardship and injustice and suffering. Paul is telling us that he has learned to keep the past in the past and move on. Being a Christ-follower doesn't mean we pretend that stuff doesn't happen. But God has put the tools at our disposal to defeat those things so that they don't hold us in bondage. The point of the cross is that we don't lead our lives as victims, but that we have been set free from anger, resentment, and bitterness. Don't be held captive to those things. Jesus wasn't—He forgave those who wronged Him, even as He was dying on the cross. Don't allow your present to be defined by your past. Forgive and move ahead. You can be free! Press on!

• THINK ABOUT IT •

What is your attitude toward your past? Do you drag life's hardships around in a box that you open and grieve over, or do you chalk those things up as life experience and follow Jesus confidently into the future?

Prayer

Heavenly Father, I rejoice in the protection of an Almighty God—my shield and strength. Your grace and mercy sustain me. Your Holy Spirit is my Helper. Through Jesus' blood, I am delivered out of the hand of the enemy and am secure in the hands of my Creator. My hope is anchored in the faithfulness of my Lord and Redeemer. In Jesus' name, amen.

INVITATIONS ACCEPTED

The Lord had said to Abram, "Leave your country, your people and your father's household and go to the land I will show you. I will make you into a great nation and I will bless you; I will make your name great, and you will be a blessing."

GENESIS 12:1-2

Almighty God revealed Himself to Abram and said, "I want you to leave your home and your people. I'll show you where to go, but the destination isn't nearly as important as your willingness to obey me." So Abram said to his wife, "We're leaving, honey. I'll start loading up." What staggers me isn't Abram's willingness to go—God spoke to him directly, after all—it's that everyone didn't want to go with him. Surely they were curious and asked him, "Why are you leaving?" and he answered, "God spoke to me." But even then they weren't interested. They probably said, "Nah, we've finally got the tent just like we want it." It's wrong to assume that everyone will be interested in pursuing God's purposes. Abram did say yes to God's invitation, and his response changed the course of history and made possible a completely different outcome for innumerable people.

• THINK ABOUT IT •

Can you identify a time when you or someone you know said yes to God's invitation and made possible a new outcome for someone else?

Prayer

Heavenly Father, I commit myself into Your care—Your wisdom and strength watch over me. Give me boldness to follow You with joy and say yes to Your invitations. Thank You for hearing my prayers and teaching me Your ways. I desire to be pleasing in Your sight. Your great love has delivered me, giving me a hope and a future. In Jesus' name, amen.

TRUE BEAUTY

Your beauty should not come from outward adornment, such as braided hair and the wearing of gold jewelry and fine clothes. Instead, it should be that of your inner self, the unfading beauty of a gentle and quiet spirit, which is of great worth in God's sight.

1 PETER 3:3-4

Rather than suggesting godly women shouldn't care much about their appearance, I think it is advice for all of us that we should be more concerned with our inner selves than our outer selves. But if our goal is "unfading beauty," how do we acquire that? Almost every beautiful thing fades—flowers, physical attractiveness, material possessions, even memories. Time causes those things to diminish. So what can we do with our physical strength, talents, energies, and resources that will not fade with time? This passage gives us a shockingly simple answer: Cultivate a gentle and quiet spirit. This doesn't mean you should be a pushover who agrees with everyone on everything. Your quiet and gentle spirit is of "great worth" in God's economy because it will show others the love of Christ and draw people to Him.

• THINK ABOUT IT •

Which is greater, the amount of time you spend on your outward self or the time you spend on your inner self? What are you doing to acquire "unfading beauty"? Can the love of Christ and the peace it brings be seen in your life?

Prayer

Heavenly Father, may fear and reverence of You flourish in my heart. Lord, deliver me from the bondage and limitations of selfish ambition and "me-centric" desires. Let new expressions of faith and courage arise within me that I might reflect Your peace, joy, and love, drawing many to You. In Jesus' name, amen.

DAY 99

RESCUED

The grace of God that brings salvation has appeared to all men.

TITUS 2:11

"Salvation" is a wonderful word. Have you ever been saved, not in the religious sense? Have you ever had a deadline at work and a coworker helped you finish on time? Perhaps you had a fussy baby pushing you to the brink of exhaustion and a friend brought a meal and took care of your little one so you could go to the grocery store or take a nap. Maybe you had car trouble and someone loaned you a vehicle. You might have had unforeseen expenses and someone gently pushed a few bills into your hand. It's a wonderful but humbling feeling when someone saves you from a difficult situation. That's true in the context of spiritual things as well. "Salvation" is the word God chose to describe His intervention on our behalf—His power exerted for us. Through His grace, He offers salvation that is much more than a ticket to Heaven. He is rescuing our total person—body, soul, and spirit—from a life of sin and giving us a fulfilling life on the earth and a glorious future with Him for eternity. The reasonable response to such a gift is an attitude of humility and gratitude toward Almighty God.

• THINK ABOUT IT •

Has there been a time when someone rescued you from a situation that you felt powerless to rescue yourself from? How did that make you feel? How did you respond?

Prayer

Heavenly Father, I am a sinner, and I need a Savior. I believe Jesus is Your Son. I believe He died on a cross for my sin. I believe You raised Him to life for my justification. Jesus, be Lord of my life and forgive my sin. I forgive any who have sinned against me. I choose to yield to You with all that I am. In Jesus' name, amen.

TOTALLY WORTH IT

Turn from evil and do good; then you will dwell in the land forever. For the LORD loves the just and will not forsake his faithful ones.

PSALM 37:27-28

This short sentence packs a powerful message that can be challenging to live out. When you begin to live according to God's plan, it will have an impact on your life. When you strive to avoid evil and do good, not everyone will understand or appreciate your efforts. You may have to turn down lucrative business opportunities. You may lose friendships. You may not be invited to all of the social events you were before. But I want you to know that it's still worth it. God has promised to reward those who seek Him, so He will take care of any lost opportunities. Your actions will speak louder than your words about your relationship with the Lord. People will see that He is more important to you than financial gain and shallow friendships. They will see that He really does make a difference in your life.

• THINK ABOUT IT •

Have there been times when you have sacrificed professionally or personally in order to honor the Lord? What were the results?

Prayer

Heavenly Father, I want to serve You with all I am and with all I have. I will strive to avoid evil at all costs. I will seek You and look for the opportunities You provide for me with a grateful heart. I choose to be a light among my friends and acquaintances so that they can see Jesus Christ is Lord of all my life. In Jesus' name, amen.

REDEEMED AND FORGIVEN

In him we have redemption through his blood, the forgiveness of sins, in accordance with the riches of God's grace.

EPHESIANS 1:7

"Redeem," in the spiritual sense, means to free from the consequences of sin. We weren't redeemed by some arbitrary decision of God. We were redeemed by Jesus coming to the earth, then being crucified and raised to life again to pay the price for our sins. Jesus' earthly life was nothing less than the power of God demonstrated on our behalf. If you will just believe that truth, all of the benefit of that redemptive work comes toward you to change your life in time and for eternity. It is a free gift. Because of God's unmerited grace, we don't have to earn it or try to be good enough. You may be the most resistant, unrepentant, hard-hearted, evil, obsessed person on the planet; but if you will choose Jesus as Lord, you can be redeemed and forgiven.

• THINK ABOUT IT •

Have you accepted Jesus as Savior and asked Him to be Lord of your life? If you have, consider the magnitude of His power at work on your behalf. If you have not, won't you do that now?

Prayer

Heavenly Father, I believe Jesus is Your only Son and the only way to You—that He died on the cross for my sin and rose again from the dead by the power of Your Holy Spirit. I choose to turn from my sin. I now invite Jesus into my heart and life. I choose to trust Him as Savior and follow Him as Lord of my whole life. In Jesus' name, amen.

DAY 102

TERMS OF SERVICE

*"If anyone comes to me and does not hate his father and mother, his wife and children, his brothers and sisters—yes, even his own life—
he cannot be my disciple."*

LUKE 14:26

This verse seems very extreme, doesn't it, asking us to hate our families and even ourselves? Marriage and family were God's ideas, after all, and there are other passages that instruct us to cherish those people and guard those relationships. This instruction is simply Jesus' reminder of what our priorities should be when we choose to follow Him. He did not want anyone to choose Him as Savior and Lord with an idealistic vision of what would be required. He wanted to make sure we knew that being a Jesus-follower could be difficult, inconvenient, and perhaps even dangerous. But neither does He ask us to follow Him without reward, because He has promised His provision and blessing when we make Him our first priority.

• THINK ABOUT IT •

Have there been times when following Jesus has been difficult or inconvenient for you? How did you respond? What was the result?

Prayer

Heavenly Father, only You know my heart's intentions. I humbly ask You to reveal to me the true intentions of my heart and mind. I choose to submit myself to You for examination. Your Word is clear about what I should value as Your child and disciple. Teach me to walk in obedience and deny myself by taking up my cross daily. In Jesus' name, amen.

IN PURSUIT OF FAITH

As iron sharpens iron, so one man sharpens another.

PROVERBS 27:17

We need godly people in our lives. If you want to learn to be a better fisherman, you need to spend time with people who know how to catch fish. If you want to learn to be a better musician, you need to hang out with people who know how to make beautiful music. If you want to learn how to have a fulfilling and productive Christian life, you need to spend time with people who already have fulfilling and productive Christian lives. It's likely that they will point out some things that you could improve on, and that's okay because they have been on the journey longer and have more experience with the Lord. They just know some things you don't know. I want to encourage you to consider being involved in a community of believers—routinely, consistently being engaged with other people who are in pursuit of faith. Being sharpened by others is not always a painless process, but there is nothing quite like it for growing in maturity in your walk with Jesus.

• THINK ABOUT IT •

Have you been in a position where you were "sharpened" by another believer? How did that process change you?

Prayer

Heavenly Father, thank You for relationships with fellow believers, even when painful. I learn much from those You have placed around me, bringing eternally significant purpose to my life. Surround me with those who will help me gain momentum in my faith. May I also help others grow toward You as they have helped me. In Jesus' name, amen.

TRAIN NOT TRY

In fact, though by this time you ought to be teachers, you need someone to teach you the elementary truths of God's word all over again. You need milk, not solid food! Anyone who lives on milk, being still an infant, is not acquainted with the teaching about righteousness. But solid food is for the mature, who by constant use have trained themselves to distinguish good from evil.

HEBREWS 5:12-14

You can try to be more godly with the best intentions and not accomplish what you can by training. Training is about repetitive behaviors that, once instilled, result in a completely different result. Ask an NBA player how many hours he has worked on his jump shot or a Major League slugger how often he takes batting practice. In order to master the skill, they committed to the training it would take for them to achieve their goals. If we will allow ourselves to be trained, we will learn about God and acquire spiritual skills we don't currently have. God does not want us to live our lives as spiritual infants. He wants us to have spiritual goals and gain spiritual maturity so that we will be able to "distinguish good from evil" and exhibit righteousness that glorifies and pleases Him.

• THINK ABOUT IT •

Have you committed time to learning some skill? How has that affected your ability to perform that task? Have you committed time to learning about God and growing in spiritual maturity?

Prayer

Heavenly Father, I desire my life to please You. Thank You for the gifts and talents You have given me to better serve You and Your people. I know if You call me to a task You will equip me to perform it. Help me make time to know You, know Your Word, and grow in spiritual maturity. I want to give You my best. In Jesus' name, amen.

STEP OUT

Jesus went out to them, walking on the lake. When the disciples saw him walking on the lake, they were terrified. "It's a ghost," they said, and cried out in fear. But Jesus immediately said to them: "Take courage! It is I. Don't be afraid." "Lord, if it's you," Peter replied, "tell me to come to you on the water." "Come," he said.

MATTHEW 14:25-29

The disciples were crossing the Sea of Galilee late at night, and Jesus began to walk across the water toward their boat. They naturally were terrified to see a man striding across the water. When Jesus identified Himself, Peter spoke up and made one of the most famous requests in the Bible: "Lord, if it's you, tell me to come to you on the water." Jesus said, "Well, come on." We usually hear this story in the context of Peter's trust in Jesus that surged then faltered. But I'd like for you to think about the other men—the ones who didn't ask to go to Jesus and stayed in the boat because they didn't think or weren't sure that Jesus had the power to bring them across the waves. What were they thinking as Peter stepped out and started walking? Did they regret they hadn't asked too? Let's not be the ones who stay behind in the boat. Let's be the ones who step out and trust Jesus to do the miraculous.

• THINK ABOUT IT •

Do you have the faith of Peter, or the faith of the men in the boat? How does that impact your life?

Prayer

Heavenly Father, here I am. Prepare me to do my best for Your Kingdom. I want to see the Holy Spirit's power living in and through my life. When You invite me to do the impossible, help me to remember that it is in the impossible that I see Your power living in me. I believe that when I am afraid, You will give me courage. In Jesus' name, amen.

STOP FOR DIRECTIONS

Be strong and take heart, all you who hope in the LORD.

PSALM 31:24

Psalm 31 was written by David, who in his youth had assured King Saul that the warriors who were hiding from Goliath in their tents should not lose heart. David, who had the least experience and should have been the most frightened, said, "Cheer up! God is on our side!" David's life illustrates the fact that victories usually do not come without a struggle. We would prefer that God just fix things or make the problem go away, but His method more often is to do something inside us so that we can address it ourselves. God knows how to deliver His people. He will give you the strength to overcome life's difficulties if you will ask Him to show you how to respond and obey when He tells you what to do. God is faithful, and you will gain experience that will cause you to be stronger and more steadfast than when you began this season of your journey. Be strong. Take heart. You can trust Him.

• THINK ABOUT IT •

Have you gone through a season when you were completely dependent on God's power to deliver you from something? What did God accomplish in you and through you?

Prayer

Heavenly Father, many opportunities require Your supernatural power for the best outcome. Holy Spirit, please guide me through each of these opportunities. I choose to cooperate with You in order to be an instrument for righteousness. Thank You for the strength to confidently walk both in the valleys and on the mountain tops. In Jesus' name, amen.

BEST FRIENDS

I want to know Christ and the power of his resurrection and the fellowship of sharing in his sufferings, becoming like him in his death, and so, somehow, to attain to the resurrection from the dead.

PHILIPPIANS 3:10-11

I have lived for several years with a rather simple idea: I want to be Jesus' friend. You and I know what it means to be a true friend. We want to really know the other person. We learn what is important to them and try not to intentionally aggravate them. We learn what they like and what they don't like, and we try to do things that make them happy. Being Jesus' friend is similar to that notion. We want to live in a way that pleases Him and respects what He thinks is important. Someday when I see Jesus face to face, I want Him to be glad to see me. I want Him to smile at me, not the polite smile of a casual acquaintance, but the huge smile we give a friend. For me, that is the essence of being a Christ-follower. It's not about a set of rules or a building I go to on the weekends. I just want to be Jesus' friend.

• THINK ABOUT IT •

Is your relationship with Jesus a real friendship? What do you imagine Jesus' expression will be when you see Him face to face?

Prayer

Heavenly Father, I want to be a friend to Jesus. Teach me to sit quietly before You, listening to what Your Word says. Help me do the things I say I believe—loving my neighbor, being truthful, and giving with a cheerful heart. Thank You for the suffering Jesus chose that I might have a relationship with You and be His friend. In Jesus' name, amen.

UNLIMITED ACCESS

After they prayed, the place where they were meeting was shaken. And they were all filled with the Holy Spirit and spoke the word of God boldly.

ACTS 4:31

There is a parallel between the Spirit of God and the power of God; where you find one, you find the other. In this case the early Church was being pressured by the religious establishment to quit talking about Jesus. Instead of backing down, they prayed, were filled with the Holy Spirit, and continued telling people about God with boldness. This powerful principle runs throughout Scripture. It is important, because every one of us needs more than doctrine or religious activity or a sense of cultural faith; we need God's power to help us, and we cannot have that power without the presence of the Holy Spirit. When you limit the access you give the Spirit of God to your life, you limit the power of God at work on your behalf. I tell you that because it's common to begin a discussion of the Holy Spirit talking about limits—what we don't believe or won't embrace. I want to invite you to lay aside those preconceptions and simply say to the Holy Spirit, "I need You. You are welcome in my life."

• THINK ABOUT IT •

What is your relationship with the Holy Spirit? Have you invited Him into every part of your life?

Prayer

Heavenly Father, thank You for sending Your Holy Spirit to help and comfort me as He directs, guides, convicts, and course-corrects my heart. Thank You that the power that raised Jesus Christ from the grave is helping me be more committed to Your purposes. I welcome Your Spirit afresh into my life that You might be glorified. In Jesus' name, amen.

FAITH ABOVE FEAR

When I am afraid, I will trust in you. In God, whose word I praise, in God I trust; I will not be afraid.

PSALM 56:3-4

God created us to feel and show emotions, but they are not good guides for life. If you follow your emotions—if they are controlling your internal GPS, they will lead you into roadblocks and collisions. Emotions are just not reliable. So we have this problem—we feel fear, sometimes appropriately so, and have to decide what to do with it. In our spirit there's a deeper level where we can choose to trust God. While my emotions may be saying, "You should be afraid right now," deeper within myself I can say, "I will trust what God has said, and fear will not rule me." This will take determination, courage, and practice on your part. But your life will begin to change as you learn to monitor your fearful thoughts and subject them to God's Word and the direction of the Holy Spirit. You will have a different emotional response to life, one that is more stable and more triumphant.

• THINK ABOUT IT •

Do you believe that you can trust God with your fears? Does that knowledge show itself in your actions?

Prayer

Heavenly Father, I thank You that through the cross, I do not have to be ruled by unhealthy emotions. I submit my head and my heart to You, Lord, and yield myself to the working of Your Holy Spirit to sanctify my life. In Jesus' name, amen.

NO WORRIES

"Therefore do not worry about tomorrow, for tomorrow will worry about itself. Each day has enough trouble of its own."

MATTHEW 6:34

Jesus said it plainly: "Don't worry about tomorrow—just don't do it!" He wouldn't have told us not to worry if He didn't know that worry was going to be a struggle. Life at the best of times is challenging, and sometimes life can be very difficult. Jesus said so. He told His disciples, the people who knew Him best, "I want you to know you're going to have trouble in this world" (John 16:33). But He also wanted us to know that it's not helpful or productive to allow anxiety and worry and stress to fill our lives, and tomorrow will be here soon enough. He's not condemning planning and preparation; He's simply saying not to anticipate the problems that may or may not come. God will give you all the strength you need for this day today and for tomorrow when it arrives.

• THINK ABOUT IT •

Are you prone to worry about tomorrow? If so, how can you change your thinking to depend on God?

Prayer

Heavenly Father, I cast all my cares on You. I know that You care about me, and I trust Your character to work out the circumstances in my life. Thank You for Your Word that shows me repeatedly why I can trust Your ways. Help me to put Your Word in my heart for the unexpected turns in life, that I might not sin against You. In Jesus' name, amen.

WALK PROTECTED

Be self-controlled and alert. Your enemy the devil prowls around like a roaring lion looking for someone to devour. Resist him, standing firm in the faith. . . .

1 PETER 5:8-9

Occasionally a news report will come out of Africa about an inexperienced big game hunter who decided to get too close to a lion and paid a price for that decision. The guy had probably invested a lot of time and money to be on safari, and in his excitement and bravado he had climbed out of his vehicle. He probably said, "Hey, watch this!" I have been to some of those game parks, and I have seen the wildlife. It has never occurred to me to climb out of the safety of the vehicle and get closer because I know the damage those animals can inflict. It is no game to them—they are looking for a meal. Peter is cautioning us to be alert because the devil is like a roaring lion that is looking for someone to devour. It is not a cowardly act when we avoid those things that might lead to an encounter with evil. In fact, it is a brilliant move to "be self-controlled and alert" and do everything in our power to resist evil by staying within the protective boundaries of our faith.

· THINK ABOUT IT ·

What is your action plan for staying away from evil and inside the protective boundaries of your faith?

Prayer

Heavenly Father, there are days when I feel like prey for the enemy. I know the fruit of Your Holy Spirit includes self-discipline, which can help me walk protected wherever You call me. Help me cultivate a fruitful life, self-controlled and alert. May I not underestimate the power of either evil or Your protective boundaries. In Jesus' name, amen.

GOD KNOWS

If you accept my words and store up my commands within you, turning your ear to wisdom and applying your heart to understanding . . . then you will understand the fear of the LORD and find the knowledge of God.

PROVERBS 2:1-2, 5

People ask pastors some interesting questions, and I'm no exception. I'm not sure why someone would ask me about diaper rash or cooking, but I've heard those and a lot more. I'm the first to admit that there are all kinds of questions I don't have the answers to and lots of things I don't know anything about at all. I'm okay with that. There is great freedom in admitting that I am not all-knowing. Neither are you, so don't pick that burden up. But we do have this promise from God, that if we will diligently seek Him, storing up His commands and seeking His wisdom through Bible study and prayer and relationships with more experienced Christians, then we will grow in our understanding of Him. I'm not sure that every one of life's questions will have a direct answer, but I do think that the Holy Spirit will pour His wisdom into every area of our lives.

• THINK ABOUT IT •

How do you feel that the wisdom of God affects areas of your life such as work and parenting and other relationships?

Prayer

Heavenly Father, Your Words light my path. When I struggle with discouragement and a lack of understanding, it is comforting when a friend of Yours stands with me, assuring me I will find peace as I wait on You. Thank You for those You have sent my way. I believe You are able to keep me through the hard times. In Jesus' name, amen.

RAISE THE BAR

Finally, brothers, whatever is true, whatever is noble, whatever is right, whatever is pure, whatever is lovely, whatever is admirable—if anything is excellent or praiseworthy—think about such things.

PHILIPPIANS 4:8

What is your daily protocol for guarding your thoughts, your emotions, and your will? This verse gives us a starting place: Think about things that are true, noble, right, pure, lovely, admirable, excellent, and praiseworthy. That's quite a list, isn't it? It will require some maturity on our part to filter the massive amount of information and entertainment and conversation that comes our way through it. When we discipline ourselves to begin that process, it will change what we watch and what and whom we listen to. Some things will cause us to say, "You know, I could use more of that." Other things will cause us to change the channel or even choose other close friendships to invest in. This is one of those areas where practice helps. The more we consume the things that stay within the boundaries set out in this passage, the more we will want to say no to the things that don't.

• THINK ABOUT IT •

Do your usual choices of information, entertainment, and conversation meet the criteria of Philippians 4:8? If not, what changes can you make?

Prayer

Heavenly Father, critics, grumblers, and negative voices tear down my hope and faith. I choose, therefore, to listen and look to what is true, noble, right, pure, and whatever is lovely and admirable. Help me to guard my heart and mind effectively and hide under the protection of Your wing. Keep me in the palm of Your hand. In Jesus' name, amen.

DEPOSIT SLIPS

"You have heard that it was said, 'Love your neighbor and hate your enemy.' But I tell you: Love your enemies and pray for those who persecute you, that you may be sons of your Father in heaven. . . . If you love those who love you, what reward will you get? Are not even the tax collectors doing that?"

MATTHEW 5:43-46

It's easy to love and pray for the people who love and pray for us. But why should we love and pray for people who don't like us, even the ones who intentionally try to do us harm? Because we get a reward! Make a list of those who cause you pain and begin to pray for them—not that they would do what you want, but that God would show them mercy and shower them with blessings. Love them with the strength that God will give you. Pray for them until you can do it with the compassion that Jesus modeled as He looked down from the cross and said, "Father, forgive them. They don't know what they're doing." The soldiers certainly knew what they were doing as they tortured Him. But they didn't realize the full ramifications of what they were doing, so Jesus interceded for them. Love and pray for those who persecute you and trust that you are stacking up deposit slips in God's economy.

• THINK ABOUT IT •

What is your attitude toward those who cause you pain? Do you love them and ask God to shower them with blessings?

Prayer

Heavenly Father, forgive me when I have dismissed Your command to love my enemy. I choose to begin loving others above myself. Help me see the God-opportunity in responding that way to those who have hurt me or cannot return the same kindness to me. Show me those who need expressions of Your love today. In Jesus' name, amen.

DAY 115

ENOUGH IS ENOUGH

I am the LORD your God, who brought you up out of Egypt. Open wide your mouth and I will fill it.

PSALM 81:10

Much of the stress in our lives comes from anxiety about having enough for tomorrow. Sometimes having enough can be a very real challenge, but we need to remind ourselves that the earth and everything in it belongs to God. It's not like He doesn't have the resources or He's not interested in our well-being. Jesus said that if we would put God first and make His priorities our priorities, He would give us what we need. In this verse God reminds us that the same power and provision He demonstrated in bringing His people out of slavery and providing for them in the desert is available to us. We can find tremendous peace and rest in God's promise. If worry about tomorrow is filling your thoughts, I want you to know you can trust the Lord to take care of it. Give it to God in prayer, believing that He will provide in every area of your life.

• THINK ABOUT IT •

How does God provide for your needs? Do you freely acknowledge His provision, both to yourself and as a witness to others?

Prayer

Heavenly Father, I am grateful for Your plans and provision, and I trust Your oversight over my life. If I am afraid I will not have enough, remind me about Your generosity. When I am tempted to be envious or anxious about my circumstances, give me a spirit of peaceful contentment. I will trust in You, my Lord and my Redeemer. In Jesus' name, amen.

BETTER OFF

"I tell you the truth: It is for your good that I am going away. Unless I go away, the Counselor will not come to you; but if I go, I will send him to you."

JOHN 16:7

Jesus' life on earth was filled with purpose. We don't know much about His early years, but when we meet Him as an adult, it's obvious He's not just drifting along; He is focused on fulfilling God's plan for Him. Just as Jesus lived among people with a purpose that brings benefit to you, the Holy Spirit is active in the earth with a purpose of equal benefit to you. Jesus said we were better off with the Holy Spirit than if He Himself stayed, and Jesus always told the truth. So we might need to rethink our attitude toward the Holy Spirit and think about some simple ways the Holy Spirit will help you. He will give you knowledge and insight, not just information. He will give you understanding into who you are and how you can effectively engage the world to advance His Kingdom-purposes. The Holy Spirit is your Helper, and He wants to help you live with a God-perspective that will make a difference for good, in your life and in the lives of others.

• THINK ABOUT IT •

What is your understanding of the work of Jesus and the Holy Spirit? How does your understanding of their roles impact your relationship with each?

Prayer

Heavenly Father, thank You for the gift of Your Holy Spirit through whom Your steadfast love is proven by His help and comfort to Your people. Thank You, Holy Spirit, that You are in our midst—guiding, convicting, and turning our hearts toward honoring the Lord. Help me be increasingly committed to Your Kingdom and purposes. In Jesus' name, amen.

DAY 117

A CHANGE IN PERSPECTIVE

He said to them: "You are well aware that it is against our law for a Jew to associate with a Gentile or visit him. But God has shown me that I should not call any man impure or unclean. So when I was sent for, I came without raising any objection. May I ask why you sent for me?"

ACTS 10:28-29

God had just shown Peter in a vision that the Jewish dietary laws he had known and followed all his life were no longer in force. As he's processing that, a group of non-Jewish men came to his door, asking him to come home with them. Recognizing the God-opportunity, Peter left without question. The amazing result of his journey was that the same Holy Spirit that had been poured out on Jesus' most trusted followers was poured out on a Roman soldier and his household. The Holy Spirit intersected Peter's life and radically changed his spiritual perspective. If Peter, one of Jesus' closest followers and dearest friends, needed the help of the Holy Spirit, don't you think we do too? Begin by saying, "God, I don't want to miss what You've created me for. If I hold any idea that limits me, help me." He will. The Holy Spirit will give you insight and understanding. He may bring it in a vision, or there may be a knock at your door. I don't know how He will do it, but He will.

• THINK ABOUT IT •

How do you allow the Holy Spirit to speak to you? Through reading Scripture? Prayer? Other believers? A knock at your door?

Prayer

Heavenly Father, help me embrace Your Holy Spirit every day, inviting Him to be in charge of my thoughts and actions. Teach me to regard Your ways above my own. Turn me toward Your perspective and away from unfruitful and limiting traditions. I choose to submit to Your Word and Holy Spirit, allowing You to transform me. In Jesus' name, amen.

DESIRE OF THE HEART

LORD, walking in the way of your laws, we wait for you; your name and renown are the desire of our hearts. My soul yearns for you in the night; in the morning my spirit longs for you.

ISAIAH 26:8-9

What do you aspire to? In the quiet places of your life, what do you really long for? For many of us, our desires tend toward the material—the right vehicle parked on the right street in the right neighborhood in the right zip code. Or perhaps your desires are relational—to be seen with the right people or have your child get into the right school so they will make the right connections. Jesus-followers are not immune to these longings. We can have stacks of Bibles, sit in church, and volunteer to serve but still have a heart that is filled with this world. If you examine your deepest desires and see that they are predominantly focused on things other than the Kingdom of God, I would encourage you to ask Him to help you. He wants to be your first priority, and He will help you make that the reality of your life.

• THINK ABOUT IT •

What do you desire most? Material things? Relationships with the right people? Or to know God more fully and serve Him more earnestly?

Prayer

Heavenly Father, forgive me when my heart's desires do not align with Your priorities. I long for Your presence and joy every morning, Your faithfulness at the end of the day. Help me guard my heart from the world's cares and desires. I commit to seek You every day in repentance and humility. In Jesus' name, amen.

DAY 119

HOME-MADE COOKIES NOT REQUIRED

"He who receives you receives Me, and he who receives Me receives Him who sent Me. . . . And whoever in the name of a disciple gives to one of these little ones even a cup of cold water to drink, truly I say to you, he shall not lose his reward."

MATTHEW 10:40, 42 • NASB®

Hospitality is a characteristic of Christ-followers, and the blessing that comes from showing hospitality is shown throughout Scripture. Hospitality is not about your home being beautifully decorated—you're probably not the next home design celebrity. It's not about being a perfect housekeeper—when I was a young man I hosted a Bible study and hoped folks wouldn't notice the empty pizza boxes. You don't have to cook like a chef—Jesus said we'd be rewarded for giving even a cup of cold water in His name. Open your life and your home to people. You will give them a safe place to share their victories and struggles, and you will probably make some lasting friendships. Sure, you'll entertain a few who are harder to love along the way, but that's all right because you'll probably be entertaining a few angels too (Hebrews 13:2).

• THINK ABOUT IT •

Do you practice hospitality in your home? If you do, how might you mentor others to do the same? If you don't, what steps might you take to open your life and home to others?

Prayer

Heavenly Father, thank You for making Your home in me. May I, in turn, open my life and my home to others, receiving them with joyful acceptance. May Your grace be evident in my every act of hospitality. Reveal Yourself to each one we host. May my choices today have an impact for good, both in time and for eternity. In Jesus' name, amen.

DAY 120

A BRIGHT FUTURE

*When you were dead in your sins and in the uncircumcision of your sinful
nature, God made you alive with Christ. He forgave us all our sins. . . .*

COLOSSIANS 2:13

This is very graphic language, isn't it? Existence without Christ is
described as dead; existence with Christ is described as alive. We all
know the difference between being dead and being alive. A dead body
is an empty shell, a cold and expressionless container that once held a
living person. Our cultural tradition is to make a dead body look as alive
as possible, but it is obvious that it is a vacant earth suit. In contrast,
the body that is alive is full of emotion, expression, thoughts, and plans.
Those of us who are "alive with Christ" are in an even greater state of
awareness because we are in touch with spiritual things. We know
what it feels like to be forgiven and freed from the bondage of our sin.
Because of our relationship with Jesus of Nazareth, we can look forward
to our days in the earth and our eternity in Heaven. Death or life: It is
our choice to make.

· THINK ABOUT IT ·

Are you looking forward to your future after death? Why or why not?

Prayer

Heavenly Father, thank You for Jesus—that He died for me, rose from
death, and now sits at Your right hand in Heaven interceding for me.
I can live victoriously because of His finished work on the cross, and
also joyfully anticipate my eternal home in Heaven with You. This is my
heritage as a servant of the Lord! In Jesus' name, amen.

ONE OF THEM

When the servant girl saw him there, she said again to those standing around, "This fellow is one of them." Again he denied it. . . . "Surely you are one of them, for you are a Galilean." He began to call down curses on himself, and he swore to them, "I don't know this man you're talking about." Immediately the rooster crowed the second time. Then Peter remembered the word Jesus had spoken to him: "Before the rooster crows twice you will disown me three times." And he broke down and wept.

MARK 14:69-72

Jesus was the most remarkable man Peter had ever known. He taught Peter things that changed his life in unimaginable ways. But when Jesus needed his love and loyalty the most, he bailed. When Peter realized what he had done, his heart was broken. Have you ever failed the Lord? I have. There have been circumstances when I wanted someone's approval so much that I shoved Jesus away, acting like I didn't know Him. When I came to my senses and sought the Lord's forgiveness, He was faithful to restore and renew me. Jesus is worthy of every ounce of love and loyalty we have. Let's remember that when we are asked, "Are you one of them?"

• THINK ABOUT IT •

Have you ever wanted someone's approval enough that you knowingly acted in a way that you knew Jesus would not approve of? What were the consequences?

Prayer

Heavenly Father, forgive me for when I have denied You or lacked commitment to Your purposes. I want to faithfully obey Your agenda and plans. Help me use my time wisely and serve You and Your Church instead of resisting You. In Jesus' name, amen.

NOT BEYOND HOPE

For since in the wisdom of God the world through its wisdom did not know him, God was pleased through the foolishness of what was preached to save those who believe.

1 CORINTHIANS 1:21

Do you know people who are ungodly? I don't mean people who waffle spiritually; I mean people who are far from God and are completely unconcerned about it or even proud of it. Did you know that it would please God to see them saved? Do you pray for those people? What do you pray for them? Do you pray that the earth would open up and swallow them? Or do you pray that God will deliver them? Sometimes our human nature wins, and we selfishly think that God's blessings are for people who are like us. But that's not the attitude God has or wants us to have. God is pleased to see people move toward Him and come into His Kingdom—all people, even the ones some might think are beyond hope. One of the ways we know that God's character is growing in us is when that pleases us too.

• THINK ABOUT IT •

What is your attitude toward people who are far away from God? Does it reflect God's attitude toward them?

Prayer

Heavenly Father, may I be one You can trust with Your message of love and forgiveness. Forgive me for carelessness toward the ungodly. Help me reflect Your character in ways that attract the lost, extending Your grace and truth. In Jesus' name, amen.

A DAILY ADVOCATE

Justice is driven back, and righteousness stands at a distance; truth has stumbled in the streets, honesty cannot enter. Truth is nowhere to be found, and whoever shuns evil becomes a prey. The LORD looked and was displeased that there was no justice.

ISAIAH 59:14-15

This is a pretty accurate description of the world we're living in, isn't it? You can choose ungodliness and be celebrated. But if you choose to honor God, you're often mocked and ridiculed. Holiness and righteousness and God's justice are not held in high esteem. Truth has not stumbled in private; it has stumbled in public, in full view of everyone. Scripture says there is a God, and He can be known. His way is truth, and it can be known. There is right and wrong in our world, and it can be understood. God's desire and intent is to give insight and understanding to humanity. If we seek Him and cooperate with Him, we can know the truth so that we might live with honesty and integrity and be advocates for God's justice as we flourish in our days under the sun.

• THINK ABOUT IT •

Are you an advocate for God's truth and God's justice? What does that look like in your daily routine?

Prayer

Heavenly Father, You are the Truth—all truth comes from You. Grant me deeper understanding of Your character and help me be a person of truth, modeling You in all I do. May I lift Your name so others will know and honor You. In Jesus' name, amen.

THE WINNING TEAM

"They will make war against the Lamb, but the Lamb will overcome them because he is Lord of lords and King of kings—and with him will be his called, chosen and faithful followers."

REVELATION 17:14

I don't know if it was my upbringing or if I was hardwired this way, but I'm a little competitive. We've all heard people say, "It doesn't matter whether you win or lose. It's how you play the game." If you believe that, I hope you're on the other team. I've won and I've lost, and winning is better. One of the pieces of my faith that I cling to with the greatest tenacity is that, ultimately, righteousness will prevail. I've read the end of the Book, and we win. Just when it looks like Jesus' adversaries have eclipsed His name in the earth and despair is universal, the eastern sky will split and a trumpet will sound. The Lord of lords and the King of kings will be back, and He will set things right. He tells us this in advance so that we can be ready; when that time comes, it's too late to change teams. Choose your allegiance carefully, because God's righteousness will prevail.

• THINK ABOUT IT •

Are you ready for the return of the Lord? If not, what should you do to prepare for that day?

Prayer

Heavenly Father, Your righteousness prevails over all Your adversary's plans—against Your people individually or on a global scale. My hope is in You, Lord, and I eagerly await Jesus' triumphant, glorious return. Come, Lord Jesus! In His name, amen.

BONDAGE IN DISGUISE

It is God's will that you should be sanctified: that you should avoid sexual immorality; that each of you should learn to control his own body in a way that is holy and honorable. . . .

1 THESSALONIANS 4:3-4

Sexual freedom has been talked about a lot during my lifetime, but the discussion has led to more confusion than clarity. God is not opposed to sexual activity, but He also defined the context in which it is appropriate—in the context of marriage between a man and a woman. But sexual immorality, which is any sex outside of marriage, is destructive—to our emotions, families, and the larger society—and there is overwhelming evidence to support that. We tend to push against boundaries, especially when we think someone is trying to limit our freedom. But some of what we call freedom is, in reality, rebellion. We see the Designer's intentions and say, "No thanks. You're limiting my freedom. I'm going to do what makes me happy." Remember, not all freedom brings liberty. We need the perspective of Almighty God to help us realize what true freedom is.

• THINK ABOUT IT •

Do you share God's perspective about sex outside the context of marriage between a man and a woman? How does that influence what you think, what you say, what you read, and what you watch?

Prayer

Heavenly Father, may Your perspective inform all my gifts, talents, time, and resources. Help me honor Your protective boundaries with the help of Your Holy Spirit. Forgive me if I fail, Lord, and renew a right spirit within me. In Jesus' name, amen.

PRAISE HIM

I will exalt you, O LORD, for you lifted me out of the depths and did not let my enemies gloat over me. O LORD my God, I called to you for help and you healed me. O LORD, you brought me up from the grave; you spared me from going down into the pit. Sing to the LORD, you saints of his; praise his holy name.

PSALM 30:1-4

None of us makes it through life without facing challenges. Sometimes challenges are the result of our own life choices. We've done something we shouldn't have, and we pay the price for it. Sometimes challenges come as the result of other people's choices. We didn't ask for them or deserve them, but they arrive on our doorstep anyway. In either case, praise is a powerful response. Praise Him for who He is. Praise Him for lifting you out of the depths. Praise Him for His healing power. Praise Him for His provision in your life. Let the people around you see your dependence on the Lord as an expression of praise to Him. Be a person with praise on your lips—it will open doorways for the Lord to work in your circumstances and change the trajectory of your life.

• THINK ABOUT IT •

What is the first thing on your lips when you address Almighty God? Do you spend more time making requests of Him or praising Him?

Prayer

Heavenly Father, You are worthy of all my praise in times of both ease and difficulty. I praise You for the cross and all You have provided—salvation, deliverance, and healing. May my words reflect the praise in my heart so others will see You in my life. In Jesus' name, amen.

CREDIT WHERE DUE

Command those who are rich in this present world not to be arrogant nor to put their hope in wealth, which is so uncertain, but to put their hope in God, who richly provides us with everything for our enjoyment.

1 TIMOTHY 6:17

The Bible warns us wealth is deceptive. To be deceived is to believe something is true that in reality is not. Wealth can cause you to believe untrue things about yourself, making you think you earned it. But the Bible very clearly says God is the One who gives us the ability to accumulate wealth—that all of the gold and silver belongs to Him and that your blessings are a result of God's involvement in your life. I cannot tell you how many people have come to me and said, "Pastor, I hear what you're saying, but I've worked hard. I got a good education, got up earlier and stayed up later, invested wisely, taken greater risks." I believe that all of those factors contribute to your ability to do well. But the reality is that you can do all of those things and still struggle to accumulate wealth. Work hard, certainly, but then ask God to bless your efforts and thank Him for His provision.

• THINK ABOUT IT •

Do you tend to claim credit for your material blessings, or do you thank God, privately and publicly, for His provision?

Prayer

Heavenly Father, forgive me for when I have either taken credit for success and blessings or taken Your provision for granted. May Your truth be more precious than the things of this world, and may I continually praise You for both. In Jesus' name, amen.

A DEFEATED ADVERSARY

Submit yourselves, then, to God. Resist the devil, and he will flee from you.

JAMES 4:7

We need to be aware that we inherit an adversary when we become Jesus-followers. We first meet Satan early in the book of Genesis, in the Garden of Eden. We see him at work in Bethlehem when the baby boys in the city are slaughtered after Jesus' birth. We see him tempting Jesus in the wilderness and possessing Judas before his betrayal. He is still at work in the earth, and he stands opposed to you and me because of our alignment with the Kingdom of God. The good news of the gospel is that through the redemptive work of Jesus, our adversary has been defeated. That doesn't mean he can't challenge us, but God's power at work on our behalf strengthens us to resist him and any temptation he sends our way.

• THINK ABOUT IT •

Do you depend upon the power of God to confront temptation, or do you attempt to resist it in your own strength?

Prayer

Heavenly Father, temptations present themselves, but through the cross, Your Kingdom is within me, and I am rescued from darkness—forgiven and reconciled to You. Thank You for Your merciful provision that purchased my victory over evil. In Jesus' name, amen.

DAY 129

FAITH NOT WORRY

"Do not fear, for I am with you; do not be dismayed, for I am your God. I will strengthen you and help you; I will uphold you with my righteous right hand."

ISAIAH 41:10

Worry has to do with fearing the future; it is anticipating that something bad will happen. There is an inverse relationship between faith and worry: Faith diminishes as worry flourishes, and worry diminishes as faith flourishes. Worry is saying, "I don't think God can handle this, so I am going to pick it up. I am going to invest time and emotional energy in my fear and anxiety, even knowing that I am not going to change the outcome one bit." Scripture has much to say about worry, with the overarching message being "Don't do it!" What Scripture does tell us to do is cast our cares upon God and trust Him with the future. He has promised to not abandon us, but to strengthen us, help us, and uphold us. What do we have to fear when the God of the universe is on our side?

• THINK ABOUT IT •

What is your response to challenging situations? Do you make worry a habit, or do you trust the Lord with your cares and concerns?

Prayer

Heavenly Father, when I am tempted to worry, may Your Holy Spirit help me to recognize worry as sin, and confess it to You. Help me transfer my trust from anyone or anything else other than You. You alone are my source and security. In Jesus' name, amen.

BEFORE AND AFTER

*If anyone is in Christ, he is a new creation; the old has gone,
the new has come!*

2 CORINTHIANS 5:17

Many people think that becoming a Christ-follower is mainly about finding a new destination for a few minutes on the weekend where you can sit and watch, and perhaps transform into a kinder and gentler person along the way. Those things are true, but they are only small pieces of what it means to be "in Christ." To become a Christ-follower means that we are made alive to things of which we were previously unaware. It means that the Spirit of God has set us free from our old nature—body, soul, and spirit—to do the very thing for which we were created: to bring glory and honor to Almighty God. We may hesitate to give up the "old" because we cannot imagine what the "new" will be like, but our lives will never be more vibrant and fulfilling than when the Spirit is working in us to make us more like Christ.

• THINK ABOUT IT •

How do you compare your life before Christ to your life after Christ? How do you tell others about the difference He has made in your life?

Prayer

Heavenly Father, my life is a new creation, fresh and new in You. I welcome You into every corner of my life. Search and show me if there is anything separating me from You. Teach me what is right and just. May discretion and understanding guard my heart. In Jesus' name, amen.

DAY 131

A PERSONAL RELATIONSHIP

"For God so loved the world that he gave his one and only Son, that whoever believes in him shall not perish but have eternal life.

JOHN 3:16

How do you become a participant in the Kingdom of God? Perhaps you think you must have inherited Christian faith from your parents, like your eye color, or because you visit a church on Easter and Christmas and know all the songs. Actually, none of those things make you a part of God's Kingdom. Unlike other faiths, the Christian faith is intensely personal—the decision to make Jesus Lord of your life is yours alone. It is about your relationship with Jesus of Nazareth. Scripture tells us that God loved the world so much that He gave His only Son to live with us and die for us. If you believe that is true and choose to make Him Lord of your life, you can have a joyous, eternal life with Him. I believe that His claims are so compelling that you will want to choose Him as Lord. The rewards during your days under the sun will be incredible, and your eternal life with Him will be wonderful beyond your imaginings.

· THINK ABOUT IT ·

Is your relationship with Jesus one you feel you inherited, or is it one you have established for yourself? If you have not made Him Lord of your life, will you do that right now?

Prayer

Heavenly Father, I choose to put my faith in both Jesus' work on the cross and His resurrection from death. I choose Jesus as Lord of my entire life. Help me receive all that the blood of Jesus purchased for my freedom and victory. In Jesus' name, amen.

DAY 132

VINTAGE TRUTH

All your words are true; all your righteous laws are eternal.

PSALM 119:160

Every day we hear messages telling us that God's words, and especially His guidelines for living, are out of date. Sometimes these cultural messages are obvious and plainly delivered; at other times they are subtle and seen clearly by those who have asked the Holy Spirit to open their eyes to the truth. If you take a stand and say you hold to a biblical worldview, the culture often will mock you and tell you that you are foolish and naïve to accept a moral perspective that comes from antiquity. I disagree with that viewpoint, however. I not only think God's rules are still relevant today, I also think they are essential to our well-being in the twenty-first century. As you ask the Holy Spirit for a greater awareness of God's ways and a greater alignment between His instructions and your behavior, you will widen the pathways for His intervention and blessing in your life and the lives of those around you.

• THINK ABOUT IT •

Do you view God's instructions as antiquated or eternal? How does this affect your thinking and your actions?

Prayer

Heavenly Father, Your Word is eternal truth—alive and powerful—inspired by Your Holy Spirit to convict, teach, and comfort Your people. May Scripture's wisdom guide me daily as I tuck it into my heart that I might honor You. In Jesus' name, amen.

DAY 133

PREPPING FOR ETERNITY

"You also must be ready, because the Son of Man will come at an hour when you do not expect him."

LUKE 12:40

Preppers, or survivalists, are a subculture that has emerged in recent years. They encourage people to become self-sufficient in order to be ready for every eventuality, from economic collapse to biologic terrorism to nuclear war. There are websites and companies that provide information and materials to help you learn how to survive various disastrous events. Certainly, reasonable care about the future is wise, but I'm more concerned about preparing spiritually than I am about building a nuclear fallout shelter in my backyard. You see, if we are unprepared spiritually, we are unprepared in the most fundamental way. While much of what people so earnestly prepare for may never happen, we know with certainty that the Son of Man will return to judge the earth. And the best way to prepare for that is to nurture a real, vibrant faith in Almighty God—who also has promised to protect you and provide for you.

• THINK ABOUT IT •

How are you preparing for your future? If a stranger reviewed your expenditures and your calendar and talked to your closest friends, what would be their conclusion?

Prayer

Heavenly Father, Jesus is returning soon as Judge and King of the whole earth. Christ-followers will rule with Him, so we must be ready for that role. Teach me to hear and obey Your voice, that a vibrant faith in You might flourish. In Jesus' name, amen.

DAY 134

THE STICKY WEB OF SIN

Let us throw off everything that hinders and the sin that so easily entangles, and let us run with perseverance the race marked out for us.

HEBREWS 12:1

This verse reminds us that sin is not something that we can easily walk into and out of—it entangles us. Sin reminds me of a cobweb. If you're like me, you've walked into more than a few cobwebs that you didn't see. In an instant, it seems, sticky filaments are wrapped around you. The threads are hard to find and difficult to pull off when they stick to your fingers. Very often you get more than a sticky web; you get the dead insects that got caught and came to a sticky end. If we had seen those webs, we would have avoided them; but we weren't paying attention, and we walked into a mess. If we are to run our life's race successfully, we need to keep our eyes open for the sin that is waiting to entangle us. It's much easier to avoid the sticky web completely than to clean ourselves up after we walk into it.

• THINK ABOUT IT •

Have there been times when you have seen the web of sin in front of you but walked into it anyway? What was the result?

Prayer

Heavenly Father, help me discard all that prevents me from persevering and running the race You have marked out for me. Help me increasingly gain the freedoms available to me, purchased through the cross and Jesus' shed blood. In Jesus' name, amen.

WINDOWS INTO THE HEART

The tongue has the power of life and death. . . .

PROVERBS 18:21

There are many ways we express ourselves—a smile or a frown, a raised or furrowed brow, a relaxed or tense posture, to name a few. But our greatest means of expression is the way we use words. Some of us mainly speak our words aloud while others communicate more often via the written word. But no matter how we communicate, our words carry authority and a tangible quality of good or evil. Our words help or hurt, build up or tear down. The more aware we are of that and the more intentionally we use words in positive ways, the more skilled we become with these tools that have been entrusted to us and the more fully we open our lives to be used by God to heal, encourage, and build up.

• THINK ABOUT IT •

Jesus said our words are a window into our hearts and the best single indicator of who we are. What do your words reveal about you?

Prayer

Heavenly Father, the power of life and death is in our words. Give me a new awareness of my words, that I might speak life for myself and those around me. May they always honor You and bring health and encouragement to all listening. In Jesus' name, amen.

UNOPENED GIFTS

Each one should use whatever gift he has received to serve others, faithfully administering God's grace in its various forms.

1 PETER 4:10

God has given every one of us strengths and gifts and abilities. It's wonderful to see God's people acknowledge and use what He has gifted us with, and it's sad to see God's people deny their gifts and abilities or let them sit unused. Sometimes people do this out of resentment that they didn't get the specific package they wanted. They were given the ability to develop a financial plan and budget when they'd rather play the guitar in the worship team. Or they were given the ability to shepherd and teach children when they'd rather be greeting people at the door. Sometimes people even deny their gifts out of fear they'll be asked to actually use them! God has given us these things in order that we might have a place of service in His Kingdom. Using our gifts and abilities wisely is not only a great responsibility; it is a great honor.

• THINK ABOUT IT •

What are your God-given strengths and gifts and abilities? How are you using them to build His Kingdom?

Prayer

Heavenly Father, thank You for the gifts and talents You have given me. Help me use them to further Your Kingdom and encourage others. Forgive me when I have lived selfishly, forgetting Your grace, which has carried me through many difficult seasons. Now let me show grace to those who need it today. In Jesus' name, amen.

DAY 137

PRIORITY CONVERSATIONS

Pray in the Spirit on all occasions with all kinds of prayers and requests. With this in mind, be alert and always keep on praying for all the saints.

EPHESIANS 6:18

I have discovered that the place where I live is a strategic center of global activity. I have deduced this by observation. When I drive the roadways, many of the cars I meet are driven by someone speaking on a cell phone. The same is true when I am in the grocery store: Many of my fellow shoppers are deep in conversation, and I can tell from their earnest facial expressions and urgent tone of voice that weighty matters are being discussed. For there to be that much conversation required of that many people, we are clearly engaged in solving issues of great importance. Yet if someone suggests that we should make conversation with the Lord a priority, the response is often, "Sorry. Not me. I don't have the time, and I'm not much of a talker." I would challenge you to make talking with the Lord a priority in your day. There are matters of great importance to be discussed.

• THINK ABOUT IT •

How does the amount of time you spend on your cell phone compare to the amount of time you spend in prayer?

Prayer

Heavenly Father, prayer is essential to my spiritual well-being. May Your Holy Spirit teach me to pray without ceasing for Your Church and purposes around the world. Help me remember time spent praying is a vital part of my relationship with You. In Jesus' name, amen.

PROMISE OF PROTECTION

Even though I walk through the valley of the shadow of death, I will fear no evil, for you are with me; your rod and your staff, they comfort me. You prepare a table before me in the presence of my enemies. You anoint my head with oil; my cup overflows. Surely goodness and love will follow me all the days of my life, and I will dwell in the house of the LORD forever.

PSALM 23:4-6

Psalm 23 is one of the most familiar psalms in Scripture. It's an amazing collection of the promises and blessings of God. One of the more interesting details here is that God doesn't seem overly concerned about my enemies. If it were up to me, I'd throw them in a pit. But He is going to set a table for me in their presence. According to this passage, I should not fear even then because He will be anointing me, blessing me, and showering me with goodness and love. Sometimes we have the notion that if we really love God we will never have to contend with opposition and never feel fear. God has created us with the capacity to fear, and some fear is healthy. But this passage reminds us that even in the midst of that our God is more than able to not only take care of us, but to bless us.

• THINK ABOUT IT •

Do you trust God with your fears? Do you allow Him to bless you even in the midst of your fears?

Prayer

Heavenly Father, in a sinful world of dark forces You are a shelter for the oppressed, a refuge in times of trouble. Forgive me when I have succumbed to fear and not cried out to You for rescue. Thank You for Your unfailing promise of protection. In Jesus' name, amen.

DAY 139

ON CONDITION

If we claim to be without sin, we deceive ourselves and the truth is not in us. If we confess our sins, he is faithful and just and will forgive us our sins and purify us from all unrighteousness.

1 JOHN 1:8-9

These are two of the best-known conditional statements in the Bible. John says if this happens, then this will happen. The first is if we claim we don't grapple with sin, then we are deceiving ourselves. It seems laughable, but there really are people who believe that they have reached such a state of sanctified holiness that they no longer sin. The second is if we confess our sins, then God will not only forgive us, He will go a step further and purify us. Pretense is very destructive, so my advice to you is to be honest with yourself. Recognize that your human nature will regularly tempt you to sin and sometimes cause you to sin. Confess your sins to God and seek the forgiveness He has promised. Finally, relish the purity that a clean heart and a clear conscience will provide. An open and honest relationship with God will bring you more happiness and fulfillment than you could ever acquire through your own efforts.

• THINK ABOUT IT •

How honest are you with yourself regarding your own sin? Do you regularly confess your sins to God?

Prayer

Heavenly Father, I am a sinner, now washed in the blood of Jesus Christ, cleansed and forgiven. When I fail, may Your Holy Spirit always guide me toward repentance. Help me honor You by walking in continual repentance and forgiveness. In Jesus' name, amen.

PREVAILING POWER

Herod, wearing his royal robes, sat on his throne and delivered a public address to the people. They shouted, "This is the voice of a god, not of a man." Immediately, because Herod did not give praise to God, an angel of the Lord struck him down, and he was eaten by worms and died. But the word of God continued to increase and spread.

ACTS 12:21-24

Acts 12 opens with King Herod, full of pomp and circumstance and power, arresting and executing a man who believed in Jesus. The chapter ends with Herod, still full of pride and unwilling to praise God, being struck down by an angel of the Lord and eaten by worms. Even as the powerful king lay dying, "the word of God continued to increase and spread." This chapter contains as profound a message for our generation as it was for the people who lived during the days of Herod: Our God reigns over all, and His Word will prevail. Earthly rulers' power is only temporary. The Most High God who spoke our world into existence, invites us to participate with Him in our days under the sun. It's the highest honor that will ever be extended to us, so let's not think of that invitation in a trivial way.

• THINK ABOUT IT •

How do you see God's Word prevailing—in your life, your church, your community, and around the world?

Prayer

Heavenly Father, Your Word is everlasting and prevails over all circumstances. Thank you for the honor of being able to serve you with my days under the sun. Please help me to approach each day with that as my goal. In Jesus' name, amen.

DAY 141

MIGHTY THINGS

Who is this King of glory? The LORD strong and mighty,
the LORD mighty in battle.

PSALM 24:8

It's tempting to try to explain God's supernatural involvement in our lives as strictly a natural phenomenon. I once read an analysis of the David and Goliath event. The author speculated that Goliath had a pituitary problem that had caused him to grow to an unusual height. One of the possible characteristics of that problem would be a protrusion on his forehead where the bone was thinner, so he would be more susceptible to a negative outcome if a stone were to hit him there. I have no problem with that. It just makes me think that David, a shepherd boy, could see all the way across the valley. He must have thought, "Wow, he has a pituitary problem! And I'm good enough with my sling that I can hit that spot!" The Lord, our King of glory, is strong and mighty and ready to do battle for us. Let's acknowledge that with awe and gratitude and give Him thanks when He acts on our behalf.

• THINK ABOUT IT •

Have there been events in your life that could only be accounted to God at work on your behalf? Did you express your praise and gratitude to Him? Did you tell others about what He had done for you?

Prayer

Heavenly Father, Your intervention in my life is always supernatural. Forgive me when I have failed to see You working on my behalf. Help me be more aware of the many expressions of Your love and provision. Thank You for watching over me and all I love. In Jesus' name, amen.

HIS TRUTH

To the Jews who had believed him, Jesus said, "If you hold to my teaching, you are really my disciples. Then you will know the truth, and the truth will set you free."

JOHN 8:31-32

It's popular today to say that truth is subjective, that there is my truth and your truth and their truth. I will concede that our life experiences are unique, and all the bits and pieces that contribute to who we are as individuals give us a perspective on life that we understand as "our truth." But the fact that we have personal experiences doesn't make us the arbiter of all truth. There is objective truth. There is right and wrong. You and I, as Christ-followers, have to have the courage to grapple with that ourselves. Say to the Lord, "Let me know the truth, about myself and about the world I'm in." Then He will show you the truth, His truth, and it will set you free.

• THINK ABOUT IT •

Which has greater impact on your view of truth—people and circumstances, or God's Word and the Holy Spirit?

Prayer

Heavenly Father, You alone hold the word of truth. Lord, let me know the truth—about myself and about the world I'm in. Through Your Son, Jesus, You have delivered me and given me hope. Knowing Him is knowing Truth, and I choose His way. In Jesus' name, amen.

DAY 143

JUSTIFIED BY FAITH

A man is not justified by observing the law, but by faith in Jesus Christ. So we, too, have put our faith in Christ Jesus that we may be justified by faith in Christ and not by observing the law, because by observing the law no one will be justified.

GALATIANS 2:16

To be justified is to be "just as if we had never sinned." The Bible says we are justified not through any efforts at law-keeping on our part, but through our faith in a Person, and His name is Jesus. When you say, "I believe Jesus is the Son of God, and I yield to Him as Lord of my life," that expression of your faith, from your heart, with your words, means that you are justified in God's sight. That is important to know because one day you and I will stand alone before Him to be judged. There will be no family history of faith to claim, no friends to call for last-minute prayer, no cell phone to search for "answers to judgment questions." If we present ourselves based on our own merits, we face condemnation. It sounds too simple to be true, but it is: we are justified through our faith in Jesus, and that is enough.

• THINK ABOUT IT •

Are you assured that faith in Jesus Christ alone is sufficient for salvation, or are you tempted to look for other means that you can accomplish on your own?

Prayer

Heavenly Father, I am only reconciled to You through Jesus. I can add nothing to His finished work on the cross for redemption or Your acceptance. Help me apply the freedom the cross offers, helping others to also trust in Jesus. In His name, amen.

UNEARNED GRACE

"Not one of the men who saw my glory and the miraculous signs I performed in Egypt and in the desert but who disobeyed me and tested me ten times— not one of them will ever see the land I promised on oath to their forefathers. No one who has treated me with contempt will ever see it."

NUMBERS 14:22-23

The greatest story of deliverance in Scripture, apart from Jesus' crucifixion and resurrection, is the liberation of the Hebrews from Egyptian slavery. But, with the exception of two families, the Hebrews who saw the miracles in Egypt and walked through the Red Sea didn't make it into the land God had promised them. They had begun to treat His grace and provision with indifference, and God caused them to wander in the desert until that generation died out. Western Christians have been uniquely blessed by God, and we also are pretty casual about it. We act as if the freedoms and material abundance we experience are our right instead of a blessing from God's hand. Let's not take God's activity among us for granted. Let's speak up when we hear His name diminished and offer Him praise when we see Him at work in our midst.

• THINK ABOUT IT •

Do you sometimes take God's activity in your life for granted? Do you ever remain silent when you hear His name diminished?

Prayer

Heavenly Father, forgive me for ever having treated Your blessings casually or grumbling in the midst of Your miraculous intervention. Help me embrace Your will for my life and trust You to fulfill Your promises. Your grace is sufficient for me. In Jesus' name, amen.

DAY 145

OUR GREAT INTERCESSOR

Since we have a great high priest who has gone through the heavens, Jesus the Son of God, let us hold firmly to the faith we profess.

HEBREWS 4:14

Jesus did not abandon us when He left the earth and ascended to Heaven. He gave us the authority of His name and sent the Holy Spirit to the earth as our helper and guide. He is our High Priest, seated at the right hand of God the Father. The Bible says that Jesus not only gave His earthly life as a sacrifice so that you and I might gain entrance into the Kingdom of God, but that He even now is taking our prayers before the throne of God Himself. Even as Jesus-followers, we are not perfect. Life can be very difficult, and sometimes our challenges seem monumental. All the while our adversary seeks to undermine our trust in God. As the storms of life are raging around you, remember that Jesus is on your side and hold firmly to the faith you profess.

• THINK ABOUT IT •

When you imagine Jesus, do you think of His earthly existence, His heavenly existence, or both?

Prayer

Heavenly Father, Jesus, Your Son, is my High Priest who intercedes for me. He has completely and perfectly fulfilled the qualifications of the Law on my behalf. May I hold firmly to Him and walk by faith in Him all the days of my life. In Jesus' name, amen.

BODY 2.0

We eagerly await a Savior from there, the Lord Jesus Christ, who, by the power that enables him to bring everything under his control, will transform our lowly bodies so that they will be like his glorious body.

PHILIPPIANS 3:20-21

When Paul says that you and I have "lowly bodies" and Jesus has a "glorious body," he's referring to the difference between our bodies in time and the resurrected bodies we will have in the future. After His resurrection, Jesus had physical abilities that He did not have before. Scripture tells us that He shocked His disciples when He suddenly appeared in the room where they were hiding. Later He was speaking to His disciples when He suddenly began to rise to the heavens and disappeared into the clouds. The Bible says that one day we'll get a resurrected body too, one that is not subject to sickness or aging or any of the other things that plague us now. It's impossible for us to know what the reality of that new body will be like, but it sure is fun to think about. In the meantime, let's do our best to keep our bodies in good working order so that we can fulfill His purposes during our days in the earth.

• THINK ABOUT IT •

How do you view your physical body? What do you do to keep it in good working order?

Prayer

Heavenly Father, I eagerly await my lowly body being transformed to be like Jesus' glorified body. Until then, help me to be disciplined and apply the Word of God to my life, maintaining strength and health in order to serve You and Your Church. In Jesus' name, amen.

DAY 147

THE DIGNITY OF WORK

Whatever you do, work at it with all your heart, as working for the Lord, not for men....

COLOSSIANS 3:23

Did you know that work is God's idea? The Bible begins with God at work. He labored for six days and was pleased with the results—at the end of each day He declared that day's handiwork "good." He took the seventh day as a rest day, not because He needed a day off, but because He was demonstrating a model for our own work lives. Our culture has twisted our ideas about work so that we expect every day's tasks to be "fulfilling" and "meaningful." Some work might be described that way, but for many of us work is hard and tedious. Work gives us dignity, however, and it is what God has ordained for us during our days in the earth. Therefore, we should do it with glad hearts, because ultimately we are working not for another person, but for the Lord.

· THINK ABOUT IT ·

What is your attitude toward work? Do you work as for the Lord rather than for men?

Prayer

Heavenly Father, thank You for significant opportunities and relationships with those who model a good work ethic. Give me the perspective and endurance to work in a way that brings honor to You and blessing to those around me. In Jesus' name, amen.

DAILY REALIGNMENT

The law of the LORD is perfect, reviving the soul. The statutes of the LORD are trustworthy, making wise the simple. The precepts of the LORD are right, giving joy to the heart. The commands of the LORD are radiant, giving light to the eyes.

PSALM 19:7-8

I read quite a bit, and I read many kinds of books. Sometimes I finish a book and feel good about the time I invested in reading it. At other times I finish a book and feel like I could have spent those hours doing something else. But I have discovered through the years that reading the Bible never disappoints—it is always a transformational thing for me. God has gifted us with a volume that is perfect, trustworthy, and refreshing. As I read the Word of God, it reads me. It exposes ideas, character traits, circumstances, and decisions I've made that need to be adjusted in the light of the truth of God's Word. I hope you will make Bible reading a regular part of your day. It will not disappoint you, and it will change you for the better.

• THINK ABOUT IT •

Do you read the Bible on a regular basis? How does Bible reading change you?

Prayer

Heavenly Father, Your faithfulness is infinite. As I read Your Word, may Your Holy Spirit teach me what I need to know for that season. Father, make Your Word effective in my spirit and allow me to see and understand it afresh. In Jesus' name, amen.

DAY 149

THE GREATEST INVITATION

"Salvation is found in no one else, for there is no other name under heaven given to men by which we must be saved."

ACTS 4:12

The redefinition of the word "tolerance" has made it nearly impossible to debate religious truth claims respectfully. Instead, this new tolerance, which seems to have become our ultimate civic virtue, requires that we abandon all truth claims lest we offend someone. The problem with that notion is that all religions make mutually exclusive truth claims. Either Jesus is the only way of salvation, or He is not. What Christians, Muslims, Jews, and Hindus say about the person and work of Jesus Christ cannot be reconciled. Jesus' assertion and the clear assertion of the New Testament is that participation in the Kingdom of God is extended to you and me by Almighty God when we personally choose Jesus of Nazareth as Lord. That invitation will be the greatest we will ever receive, and the nature of it needs to be clearly understood and communicated so that we understand the truth claims we are making.

• THINK ABOUT IT •

Do you have friends or family who make other claims about religious truth? How do you communicate the claim of Scripture that Jesus is the only way of salvation?

Prayer

Heavenly Father, I praise the name of Jesus, Your Son—the only way to You. Thank You for delivering me from emptiness to a life as a child of the Living God. May I humbly reflect the light of Christ in everything I do and everywhere I go. In Jesus' name, amen.

NURTURE FAITH

Prepare your minds for action; be self-controlled; set your hope fully on the grace to be given you when Jesus Christ is revealed.

1 PETER 1:13

I do not want you to live in fear for your place in the Kingdom of God. But neither do I want you to imagine that the decision you made years ago but have left untended is sufficient for you to reach the spiritual maturity that God has purposed for you. Scripture is full of reminders that our faith must be continually nurtured. Throughout life we will encounter those who will push or pull us toward or away from the Lord. But the process of maturing as Jesus-followers means that we must exert the self-discipline necessary to own our choices and outcomes. How do we nurture our faith? We prepare our minds for action by studying Scripture and praying for wisdom and guidance. We ask the Holy Spirit to give us self-control, which we practice in our daily lives. Then we set our hope on Jesus and His grace and live expectantly for the day He will be completely revealed to us.

• THINK ABOUT IT •

How are you nurturing your faith? Do you think about the revealing of Jesus with joyful anticipation or dread?

Prayer

Heavenly Father, thank You for Your Word, wisdom, and guidance—always drawing me toward spiritual growth and maturity. May Your Holy Spirit continue to help me practice self-control, nurturing the faith within me, as I eagerly await the appearing of Your Son. In Jesus' name, amen.

LEAN INTO GRATITUDE

In the desert the whole community grumbled against Moses and Aaron. The Israelites said to them, "If only we had died by the LORD's hand in Egypt! There we sat around pots of meat and ate all the food we wanted, but you have brought us out into this desert to starve this entire assembly to death."

EXODUS 16:2-3

We shake our heads when we read this passage, don't we? The Israelites are just a few days removed from hundreds of years of slavery—they still have calluses on their hands—and they're saying, "You know, we had it better in Egypt." God is engaged with His people, but He's leading them on a path that is harder than they would like it to be. All they remember about Egypt is the pots of food; they've forgotten what it felt like to be beaten by a slave driver. We're susceptible to that kind of attitude too. We think, "I'm in this game with God. I went to church today, and now my tire is flat!" Like the Israelites, we forget to look at the big picture. We forget the desperation and brokenness and futility we felt before we surrendered to the lordship of Jesus. Let's make a conscious decision to remember what God has done for us and rejoice in it. Let's be grateful people who lean into God instead of away from Him.

• THINK ABOUT IT •

Have you ever been tempted to grumble and lean away from God when faced with difficulty?

Prayer

Heavenly Father, help me be grateful, not grumbling. Teach me to guard my heart from attitudes that rob my peace and joy in serving You. Fill my heart with appreciation for my church and the purpose-filled life You intend me to live. In Jesus' name, amen.

GENUINE FAITH

Faith by itself, if it is not accompanied by action, is dead. But someone will say, "You have faith; I have deeds." Show me your faith without deeds, and I will show you my faith by what I do. You believe that there is one God. Good! Even the demons believe that—and shudder.

JAMES 2:17-19

Did you know that even the Devil believes in God? He has experienced the glory of God and the majesty of His dwelling place firsthand. Yet he was cast from Heaven because he would not yield to God, and he will pay an eternal consequence. Sometimes people give intellectual assent and say, "I believe in God, and I believe the Bible is true," but that's where their spiritual journey ends. Truly believing in Jesus as Lord leads to yielding and doing, and we have to choose those responses. We can never earn the grace of God or do anything to qualify for it. Yet Scripture is clear that people with genuine belief do not sit on the sidelines and watch to see what happens around them. People with genuine faith pray expectantly for God's invitations, then join Him as He extends His Kingdom in the earth.

· THINK ABOUT IT ·

Can the people you interact with on a regular basis see that you have a living, active faith? If not, what can you do to change that?

Prayer

Heavenly Father, help me see the opportunities You have presented me. Help me be humbly obedient, trusting You without reservation. Remind me You are in control. I repent for when I thought I knew what was best. Today, I yield to Your authority. In Jesus' name, amen.

URGENT ASSIGNMENT

For two whole years Paul stayed there in his own rented house and welcomed all who came to see him. Boldly and without hindrance he preached the kingdom of God and taught about the Lord Jesus Christ.

ACTS 28:30-31

The book of Acts begins with Jesus' ascension to Heaven and ends here in chapter 28, with Paul under house arrest for proclaiming salvation is found only in Jesus of Nazareth. Some Christian traditions teach that when the last apostle died the narrative of the book of Acts ended. That is as much a mistake as imagining when the book of Malachi ended the previous books were no longer relevant. The book of Acts is as significant to us as the rest of the story. God's power is still at work in the earth today. The same Spirit that raised Jesus from the dead and lifted Him into the heavens dwells in us. The same Spirit that empowered Paul to keep telling people about Jesus in the face of great persecution empowers us to tell people about Jesus. We are on assignment for Him just as Paul and the early apostles were, and we should approach that assignment with the same urgency they did.

• THINK ABOUT IT •

With how much urgency do you approach your assignment to tell people about Jesus? How much do you depend on the power of the Holy Spirit in your life?

Prayer

Heavenly Father, thank You for the gospel's good news and for those who told me about Your love. Holy Spirit, help me be a person who shares God's love by telling others about what Jesus did for us on the cross. May I be bold for You, Lord. In Jesus' name, amen.

SHOW THE RESULTS

Teach us to number our days aright, that we may gain a heart of wisdom.

PSALM 90:12

We live in a time of unprecedented cultural focus on youth, and not in a particularly good way. Instead of being taught a good work ethic and responsibility, many are swaddled and coddled and made to feel that their priorities should be fun and personal fulfillment. We hear it said to young people, "Sow your wild oats now. Live life to the fullest. Have a good time while you can." That is short-sighted because every person will only get one chance to be young for God. There will be no second chance to harness that youthful energy and excitement for Kingdom purposes. If you are a parent or grandparent, model a life that honors God. Show the good that results when we "number our days" in order to "gain a heart of wisdom." If you are a young person, do your best to honor the Lord. This season of your life will be happier and more fulfilling, and when you're older you can look back without regret for what you might have done for God.

• THINK ABOUT IT •

What messages do the young people in your life hear about honoring God? What does your life say to them about the importance you place on honoring Him?

Prayer

Heavenly Father, I want to live for You in every season of my life. I choose to reposition my goals, thoughts, and choices under the authority of Jesus. Lord, help me to live my life fully devoted to Your plans and purposes. In Jesus' name, amen.

PREPARE THE WAY

"This gospel of the kingdom will be preached in the whole world as a testimony to all nations, and then the end will come."

MATTHEW 24:14

Jesus gave more than a dozen signs that will indicate when we are at the end of the age, but the sign above all the others is that the gospel will be preached in the whole world. We are here for the purposes of the Kingdom of God, and our role is to proclaim the gospel of Jesus Christ. How many times have we read our Bibles and thought to ourselves how remarkable it would have been to have participated with God in His story in the earth? That is precisely the invitation before us! We live in a season of shaking, but it is not a frightening season. It is a season of preparation for the Lord's coming! Whatever arena of influence God has given you, use that arena to be an advocate for Jesus. When you do that, you will be preparing the way for the return of the King.

• THINK ABOUT IT •

What are you doing to proclaim the gospel of Jesus Christ, and thus prepare the way for His return?

Prayer

Heavenly Father, I yearn for Jesus' return. Help me be alert and prepared to proclaim Your gospel, even when not convenient. Convict me of any wrong motives and sins that separate me from You, that my life might be a light to others. In Jesus' name, amen.

A WAY OUT

No temptation has seized you except what is common to man. And God is faithful; he will not let you be tempted beyond what you can bear. But when you are tempted, he will also provide a way out so that you can stand up under it.

1 CORINTHIANS 10:13

If you are a tenured church-attender who reads your Bible and prays regularly, you might imagine that you have worked your way past temptation. Or maybe you think temptation is a chronological issue, and only younger people face it. We like to dress up, spray up, paint up, then come to church and act like we're not subject to all the things that everybody else is. We must remind ourselves that if the perfect, sinless, obedient Son of God faced temptation, we will as well. If you think you're not vulnerable, you're already deceived. The good news is that we have the power of the Holy Spirit in us to bear temptation without succumbing to it. Do everything you can to avoid temptation; but when you are faced with it, ask Him for a way out and He will gladly provide it.

• THINK ABOUT IT •

How aware are you of your vulnerabilities to various kinds of temptation? What is your plan to avoid them?

Prayer

Heavenly Father, when I face temptation, I will fear no evil, for I know You are with me. Give me wisdom to do all I can to avoid the places that are designed to separate me from Your best. Help me to keep my eyes on Christ, my Savior. In Jesus' name, amen.

HELD BY GOD

"Do not fear, for I am with you; do not be dismayed, for I am your God. I will strengthen you and help you; I will uphold you with my righteous right hand."

ISAIAH 41:10

We live in a world of unprecedented change, and not all of it feels positive. In fact, most people I talk to are ill at ease with many of the things that are happening around us. But the Bible says that if God shakes the earth, even if the mountains fall into the ocean, He will still be watching over His people. I want you to be assured that God is watching intently and personally over your life. He loves you and cares about you. He has plans for your good and not your harm. He does not want you to be afraid of the future. He has specifically promised to "strengthen you and help you" and hold you up with His own hand. That's an amazing promise from the very Creator of the universe to you and me.

• THINK ABOUT IT •

How have you experienced God's strength and help in times of need?

Prayer

Heavenly Father, shaking and value-change is all around me. I am often fearful, off-balance, and even angry. May I remember at those times to look to Your precepts to uphold me. Keep my path clearly marked so that I will always honor You. In Jesus' name, amen.

CAPTURE AND SUBDUE

For the sinful nature desires what is contrary to the Spirit, and the Spirit what is contrary to the sinful nature. They are in conflict with each other, so that you do not do what you want.

GALATIANS 5:17

God is our Deliverer, and He asks us to choose not to cooperate with the sinful, carnal, earthly nature that is so present in all of us. I've been following Christ for a long time and a "professional Christian" for many years, but those sinful attitudes are still present in me. It's shocking how close to the surface they are sometimes. I can worship the Lord, preach a sermon, and then think some pretty bad thoughts when I have to sit in traffic. I can be in a grocery store with the provision and blessing of God in and all around me, but when the person in front of me in the express lane has twenty items instead of fifteen, I want to swat him with a celery stalk. Those sinful attitudes will be in me for all my days in the earth. But because they are "contrary to the Spirit," I will continually work to be aware of them and learn to subdue them so that my thoughts and actions will please my Lord.

• THINK ABOUT IT •

What is your plan for recognizing and subduing the ungodly thoughts that come to your mind?

Prayer

Heavenly Father, everything necessary to overcome my sinful nature was provided through the cross of Jesus, Your Son. I receive all He accomplished for me, knowing I can do nothing to earn it. Help me cooperate with and honor You all of my days. In Jesus' name, amen.

VALUABLE TO GOD

For you created my inmost being; you knit me together in my mother's womb.

PSALM 139:13

God attaches great value to human beings. Scripture never explains why this is true, but it is. He planned for you, created you, and knew you long before you drew your first breath. It is not an insignificant thing to say that you are valuable in God's sight; that the Creator of the universe, Almighty God, looks at you and me and attaches importance to us. This principle has implications for us as individuals and how we understand ourselves, but it also brings significance to how we understand and interact with others. Not only are you valuable to God, your neighbors are too. How you relate to them is a reflection of how you relate to God. We ought to think of ourselves as God does—precious, valued, and loved. We ought to think of our neighbors that way too—whether they are across the street or across the ocean.

• THINK ABOUT IT •

Do you value yourself as God does? Do you value your neighbors as God does? How does this influence your thoughts and actions?

Prayer

Heavenly Father, thank You for Your grace and mercy in my life. You chose and created me for Your purposes. I live to serve You alone and love others the way You have loved me. May Your Word instruct me daily, helping me value life as You do. In Jesus' name, amen.

RESCUED FROM TRIAL

The Lord knows how to rescue godly men from trials. . . .

2 PETER 2:9

The depth of God's knowledge and understanding is unfathomable to us. Situations that seem difficult or even impossible to us are not difficult for God, and one of the things He knows is how to rescue His people from trying circumstances. He doesn't have to consult parents or friends or counselors to get to the bottom of the problem or ask for ideas. He's not trying to understand what makes people click, and He's not looking for new solutions. He already knows the answers to all of our problems! Since God knows how to deliver godly people from their trials, if you're in a difficult place, ask Him how to be a godly person. Remember, God is not intimidated by the things that intimidate us. Where there's a great need, He is able to deliver His people. That is really good news!

• THINK ABOUT IT •

Have there been times when God has delivered you from situations that seemed impossible? Have you acknowledged to others the way He has rescued you and worked in your life?

Prayer

Heavenly Father, only You know what I need to live a godly life. Your Word reveals Your character is unchanging, and I yield my life to You. I trust You to care for and guide me. Nothing is too difficult for You, and I will wait for You to show me Your way. In Jesus' name, amen.

DAY 161

UNEXPECTED TIMING

A thousand years in your sight are like a day that has just gone by, or like a watch in the night.

PSALM 90:4

We are eternal creatures, and we look forward to our glorious future in Heaven. But for now we are participants in time, and much of our emotional energy is invested in what happens here, especially the things that we expect to happen during certain seasons of life. We can become almost enslaved to the timelines of our lives. We get upset with God when our story isn't matching those of our peer group, when milestones such as education, career, family, and finances are not met like we thought they would be. Scripture tells us that God's timing is not like ours, and He is the one who is writing the story of our lives. He has a plan and purposes for you and is sovereign over all things, so don't allow the calendar to dictate your imagination of what He can do.

• THINK ABOUT IT •

Have you experienced seasons when God's timing was not what you expected? What did you learn about God and about yourself during those times of your life?

Prayer

Heavenly Father, forgive me when I have questioned Your timing. I submit to Your sovereignty. Give me grace to steadfastly trust Your timing in my life and never lose confidence in Your faithfulness to fulfill Your purposes for me. In Jesus' name, amen.

WEED THE HEART

See to it that no one misses the grace of God and that no bitter root grows up to cause trouble and defile many.

HEBREWS 12:15

If you have ever planted a vegetable garden you've noticed that for every plant you want to grow, there will be many unwanted things that decide to flourish there too. Sometimes keeping all those trespassers out can feel like a full-time job—and all you wanted was a tomato! My heart is like that. I have to keep careful watch or all kinds of unwanted things will take root and grow and crowd out the grace God wants to pour into my life. Anger, resentment, bitterness, hate, jealousy, lust, greed . . . they all seem to be ready to sprout at any time. I've learned to ask God on a regular basis to show me those things and help me pull them up before they gain momentum and develop deep roots. I've been amazed at His faithfulness to bring those things to the surface—through a person, or something I read, or just new insight into myself. Learning to follow the Lord is a gradual thing, and it begins with the willingness to pause before Him long enough to ask for help.

· THINK ABOUT IT ·

Is the soil of your heart fertile ground for ungodly thoughts and emotions? What is your plan for keeping them from taking root there?

Prayer

Heavenly Father, help me see and release anything keeping me from Your best, and make a plan for keeping it out. I don't want to hold onto, excuse, or justify it. Holy Spirit, fill me with God's grace, and help me be available to You. In Jesus' name, amen.

NO OTHER PATH

There will be terrible times in the last days. People will be lovers of themselves, lovers of money, boastful, proud, abusive, disobedient to their parents, ungrateful, unholy, without love, unforgiving, slanderous, without self-control, brutal, not lovers of the good, treacherous, rash, conceited, lovers of pleasure rather than lovers of God—having a form of godliness but denying its power.

2 TIMOTHY 3:1-5

Paul expresses several characteristics of a deteriorating human character, but his punchline is that these people will be deceived and deny the power of God. He tells us the power of God is inseparable from the cross of Christ. They'll have a form of godliness but deny the necessity of the cross, which is about "I'm a sinner, and I need a Savior." The cross is about Jesus, the incarnate Son of God who took away the sin of the world. The cross says there are not many paths to God, because there is only one Son of God who hung on a cross and rose again. The cross is the power of God expressed on our behalf, and it is the centrality of Jesus and His story that brings hope to every one of our lives. Don't be deceived about that.

• THINK ABOUT IT •

Have you ever sought a path to God other than Jesus? What was the result? How did you return to true faith?

Prayer

Heavenly Father, only Jesus brings hope for my brokenness, forgiveness for my disobedience, and restoration for my rebellion. Thank You for removing the veil of unbelief from my eyes, allowing me to see Jesus and the power of the cross. In Jesus' name, amen.

CHARACTER OVER COMFORT

The LORD God provided a vine and made it grow up over Jonah to give shade for his head to ease his discomfort, and Jonah was very happy about the vine. But at dawn the next day God provided a worm, which chewed the vine so that it withered.

JONAH 4:6-7

I have spent a good deal of time in the Middle East, and shade is a very important consideration there. If you need it and don't have it, you have a problem! It is worth noting in this account of Jonah's testing that the same God who provided the vine for Jonah's shady relief also sent the worm that destroyed it. God's primary concern was not Jonah's comfort; it was Jonah's character. God's agenda has not changed, and it's a perversion of the gospel to think that His primary activity in our lives is to assure our comfort. He doesn't celebrate our discomfort; but sometimes discomfort refines our character, and it can be a good thing.

• THINK ABOUT IT •

Can you remember a time when your character was refined by discomfort or hardship? What did you learn about God during that time?

Prayer

Heavenly Father, thank You for conforming me to Your image. Whatever hardship I encounter, Lord, help me submit to You. Help me be willing to persevere, remembering Your Word declares perseverance produces the character You desire. In Jesus' name, amen.

MOVE CLOSER

Some Pharisees came to Jesus and said to him, "Leave this place and go somewhere else. Herod wants to kill you." He replied, "Go tell that fox, 'I will drive out demons and heal people today and tomorrow, and on the third day I will reach my goal.'"

LUKE 13:31-32

Do you ever fear the overwhelming, unrelenting, and unreasoning violence we see and hear about, thinking, "What power do we have against this?" I believe the most powerful forces directing the lives of people and the courses of nations are spiritual. Listen to Jesus' response to this very real threat to His life. He is not fearful. I discovered as a young boy that when you are afraid, a good place to be is very close to someone who is not. Horses frightened me, but they did not frighten my father. Eventually I learned from his example how to handle both the horses and my fear. Even now I realize that when I'm afraid, I'm not as close to Jesus as I should be. If there is fear in you, move closer to Him. He's the least fearful person I know, and He will teach you how to handle your fear.

• THINK ABOUT IT •

How do you handle your fears? Do you tend to dwell on them, or do you surrender them to Jesus? If you dwell on them, what does that say about your belief in His love and power?

Prayer

Heavenly Father, forgive me when fear throttles my trust in You. No thing or one can separate me from You. Because of You I will not fear what man can do to me. I am Yours, not my own—I have been bought with a price, the blood of Jesus. In His name, amen.

IMPROBABLE PEOPLE

But Moses said to God, "Who am I, that I should go to Pharaoh and bring the Israelites out of Egypt?"

EXODUS 3:11

The Exodus is the account of God delivering the Hebrew people from Egyptian slavery and starting them on their way to the Promised Land. An interesting aspect of the Exodus is the man God selected to lead this difficult expedition. We tend to think of Moses as the baby in the basket and the great leader who confronted Pharaoh and delivered His people from bondage. But between those two chapters of his life, Moses was a murderer and a fugitive, a man who seemed to have squandered the unusual opportunities he had been given. But God always uses the brokenness of our lives for His purposes, and that's shown in the life of Moses. Our God is a God who redeems, delivers, restores, and uses the most improbable people to work His unfolding story in the earth. That was true in antiquity, and it's true today.

• THINK ABOUT IT •

God choosing people to accomplish His purposes is more than a theological principle; it's a reality that is just as true today as it was in Moses' generation. Are you making yourself available to God, to be used in His plan?

Prayer

Heavenly Father, like Moses, I feel inadequate for the job set before me. You are a redeeming and restorative God. I trust You to complete Your purposes for my life. Thank You for including me in Your unfolding story in my generation. In Jesus' name, amen.

PROMISE KEPT

"'I myself will search for my sheep and look after them. As a shepherd looks after his scattered flock when he is with them, so will I look after my sheep. I will rescue them from all the places where they were scattered on a day of clouds and darkness. I will bring them out from the nations and gather them from the countries, and I will bring them into their own land. I will pasture them on the mountains of Israel, in the ravines and in all the settlements in the land.'"

EZEKIEL 34:11-13

Count the number of times God says "I will" regarding the Jewish people. He didn't say governments would rescue them or that they would gather themselves. He said, "I am going to do this." I think we are seeing this passage being fulfilled before our very eyes—over the consternation and objections of many nations, powers, and influences. God has gathered the Jewish people from the nations of the world and has reestablished them in the land of Israel where they are flourishing. This has not come without sacrifice, and Scripture suggests there are still challenging seasons ahead for Israel. God is at work among the Jewish people, however, and it affirms our faith to see His promises fulfilled.

· THINK ABOUT IT ·

God always keeps His promises. How have you seen His promises fulfilled in your life?

Prayer

Heavenly Father, You promise to protect Your own. I, too, am a sheep of Your pasture, always in Your loving care. Even when scattered and lost from the flock, I am not lost from You. Praise and thanksgiving are Yours forevermore. In Jesus' name, amen.

NO DOUBTS

Take care that what the prophets have said does not happen to you: "'Look, you scoffers, wonder and perish, for I am going to do something in your days that you would never believe, even if someone told you.'"

ACTS 13:40-41

Paul is speaking in a synagogue in Pisidian Antioch, and he's talking to them about the power of God. He quotes Habakkuk, one of the Hebrew prophets, to warn the people to carefully consider the condition of their hearts. Like Habakkuk's audience hundreds of years earlier and Paul's audience in the early days of the Church, we too must choose what to believe. Will you sit in the seat of the scoffer, the critic, and "wonder and perish," continuing to doubt what God can do? Or will you choose to believe that Jesus of Nazareth is the Messiah and let the powerful message of His resurrection transform your life? I would encourage you to cast your lot with Jesus, because I believe God is going to do something in the season ahead of us that will exceed anything we've ever seen before, something "that you would never believe, even if someone told you."

• THINK ABOUT IT •

Have you trusted God to transform every aspect of your life, or are there parts of your life that you sometimes hold back from Him?

Prayer

Heavenly Father, help me not doubt and scoff in unbelief, but endeavor to know and trust in Your character, wisdom, and purposes. Your grace through the cross overwhelms me, and I am grateful for its perfect transformative power. In Jesus' name, amen.

A VITAL PURSUIT

Be kind and compassionate to one another, forgiving each other, just as in Christ God forgave you.

EPHESIANS 4:32

Are there people in your past whom you struggle to forgive? Maybe someone caused you to feel rejected as a child. Maybe your parents let you believe their divorce was your fault. Maybe you were denied a job opportunity because of some dishonest interaction. Maybe the relationship you thought was "the one" ended badly. These are real hurts, and burying your feelings of rejection or hurt or anger or betrayal will not eliminate the consequences of those feelings. Having a tough outer shell and saying "it doesn't matter" is not the same. They will continue to color your life and shape your future until forgiveness is achieved. How we process forgiveness defines our lives, so pursue it with determination—"just as in Christ God forgave you."

• THINK ABOUT IT •

Are there issues from your past that you have not processed, issues that keep you in the bondage of unforgiveness? Ask God for the ability to forgive, just as He has forgiven you.

Prayer

Heavenly Father, as You have forgiven me, I forgive any who have hurt or rejected me, releasing them from anything I think they owe me. Thank You for the salvation, deliverance, and restoration available through the cross of Jesus Christ. In His name, amen.

A GOD FILTER

An angry man stirs up dissension, and a hot-tempered one commits many sins.

PROVERBS 29:22

We probably have a mental picture of anger: voice raised, veins popping, and physically threatening. But that's not always the case. You can be filled with rage and yet be very calm. No matter its physical manifestation, you can recognize the fruit of anger: dissension and sin. When I see people who create unhappiness and leave division in their wake, I know that those people are filled with anger. They may have a smile on their face and speak softly, but they are filled with hostility. We have a whole vocabulary for excusing our anger. We get "frustrated" when people don't do what we want, or we have a "quick trigger" or a "short fuse." Or, "That's just the way my family is." Whatever your excuse, the truth is that if you are a habitually angry person, it will have an impact on you and on the people around you. No one wants to be a person who stirs up dissension or commits sin, so let's learn to think through what makes us angry and then filter those thoughts through God's perspective.

• THINK ABOUT IT •

How do you think through what makes you angry? Do you filter your angry thoughts in a way that honors God?

Prayer

Heavenly Father, forgive me for angry thoughts or emotions that distract me from Your purposes. I submit myself to Your Holy Spirit to examine the motives in my heart, cleanse me from all impurity, and be my ever-present filter. In Jesus' name, amen.

TEAM GROWTH

Encourage one another and build each other up, just as in fact you are doing.

1 THESSALONIANS 5:11

As a younger person I liked to participate in team sports. I enjoyed being on a team where, collectively, you could accomplish something that you couldn't accomplish individually. I still enjoy watching the dynamics of a great team: the baseball player who just tries to get on base because he knows a slugger is up next, the offensive lineman who protects the quarterback so that the wide receiver can make the spectacular catch. True team players understand that it takes the whole group to be successful, and they are grateful when every person fulfills their role. Achieving spiritual strength is also easier to achieve in a group. We each have spiritual gifts and talents and insights that help us mature as individuals but also contribute to the collective maturity of the group. God did not intend for us to "go it alone," so I'd encourage you to invest yourself in a group of people who are willing to be on your team and encourage others as they are encouraged.

• THINK ABOUT IT •

Are you a "team player" spiritually? How are you investing yourself in the spiritual lives of others? How are you allowing others to invest in you?

Prayer

Heavenly Father, teach me more fully what investing in others looks like. Help me to be consistently loving and compassionate, forgiving and encouraging to those around me so that they might be drawn into Your light and purposes. In Jesus' name, amen.

BODY, SOUL, AND SPIRIT

And my God will meet all your needs according to his glorious riches in Christ Jesus.

PHILIPPIANS 4:19

Followers of Jesus will readily declare that Jesus died on the cross for our sins and was raised to life for our redemption. But some of us struggle to realize that the redemptive work of Jesus extends beyond simply forgiving our sin. What Jesus accomplished for you and me also is a declaration of restoration. When God created the world and put human beings in the midst of it, He made abundant provision for every aspect of our existence, and Jesus restored to us all that God intended. We still live in a fallen, sin-filled world. But Jesus redeemed us totally—body, soul, and spirit. Christians are reluctant to fully believe that God wants to provide for them and comfort them and heal them, but He truly wants to meet our physical needs and emotional needs and spiritual needs. Don't hesitate to ask God for what you need and trust Him to provide it.

• THINK ABOUT IT •

Do you fully trust God to provide everything you need—body, soul, and spirit? If not, why?

Prayer

Heavenly Father, thank You for Jesus' redemptive work on the cross, and its total provision for my restoration—body, soul, and spirit. Reveal to me where I don't trust You fully to provide for my every need. Help me to trust You more each day. In Jesus' name, amen.

DAY 173

COURAGE TO TRUST GOD

I will instruct you and teach you in the way you should go; I will counsel you and watch over you.

PSALM 32:8

I became a Christian as a boy and grew up around people of faith. I had known what I wanted to do since I was a child. I charted my academic course and worked at it diligently. I had almost finished my undergraduate program and had been planning for graduate school. I had every intention of being a godly professional who would attend church and pay my tithe. I was in my dorm room, leaning against a concrete block wall when God spoke to me about my plans: "You can go," and I knew that was His permission to move ahead. But for the first time in my life that thought gave me a cold chill, because I had honestly never asked God what He wanted me to do. That's because I didn't want to know what He wanted, and I wanted to do what I wanted. A couple of weeks later I found the courage to ask the Lord, "What do You want me to do?" I hadn't had any imagination of ministry, but God began orchestrating a series of things that changed the direction of my life. I can honestly say that I don't have any regret about that.

• THINK ABOUT IT •

Do you trust God to know what is best? Do you have the courage to give Him permission to write a new future for you?

Prayer

Heavenly Father, I want Your thoughts and ways to be my own. Forgive me when I have not asked Your opinion about my plans. Your plans are always best, and I want You to always have my best in return. May my life continually honor You. In Jesus' name, amen.

DAY 174

CONVERSATION STARTERS

"She will give birth to a son, and you are to give him the name Jesus, because he will save his people from their sins."

MATTHEW 1:21

I like to go all-out in celebrating Christmas and Easter. I appreciate the privilege we have of celebrating the birth and resurrection of our Lord, and I have observed that the holidays open doors for meaningful conversation. Whether people celebrate Christmas and Easter with a secular motive or not, the reality is that Jesus is the cause of all the commotion, and it's up to us to bring the meaning to the seasons. Don't allow the commercialization and secularization to rob you of the joys and opportunities these holidays bring. Chubby guys in red suits and bunnies with eggs are good ways to begin telling the story of Jesus and the new life He brings. Yes, teach your children the real meaning behind the holidays. Then, in the midst of all the celebration, remind them, "We're celebrating what our Lord has done for us."

• THINK ABOUT IT •

Have you allowed the commercialization of Christmas and Easter to rob you of the joy of those seasons? How can you use the secular aspects of those seasons to have conversations about what Jesus has done for you?

Prayer

Heavenly Father, thank You that recognition of Jesus' birth and resurrection causes such celebration! Draw others to You as my family celebrates special times and special people. May we recognize You in all we celebrate year round. In Jesus' name, amen.

HIGHLY ESTEEMED

"This is the one I esteem: he who is humble and contrite in spirit, and trembles at my word."

ISAIAH 66:2

When God says, "I'll tell you the kind of person that I highly value," I pay attention. I would expect God to say that He values the most talented, most articulate, most intelligent, most successful, and the most prosperous. Certainly He must value the people who are the most committed or the ones who work the hardest. But this verse says something unexpected: God values humility and a repentant spirit and reverence for His Word. His criteria seem to be nearly the opposite of what our current value system is. When our world is telling us to think more of ourselves, He tells us to think more of Him. When our world tells us that sin doesn't exist, only questionable judgment, He tells us we should ask for forgiveness and show repentance. When our world tells us that the Bible is a series of myths and fables, He tells us to tremble at His Word. God is smarter than the experts telling us what to think and do, so I'm going to pay attention to what He says and try to meet His expectations.

· THINK ABOUT IT ·

How do cultural voices send us the wrong messages about the value of a person? What can we do to fill our minds with God's messages?

Prayer

Heavenly Father, I want to be one You esteem and trust. I choose to live repentantly, humbly serving Your agenda. May I honor Your character by caring for the poor and lonely, and encouraging the downcast with hope and affirmation. In Jesus' name, amen.

STORYTELLING

[The Sanhedrin] called the apostles in and had them flogged. . . ordered them not to speak in the name of Jesus, and let them go. The apostles left the Sanhedrin, rejoicing because they had been counted worthy of suffering disgrace for the Name. Day after day, in the temple courts and from house to house, they never stopped teaching and proclaiming the good news that Jesus is the Christ.

ACTS 5:40-42

What would happen if the early apostles visited your house today? Would they inquire what you have suffered in speaking of the Lord? Might they ask the results of your "teaching and proclaiming the good news that Jesus is the Christ"? I think they would be eager to talk about their experiences and compare notes to see what we did with our assignment. I hope I would have something more to say than, "Well, I read about what happened to you. You sure had it rough, but you got a lot done." Our assignment, simply to tell our Jesus-stories, is the same one Jesus gave His first followers. I hope to do it well so that I would not be embarrassed should one of them ever ask me what I accomplished for the Lord.

• THINK ABOUT IT •

What do you think the conversation would be like if some of the early apostles came to your house today? What stories of following Jesus would you be able to tell?

Prayer

Heavenly Father, help me be tenacious like the early apostles. Forgive me when I have been fainthearted in sharing Jesus Christ, afraid of consequences. Teach me to persevere in persistently sharing Your good news, even when rejected. In Jesus' name, amen.

DAY 177

NO SECRETS

"I am the good shepherd; I know my sheep and my sheep know me. . . ."

JOHN 10:14

It's a remarkable gift to be known. In fact, some say that being truly known is one of our greatest human needs. We make an effort to know the people who are important to us, and we hope that they will want to know us in return. But God takes this knowing to a completely different level. Jesus said in Matthew 10:30 that "even the very hairs of your head are all numbered." We smile at this and joke about the counting being easier on some heads than others. But God does not have to stop and count: He knew how many were there when you got up this morning, and He knows how many are there now after a few came off in your comb. This is a profound statement of God's desire to know us intimately. You are not just another one of your parents' children. You are not just another face in the yearbook of time. You are known to God.

• THINK ABOUT IT •

Consider the things that God knows about you that no one else knows. Do you desire to know Him as intimately as He knows you?

Prayer

Heavenly Father, You knew me before I was conceived and even know the number of hairs on my head. Through the cross, I am a sheep of Your pasture. Thank You for diligently, daily watching over my life. I long to know You more, even as I am known. In Jesus' name, amen.

JUST-IN-TIME PROVISION

I trust in you, O LORD; I say, "You are my God." My times are in your hands....

PSALM 31:14-15

One philosophy of modern industry is "just-in-time" manufacturing. A key principle is a manufacturer doesn't need to stockpile enormous inventories of necessary materials to maintain production. The system is designed to insure the materials will be delivered "just in time." Whatever your role in that process, you don't have to worry about the supply line and systems. You just keep doing what you're supposed to do, and everything you need to do it will be there when you need it. This reminds me of the way God asks us to trust Him for our provision. Frankly, I don't ever like to be in a position where timing is in question, because timing requires trust, and it can be uncomfortable to have to trust God. I'd much rather have everything I need stockpiled and say, "Thanks, God! I have everything I need! You can move on to someone else now!" But there are times when God needs to remind us to trust Him to meet our needs. He is more than able to give me today everything I will need for the rest of my life, but then I wouldn't need to trust Him, and that trust is His goal.

• THINK ABOUT IT •

Some of us find it harder to trust than others. How completely do you trust God to provide for you?

Prayer

Heavenly Father, I am grateful for Your timing. Strengthen me to persevere while I trust, waiting upon You. Your Word reveals the godly discipline gained by those who trusted Your timing. May I embrace Your ways as I watchfully wait. In Jesus' name, amen.

DAY 179

CHURCH-BUILDING BUSINESS

The church throughout Judea, Galilee and Samaria enjoyed a time of peace.
It was strengthened; and encouraged by the Holy Spirit, it grew in numbers,
living in the fear of the Lord.

ACTS 9:31

Contemporary Americans have been privileged to live in relative peace, imagining that the goal of the Church is our comfort and convenience. The goal of the Church, however, is to bring more people together to lift up the name of Jesus, and seek the Holy Spirit to gain greater awareness of God's purposes for our lives. A desire for that has to come from within our hearts. If we're on the wrong side of this, it will never happen. It's easy to think, "Well, I'm in. I'm good. I want my seat, and I want my parking place." We don't want to say it out loud, but our attitude is, "We've got a good thing going here. Can't somebody else build the Church?" This passage says when churches welcome the Holy Spirit and learn to fear the Lord, they will be strengthened and will grow. Don't we want that to describe our own congregation? Since Jesus is in the Church-building business, that's the business we should be in too—even if we have to find another seat.

• THINK ABOUT IT •

How welcoming are you to visitors and newcomers to your congregation? How willing are you to change in order to make room for more?

Prayer

Heavenly Father, help me love Your people and strengthen Your Church. I want to be reverently rooted in Your Word, welcoming Your Holy Spirit who helps me to be a light in dark places. May I be a faithful servant in Your Kingdom. In Jesus' name, amen.

DESERT SEASONS

The LORD will guide you always; he will satisfy your needs in a sun-scorched land and will strengthen your frame. You will be like a well-watered garden, like a spring whose waters never fail.

ISAIAH 58:11

I've learned some things from spending time in the desert: In order to survive, you need to learn to cooperate with your environment. You need to stay ahead of thirst and exhaustion, so you drink before you're thirsty and rest before you're tired. There is not a great deal of noise, so the desert's messages come to you in a gentle way . . . the sound of a rattle snake or the gurgle of running water. In the Bible, the desert is a place where God reveals Himself in new ways as people learn to trust in His provision, drink from His promises, and lean on Him for rest and shelter. If you are in one of those desert places, God has not forgotten or abandoned you; He's given you a season to learn about Him and lean into His assurances that He is all you need.

• THINK ABOUT IT •

Have you experienced a desert season spiritually? What did you learn about God's character during that time?

Prayer

Heavenly Father, wherever I am, You have prepared my way. In the heat-scorched desert or the flooded valley, You unfailingly provide shelter and protection, daily food, and sleep. You are faithful. Help me trust You at all times. In Jesus' name, amen.

DAY 181

RESISTANCE TRAINING

Do not be surprised at the painful trial you are suffering, as though something strange were happening to you. But rejoice that you participate in the sufferings of Christ, so that you may be overjoyed when his glory is revealed.

1 PETER 4:12-13

The Church's emergence in Jerusalem resulted in serious persecution. Bible scholars say Peter's strength of character and determination to follow Jesus at any cost allowed the Church to survive, even thrive, under that intense pressure. Jesus had warned and reprimanded Peter, and ultimately given him great responsibility, resulting in Peter becoming a Jesus-follower who simply would not quit. It's possible God is preparing you through various trials and difficulties—nothing builds strength like resistance. Nothing creates gratitude like awareness of our vulnerabilities being met by God's grace and mercy. Nothing creates opportunity like sharing gratitude for God's work in our lives. Christ-followers are not perfect. Like Peter, we are flawed, but God's grace is sufficient to bring us through. The strength we gain as we weather life's storms will make us even more effective ambassadors for the King.

• THINK ABOUT IT •

Remember a time when God brought you through something you thought unbearable. How did that strengthen you for greater service in His Kingdom?

Prayer

Heavenly Father, prepare me to endure throughout trials, and strengthen and equip me to honor You by helping others experiencing pain and suffering. Forgive me for any short-sighted self-interest that resists yielding to Your Holy Spirit. In Jesus' name, amen.

IN IT TO WIN IT

The weapons we fight with are not the weapons of the world. On the contrary, they have divine power to demolish strongholds.

2 CORINTHIANS 10:4

Paul wants you to know that there is warfare taking place in your heart and mind for control of your emotions and thoughts. As a Jesus-follower you are not engaged in a friendly tug-of-war or a lively intellectual debate or a Bible trivia game around the kitchen table; you are on a battlefield facing an aggressive opponent who seeks to reinforce the strongholds that challenge you and defeat you by any means necessary. Everyone who walks onto a battlefield will not necessarily leave it, and even those who leave triumphantly may bear scars. Thankfully, you are promised the "full armor of God," which enables you to "stand your ground, and after you have done everything, to stand" (Ephesians 6:10-18). Let's live with the awareness that while our spiritual battle is real, the Holy Spirit empowers us with the supernatural weapons we need to leave the field victorious.

• THINK ABOUT IT •

Are you aware of the spiritual warfare that takes place in your heart and mind? Do you depend on the power of the Holy Spirit to gain victory over the strongholds you face?

Prayer

Heavenly Father, thank You for sharing Your power to demolish evil strongholds through the cross of Jesus Christ, my Lord and Savior. I need Your Holy Spirit to help me fight and win the battles with Your enemy who seeks to destroy. In Jesus' name, amen.

DAY 183

AT THE CENTER

Then one of the elders said to me, "Do not weep! See, the Lion of the tribe of Judah, the Root of David, has triumphed. He is able to open the scroll and its seven seals." Then I saw a Lamb, looking as if it had been slain, standing in the center of the throne. . . .

REVELATION 5:5-6

The Bible concludes with John's amazing revelation of Jesus. In John's vision, he is weeping about a scroll containing the end-times story, with no one in Heaven worthy to open it. His host says to him, "Don't weep! The Lion of the tribe of Judah is worthy to open the scroll." John looks to see who has the power and authority to unleash God's perspectives for His people on the earth. He sees Jesus, the "Lamb, looking as if it had been slain, standing in the center of the throne." A lamb, still and lifeless—killed, offered as a sacrifice, its wool stained with blood. Yet this Lamb, Jesus, though bearing the marks of death, still lives and stands, triumphant in the center of the throne. What was the price that stood between our bondage to sin and our new life of freedom? The blood of the Lamb of God, Jesus of Nazareth. The image is as powerful for us today as it was centuries ago.

• THINK ABOUT IT •

What is the significance of Jesus standing in the center of Heaven's throne? What does that say to us about His deity?

Prayer

Heavenly Father, I am unworthy of the price You paid for my freedom—Jesus Christ's shed blood, paying sin's penalty for me. But today, He is alive, seated at Your right hand, interceding with absolute authority on my behalf! Worthy is the Lamb! In His name, amen.

WHAT'S THE RUSH?

I waited patiently for the LORD; he turned to me and heard my cry. He lifted me out of the slimy pit. . . he set my feet on a rock and gave me a firm place to stand. He put a new song in my mouth, a hymn of praise to our God. Many will see and fear and put their trust in the LORD.

PSALM 40:1-3

I have a hard time being patient in waiting. In fact, I try to orchestrate my life to minimize waiting. This can be a problem if I have asked God to deliver me from some situation and He hasn't done it in the timing I expected. I'm tempted to think, "Maybe I didn't pray right. Maybe He doesn't want me to be delivered from this. Maybe He doesn't really care about me after all." The Bible tells us that waiting, and waiting patiently, builds faith in us that will not be gained if our desires are granted immediately. Sometimes God wants us to wait for Him, and continue to call on Him, so that we will know that our deliverance is from Him alone. This passage assures us that He hears us and intends to rescue us. When He does we will have new reasons to praise Him, and others will be able to see what He has done for us.

• THINK ABOUT IT •

How has God changed you during times of waiting? Do you offer Him praise in private and public when He delivers you from "the mud and mire"?

Prayer

Heavenly Father, thank You for opportunities to trust You more. Help me to wait in obedient patience at every life-juncture, encouraging others to trust You. I am daily aware that all my deliverance and freedom comes from You. In Jesus' name, amen.

DAY 185

CLOSE TO THE BROKENHEARTED

As he approached the town gate, a dead person was being carried out—the only son of his mother, and she was a widow. And a large crowd from the town was with her. When the Lord saw her, his heart went out to her and he said, "Don't cry." Then he went up and touched the coffin, and those carrying it stood still. He said, "Young man, I say to you, get up!" The dead man sat up and began to talk, and Jesus gave him back to his mother.

LUKE 7:12-15

In this touching story, Jesus sees a funeral procession and immediately focuses not on the dead man but on his grieving and widowed mother. We do not know if the woman knew Jesus or how Jesus was aware of her circumstances—whether someone there told Him, or if He was given a word of wisdom. But He recognized her sadness and vulnerability, and His heart went out to her. She made no request of Him at all, yet He was moved with compassion and interrupted the procession to comfort her. Then He touched the coffin and raised the young man to life again, demonstrating His authority over even death and restoring the futures of these two people. Do you think God sees us and cares about us when we are vulnerable? I do.

• THINK ABOUT IT •

How has God demonstrated His care and concern during a time when you felt especially vulnerable?

Prayer

Heavenly Father, in heartbreaking pain, I can cry for mercy knowing You hear me. Your Word says You are close to the brokenhearted and tenderly watch over my life. Reveal Your faithfulness and provision, and I will glorify Your name. In Jesus' name, amen.

HIS BOLD PURPOSE

"If anyone is ashamed of me and my words in this adulterous and sinful generation, the Son of Man will be ashamed of him when he comes in his Father's glory with the holy angels."

MARK 8:38

The rise of anti-Christianity in America is evident. First, people said we shouldn't pray in public schools, and then we shouldn't pray in other public places. Now we're told we should be careful about mentioning the name of Jesus at all so that no one is offended. We now accept this longtime bias as normal. We are a Christian nation with a Christian heritage, but we have become embarrassed by Jesus—reluctant to assert His supremacy, His uniqueness, and His graciousness toward our country. We enjoy liberties, freedoms, and opportunities unique in the world, but hesitate to state they emerge from our Christian worldview. According to this Scripture, being ashamed of Jesus is a very dangerous attitude. I pray the Church in our nation will be awakened to Almighty God's grace, love, and power. I pray that once again we will be a people with His purposes in our hearts and His name on our lips, no matter the setting.

• THINK ABOUT IT •

Do you publicly acknowledge the grace and love and power of God? Have you told your coworkers and others that He is the source of all that is good in your life?

Prayer

Heavenly Father, forgive me for hesitantly speaking Your name—at home, across the back fence, or in my community. Awaken me fully to Your grace, love, and power that I might have Your perspective firmly established in my heart. In Jesus' name, amen.

DAY 187

JUST THE BEGINNING

"Do not worry, saying, 'What shall we eat?' or 'What shall we drink?' or 'What shall we wear?' . . . But seek first his kingdom and his righteousness, and all these things will be given to you as well."

MATTHEW 6:31-33

The general evangelical expectation of many Christians begins with a conversion point—a prayer acknowledging your need of a Savior and welcoming Jesus into your life, followed by water baptism or sprinkling. Then occasionally attending church and "tipping" God concludes your God-business. Don't misunderstand: I fully affirm conversion and the sinner's prayer, water baptism, and church attendance, but those things don't make a complete Christian life. Jesus wants to see transformation in which our hearts and minds are more focused on His eternal Kingdom than on the matters of daily life. It is hard to make Him our first priority. But if we are more worried about what we will eat, drink, or wear than about our relationship with Jesus, we will miss the Kingdom of God. This passage tells us clearly that when we put Him first, He will take care of the rest.

• THINK ABOUT IT •

How much time do you spend thinking about spiritual things? How much time do you spend thinking about what you will eat, drink, and wear? What do your answers say about your priorities?

Prayer

Heavenly Father, forgive me for when my priorities have not reflected Jesus as Lord of my life. Help me diligently seek Your Kingdom and prioritize my relationship with Jesus. I want to know and serve Him all my days, living as Your Word instructs. In Jesus' name, amen.

KNOW JESUS BETTER

"Do not tremble, do not be afraid. Did I not proclaim this and foretell it long ago? You are my witnesses. Is there any God besides me? No, there is no other Rock; I know not one."

ISAIAH 44:8

Biblical prophecy can be intimidating. We know it's in the Bible, but it's not as simple as some of the other writings and requires a little more effort to understand. "Just tell me what I need to know," we think. "Is Jesus coming back today? Am I going to be airlifted out before any trouble comes?" We think that to our own disservice. The Bible says that we would do well to pay attention to the prophets because the heart of prophecy, simply put, is Jesus. Much of the prophecy prior to His first coming was to help us recognize Him when He came and affirm what He was saying and doing. An enormous amount of the prophetic material is given to help us be prepared for His second coming. We were given prophecies to help us know Jesus better.

• THINK ABOUT IT •

Jesus warned about the dangers of being deceived, and understanding God's plan for the future is a way to guard against that. If you are intimidated by the thought of biblical prophecy, ask the Holy Spirit for a greater desire to understand what God has made available to us in His Word.

Prayer

Heavenly Father, biblical prophecy reveals that You know the end from the beginning, and that You have a plan and purpose for my life. Help me better understand Your perspective through Your prophetic word. Your Word is truth, and Your truth sets me free. In Jesus' name, amen.

DAY 189

COMPLETION PLAN

"I persecuted the followers of this Way to their death, arresting both men and women and throwing them into prison. . . I even obtained letters from them to their associates in Damascus, and went there to bring these people as prisoners to Jerusalem to be punished."

ACTS 22:4-5

Paul tells his life-story with brutal honesty. He could have bragged, "I was a rising star in the Jewish religious community—studied with the best rabbis, fast tracked in the training program with a bright future." Instead he confessed, "I was a bully, filled with hate and anger. I looked for Jesus-followers, tried to make them blaspheme His name, and cheered while they died." Paul's testimony provides a lesson. Often we portray our ungodly past like the best of times—what we left behind to follow Jesus—rather than telling the truth about how sin caused pain and suffering to us and others. Part of recognizing the miracle of God's redemptive intervention in our lives is acknowledging we did not outsmart evil. We need a power greater than the power of evil to defeat it, and God has made that power available to us.

• THINK ABOUT IT •

How do you plan to complete the course God has laid out before you? How do you aim to finish well? Thank the Lord for what He has delivered you from through the redemptive work of Jesus.

Prayer

Heavenly Father, self-interest once consumed me, but through the cross, I have been reconciled to Your plans and purposes. I need the grace, mercy, and hope that only You can give. Thank You for Your transforming power at work in me. In Jesus' name, amen.

IT'S NOT ABOUT YOU

I have been crucified with Christ and I no longer live, but Christ lives in me. The life I live in the body, I live by faith in the Son of God, who loved me and gave himself for me.

GALATIANS 2:20

Often when I begin to pray I am bombarded with reasons why I am not qualified to ask God for anything. Sometimes memories play in my head of every less-than-godly thought or word or action—whether or not I actually said or did them. Thankfully, Jesus addressed every one of my weaknesses on the cross. Has the reality of the cross settled into you? It is more than a "get out of Hell free" card, because it certainly was not free. When tempted to think you are not worthy to approach God, remember what Jesus endured that you might. He accomplished for you what you could not do for yourself. You did nothing to deserve or earn righteousness. You have been crucified with Christ. He lives in you. Your righteousness—your ability to come before the throne of God—was purchased with His blood. When you are overcome with thoughts of your inadequacies, remember: It's not about you. It's about Jesus.

• THINK ABOUT IT •

How do you understand the cross? Do you think of it as a "get out of Hell free" card, or a gift that totally transforms your life from the inside out?

Prayer

Heavenly Father, I stand before You only because of Jesus' sacrificial death and resurrection for me, that I might receive and walk in Your forgiveness, cleansing from sin, and transforming power. Thank you that Jesus lives in me! In Jesus' name, amen.

DAY 191

KEEP CALM AND CARRY ON

Consider him who endured such opposition from sinful men, so that you will not grow weary and lose heart.

HEBREWS 12:3

If the Son of God endured opposition from sinful people, we surely will too. Even after many years as a Jesus-follower, I'm still surprised when it happens. As this verse implies, when I look at myself and others, it seems that over time we get weary from facing subtle resistance and outright opposition. Weariness brings discouragement; it can snatch the heart right out of us. But if we understand the nature of the conflict, then we can be prepared for it and not be so discouraged by it. The purpose of life for a Christ-follower is to glorify God: to see His Kingdom come and His will be done on earth as it is in Heaven, and opposition from people who do not intend to honor God is part of the journey. When that opposition comes, let's consider Jesus and all He endured for us. Then let's carry on . . . in Jesus' name.

• THINK ABOUT IT •

How have you prepared for the subtle resistance and outright opposition you will face as a Jesus-follower? How do you focus your thoughts on Jesus?

Prayer

Heavenly Father, help me to be a trusted friend to You—constant and faithful. May I increasingly yield to Your Holy Spirit with willingness to acknowledge my true condition. Help me not grow tired of serving You and Your people. In Jesus' name, amen.

GOD OUR PROVIDER

"During the forty years that I led you through the desert, your clothes did not wear out, nor did the sandals on your feet. You ate no bread and drank no wine or other fermented drink. I did this so that you might know that I am the LORD your God."

DEUTERONOMY 29:5-6

The Israelites had been slaves in Egypt for hundreds of years when God sent Moses to orchestrate their exit strategy. Negotiation took a while, but ultimately the Egyptians were so glad for them to leave that they gave them their gold and silver! God provided for them in every way: They were healthy, their clothing and shoes did not wear out, and they had food and water in the desert. They lacked for nothing for forty years! It is an amazing picture of God caring for His people. Were the Israelites so righteous that they deserved all of these blessings? Hardly. They disappointed God again and again. They were not a consistent crew, yet they were His people and He provided for them in order that they would know He was "the Lord your God." We too are an inconsistent lot, but we are His people and He will provide for us too.

• THINK ABOUT IT •

Consider specific ways that God is providing for you. Have you thanked Him for being "the Lord your God" who provides?

Prayer

Heavenly Father, thank You for providing for and sustaining me. May I recognize that only You know what is best for my life. Help me allow Your Holy Spirit to reveal who I am and on what I depend, especially if there is any false way in me. In Jesus' name, amen.

DAY 193

FOR THEY KNOW NOT

When they came to the place called the Skull, there they crucified him, along with the criminals—one on his right, the other on his left. Jesus said, "Father, forgive them, for they do not know what they are doing." And they divided up his clothes by casting lots.

LUKE 23:33-34

You are probably familiar with this scene from Jesus' life. He was arrested and beaten almost to death. Then he was forced to carry His cross through the streets of Jerusalem until He physically collapsed. Help was recruited, and His cross was carried to the brow of a hill just outside the city walls. They nailed His hands and feet to the cross and lifted Him up in the air, where He was mocked and ridiculed through the agonizing hours until His death. What do you think you would have said about those who were responsible for carrying out this travesty of justice against you? I think I would have said, "Get 'em, God!" But Jesus did the unthinkable and said, "Father, forgive them, for they do not know what they are doing." Let's ponder that the next time we think how hard it is to forgive someone who has done something that seems unforgiveable.

• THINK ABOUT IT •

Has someone committed a seemingly unforgiveable deed against you? Have you forgiven that person? How has granting forgiveness changed you?

Prayer

Heavenly Father, I am a sinner who needs a Savior. Please forgive me for my rebellion and for living life my way instead of Yours. I forgive anyone who has ever hurt or harmed me. Today, I forgive _____ for making me feel _____. They owe me nothing for their offense, and I ask You to bless them. In Jesus' name, amen.

REVIVE, RENEW, AND REFRESH

We also rejoice in our sufferings, because we know that suffering produces perseverance; perseverance, character; and character, hope.

ROMANS 5:3-4

We need hope in order to survive and thrive. If you have little hope, you are in a desperate place. We lose hope the same way we gain weight—one bite at a time. In the process, we aren't really conscious of the small changes that are taking place. We can lose hope the same way—one challenge at a time, one disappointment at a time, one hurtful conversation at a time, one offense at a time—until finally our hope is just about gone. That's a desperate feeling, but we serve a God of hope, a God who can turn those hard places around and use them for gain. If you will ask Him to, He will use your suffering to produce perseverance, your perseverance to produce character, and your character to produce hope. The Holy Spirit is within you to revive and renew and refresh. Ask Him to give you hope, not through your own strength or because of anything you have done, but because of the One we have chosen to put our faith in.

• THINK ABOUT IT •

Are you in a season when you are feeling hopeless? Think about a time when God used your suffering to produce character and hope. Ask Him to do that again.

Prayer

Heavenly Father, You are the source of my hope, and I trust in You. When I am afraid, I will seek You for comfort, peace, and contentment. Thank You for delivering me, through the cross of Jesus, from every destructive scheme. In His name I pray, amen.

DAY 195

A WILLING FOLLOWER

Teach me to do your will, for you are my God; may your good Spirit lead me on level ground.

PSALM 143:10

"God, teach me to do your will." That seems like a big request, doesn't it? Here are a few simple steps to use when you are seeking to understand and do God's will. First, tell God exactly how you feel. Whether you are happy or sad or prideful or insecure, tell Him; He can stand it. Then say, "God, this is who I am; this is what I am. But I am willing to change if You will help me." Be mature enough to understand that there could be some consequences to that statement, and He may actually ask you to change. Then thank God for who He is and what He has done. God does not need our recognition of who He is; His ego is secure. But He is worthy of that. When you verbalize who God is, it helps bring your thoughts and emotions in line with His perspective. Finally, ask God to lead your life and be willing to follow Him. This is a tough one because most of us would rather lead than follow. But we can trust Him—always—to take us to a place that is better than we would take ourselves.

• THINK ABOUT IT •

Are you more comfortable leading or following? How does your personality influence your willingness to seek and follow God's will?

Prayer

Heavenly Father, forgive me for doubting and hesitating to follow You, trusting my own path. Your Holy Spirit reveals Your will—help me yield more fully to Him. Grant me understanding of Your Word, and help me plant it deep in my heart. In Jesus' name, amen.

ONE PEOPLE, ONE LORD

On their release, Peter and John went back to their own people and reported all that the chief priests and the elders had said to them.

ACTS 4:23

Peter and John, both observant Jewish men, had been arrested by Jewish religious leaders and threatened with death if they ever mentioned the name of Jesus again. So when Luke says they went back to "their own people," who was He talking about? The believers in Jesus. This is a profound shift in Scripture, because for hundreds of years God's people were understood to be the descendants of Abraham, Isaac, and Jacob—a holy nation, a unique people, a people through whom God promised to bring deliverance for the whole world. That promise has never been set aside or diminished, but Luke expanded on the idea. He said God's people are no longer defined by ethnicity, but by believing Jesus of Nazareth is the Son of God and choosing Him as Lord. In a day when divisions abound, the Church of Jesus Christ is open to people from every nation, race, language, and tribe—brothers and sisters in Christ—one people serving one Lord. Now that is wonderful news!

• THINK ABOUT IT •

Without anchoring your identity in Christ, it's easy to put national, cultural or political affiliations before who you are in the Kingdom of God. Determine to live like a Christ-follower before all else.

Prayer

Heavenly Father, thank You for calling me into Your Kingdom by the power of the Holy Spirit to become a child of God through Jesus Christ, Your Son. Jesus is my Savior, and I call Him Lord. May my life honor Him in all I do. In Jesus' name, amen.

HEAD OF THE CLASS

Jesus and his disciples went on to the villages around Caesarea Philippi. On the way he asked them, "Who do people say I am?" They replied, "Some say John the Baptist; others say Elijah; and still others, one of the prophets." "But what about you?" he asked. "Who do you say I am?" Peter answered, "You are the Christ."

MARK 8:27-29

Even though Peter was observantly Jewish, he wouldn't have made a habit of sitting around discussing the intricacies of Jewish teaching. When Jesus asked His disciples "Who do you say I am?" nobody wanted to get it wrong. They offered a few "some say" answers, then Peter stated boldly: "You are the Christ." The significance of this declaration is almost impossible for us to grasp. The Jewish power structure certainly had not admitted to the possibility that Jesus was the Messiah, yet Peter recognized He was the One foretold of by the prophets—the One the entire nation was longing for. Peter probably knew more about the Sea of Galilee than he did the words of the Law and Prophets, yet God gave him spiritual insight that even the religious elites did not have.

· THINK ABOUT IT ·

Very few of us have formal religious education. Do you ever let that inhibit your willingness to be taught by the Spirit of God?

Prayer

Heavenly Father, thank You for Your Son, Jesus—the Messiah, Lord, Savior, and Healer. May I know Him and the power of His resurrection. Lord, give me the insight that I will need to fulfill Your plans for me and the skills I need to serve and glorify You. In Jesus' name, amen.

WORK VALUES

Train a child in the way he should go, and when he is old he will not turn from it.

PROVERBS 22:6

I remember the first time my parents said, "You have a job this summer." I thought, "No, I'm good, thank you. I don't want a job. I have plans for the summer." But they had this crazy notion that I was going to get up early every morning and go work in the barn! My friends were sleeping late, going swimming, skiing—and I was mucking out stalls? They expected me to do this every day. When I showed my dad the blisters on my hands, he said, "Work is good for you. Put a bandage on that." They were determined I was going to learn to work. Working that summer and the following summers did not make me particularly happy. Many of my friends were leisurely working on their tans. But when I look back on it, I realize it made me a better person. We usually think of this proverb in the context of spiritual training, and that's certainly important and true. But it has a practical application as well. Teach your children the value and dignity of work. They will thank you for it—someday. Thanks, Mom and Dad!

• THINK ABOUT IT •

Did you learn the value and dignity of work as a young person? How has that shaped your feelings about work as an adult? Are you teaching the young people in your life how to work?

Prayer

Heavenly Father, thank You for those who have taught me the value of hard work. Help me be a person of integrity like them. Thank You for entrusting me with the opportunity to diligently serve You and bear good fruit for Your Kingdom. In Jesus' name, amen.

DAY 199

SEEING GOD

I pray also that the eyes of your heart may be enlightened in order that you may know the hope to which he has called you, the riches of his glorious inheritance in the saints. . . .

EPHESIANS 1:18

When you read the definition of "vision," you'll see it is more than your physical ability to see. Your vision has intellectual and emotional aspects as well, like your ability to think, imagine, and discern. Two people can be in the same place and have the same experience but see things completely differently. We train ourselves to be aware and alert to things that matter to us. The "eyes of your heart" will not be fully opened to all that God has for you unless you learn to value spiritual things and seek them out. Let's pray that we will be able to see beyond the physical into the spiritual realm. When we do that we will have a greater awareness of the hope we have in Jesus and assurance of the glorious inheritance that is ours.

• THINK ABOUT IT •

Are you able to see the world with spiritual eyes? When you see a rowdy preschooler do you pray that he or she will grow up to live for God? When you see the food in your cabinets do you see God's provision? When the church parking lot is crowded do you thank God that so many have come to worship Him?

Prayer

Heavenly Father, I yield to You—open my eyes and ears to Your Word and Your Holy Spirit. I ask You to help me guard my heart. I thank You for new routines to practice daily to ensure that I will find times abide in Your presence. In Jesus' name, amen.

UNSHIFTING TRUTH

Guard what has been entrusted to your care. Turn away from godless chatter and the opposing ideas of what is falsely called knowledge, which some have professed and in so doing have wandered from the faith.

1 TIMOTHY 6:20-21

"Apostasy" means "a falling away." We typically view it as a Christian turning from their faith and declaring, "I do not believe Jesus is the Son of God." But typically it is a more gradual process. The children of Israel struggled with falling away, but they didn't stop worshipping God. They just included worshipping Baal and other Canaanite gods. That's apostasy—not rejecting Christianity, but beginning to say, "We don't want to be hardcore about it." This is a time of unprecedented apostasy with more professing Christians turning from the authority of Scripture as their rule of faith and practice. In these confusing times, ask the Holy Spirit to help you guard your heart. Turn away from teachings and practices that oppose the truth of Scripture. You may have to choose different friends, read different books, listen to different preachers, but it will be worth it if it keeps you from wandering from the faith.

• THINK ABOUT IT •

Do you recognize statements or signs of apostasy around you? What is your plan for avoiding those subtle messages and staying true to biblical teaching?

Prayer

Heavenly Father, I choose to humbly serve You and consistently give You priority. Please help me to know and honor Your truth that I might be protected from deception. Help me to cooperate with the great promises You have extended. In Jesus' name, amen.

DAY 201

INVESTMENT PRACTICES

I meditate on your precepts and consider your ways. I delight in your decrees; I will not neglect your word.

PSALM 119:15-16

I've discovered taking a few minutes every day to invest in the Word of God has a positive effect on my life. Routinely spending time with the Lord gives you a different set of thoughts and emotions and changes your imagination of God's character and power. You will begin to see yourself and the people around you differently. Occasionally people say, "I said the sinner's prayer and changed overnight. I slept with my Bible under my pillow and read it every chance I got. I just couldn't get enough." That wasn't my experience. I've had to learn how to grow in the Lord. I've had to struggle to establish the habit of taking time away from something else and spending it with God. Not every passage will leap off the page with spiritual insight—it will take God's Spirit to keep you awake in Leviticus. But when you engage in the discipline of Bible reading on a regular basis it will change you, and your relationship with God, in ways that will surprise and benefit you.

• THINK ABOUT IT •

Do you have a daily routine of reading and meditating on God's Word? If so, how has it changed you? If not, what do you need to change in order to establish this new pattern?

Prayer

Heavenly Father, thank You for the unchanging truth of Your Word that leads to abundant life and blessing beyond what I can see. Help me be disciplined to give precedence to You and Your Word each day. May I guard my mind so that I might honor You. In Jesus' name, amen.

COPYCAT

In all things show yourself to be an example of good deeds, with purity in doctrine, dignified, sound in speech which is beyond reproach. . . .

TITUS 2:7-8 • NASB®

Many people in the Bible played an important role in God's unfolding plan yet were anonymous in the pages of Scripture. Pharaoh's daughter, the shepherds who celebrated Jesus' birth, the woman at the well—they all were a part of God's interactions with people. Perhaps we are not given their names because their stories and the lessons we can learn from them are more important than their identities. In some we see attitudes and actions we should imitate, like the humility of the thief on the cross who asked for admittance into Jesus' Kingdom (Luke 23). In others we see what we should not imitate, like the disobedience of Lot's wife, who ignored an angel's message from God and paid a terrible price (Genesis 19). Whether we are known to only a few or many, our responses to God's invitations will often be noticed and sometimes imitated. Let's work to be worthy of imitation.

• THINK ABOUT IT •

As people, both friends and strangers, observe your attitudes, words, and actions, what conclusions can they draw about your relationship with the Lord? Are your attitudes, words, and actions worthy of being imitated?

Prayer

Heavenly Father, give me ever increasing faith—a faith that draws others to You. I pray that all who know me can see that I love You and love Your people. Let every area of my life be tremendously fruitful as a result of my faith in You. In Jesus' name, amen.

ACCESS GRANTED

What, then, shall we say in response to this? If God is for us, who can be against us? He who did not spare his own Son, but gave him up for us all—how will he not also, along with him, graciously give us all things?

ROMANS 8:31-32

What price had to be paid for us to qualify for God's Kingdom? Our sin separated us from God, and He offered Jesus as the sacrifice—the complete, sufficient, one-time sacrifice. When Jesus was arrested and the Romans beat Him beyond recognition, what did God do? Nothing. They stretched Him out on a Roman cross and drove spikes through His hands and His feet. What did God do? Nothing. The God who parted the Red Sea could have destroyed them all, yet He did nothing. Why? Because He loves us enough to sacrifice His own Son. Paul says, "If God did not spare His Son for you, do you think He will withhold anything else from you?" The next time you doubt God's love and His desire to provide for you, think about the sacrifice that was made on the cross—for you.

• THINK ABOUT IT •

Do you ever avoid bringing a concern to God because you don't want to intrude on His time? Do you ever wonder if your concerns are too small for His attention? Consider the totality of Jesus' sacrifice made for you and the access to God He bought for you.

Prayer

Heavenly Father, You have made a way for me to be reconciled to You through the sacrifice of Your own Son. Thank You that I can live in forgiveness, peace, and joy through Christ, the Savior. Help me never doubt Your love. In Jesus' name, amen.

LASER FOCUS

Elijah said to Elisha, "Tell me, what can I do for you before I am taken from you?" "Let me inherit a double portion of your spirit," Elisha replied. "You have asked a difficult thing," Elijah said, "yet if you see me when I am taken from you, it will be yours—otherwise not."

2 KINGS 2:9-10

Before Elijah the prophet's days were over, he said to his helper Elisha, "I am about done here on earth. What can I do for you before I go?" Elisha responded, "I'd like twice the spirit you have." Elijah replied, "If you are around when the Lord comes for me, you can have what you asked for. But if not, you're out of luck." Elisha's extraordinary blessing was totally dependent upon never losing sight of Elijah. Elisha persisted, gaining him that blessing. God's best things will not come to you if you are a casual inquirer. Scripture says that God "rewards those who earnestly seek him" (Hebrews 11:6). Most of us begin our spiritual journey with a sense of inquiry and curiosity, but at some point that wears off and we have to make a commitment to seek Him. I'd encourage you to keep the Lord in sight at all times.

• THINK ABOUT IT •

Are you laser-focused on God, or are you a casual inquirer? What can you do in order to focus more intently on the Lord and His purposes for you?

Prayer

Heavenly Father, I want to receive all You desire and accomplish all Your plans for my life. Help me turn from any casual walk with You and commit afresh to diligently seeking You and Your truth, that I might have Your power in my life. In Jesus' name, amen.

SOLID INVESTMENTS

I heard behind me a loud voice like a trumpet, which said: "Write on a scroll what you see and send it to the seven churches: to Ephesus, Smyrna, Pergamum, Thyatira, Sardis, Philadelphia and Laodicea." . . . And when I turned I saw seven golden lampstands, and among the lampstands was someone "like a son of man," dressed in a robe reaching down to his feet and with a golden sash around his chest.

REVELATION 1:10-13

The book of Revelation reveals Jesus standing in the midst of seven lampstands, which represent the local churches of seven cities—His churches. Jesus' attention has always been focused upon His Church. He said that He would build His Church so that Hell would not be able to overcome it. If you sit in the seat of the skeptic regarding the Church—the Body of Christ—remember the Church's great weakness is also its great strength: It's made up of people. We are an imperfect, disappointing lot. But we also are the image-bearers of Almighty God, and He loves us beyond our understanding. If you want to invest yourself in something of eternal significance, be a person who strengthens the Church.

• THINK ABOUT IT •

Have you invested yourself in a Bible-believing local congregation? If so, how has it strengthened you? If not, won't you consider doing so?

Prayer

Heavenly Father, I am grateful for Bible-believing churches that proclaim Your transforming message of redemption, repentance, and forgiveness. Help me love Your Church the way Jesus does and honor You by being a strength to Your people. In Jesus' name, amen.

A WATCHMAN AT THE GATE

"When you see Jerusalem being surrounded by armies, you will know that its desolation is near. Then let those who are in Judea flee to the mountains, let those in the city get out, and let those in the country not enter the city. For this is the time of punishment in fulfillment of all that has been written. . . . They will fall by the sword and will be taken as prisoners to all the nations."

LUKE 21:20-24

This prophetic statement from Jesus was fulfilled about forty years after His death when Roman legions marched to and surrounded Jerusalem. They laid siege to the city to starve it into submission. When the siege was lifted, Jesus-followers fled Jerusalem because of His prophetic warning, causing a significant rift between the Jewish people who believed in Jesus and those who didn't. When the political issues were settled in Rome, the siege was put back in place; this time it held until Jerusalem was broken. The population was slaughtered, and the slave markets of Rome were filled with the Jewish people. Jesus' prophetic words came true. He could be trusted then, and He can be trusted now.

· THINK ABOUT IT ·

Read Luke 21:5-36 to learn some of the things Jesus prophesied would happen before the end of the age. Which of His statements can you see being fulfilled around you?

Prayer

Heavenly Father, the unprecedented turmoil in our world causes fear or grows faith. Help me transfer my trust from all else to You, whose warnings and promises never fail. May I be found alert and watching, keeping my eyes focused on You. In Jesus' name, amen.

LIVE WITH THE END IN MIND

One thing I ask of the LORD, this is what I seek: that I may dwell in the house of the LORD all the days of my life, to gaze on the beauty of the LORD and to seek him in his temple.

PSALM 27:4

A tremendous beginning alone is not cause for enduring celebration. We have all seen businesses, ministries, sports seasons, and lives begin with enormous promise but fail to fulfill their potential. In spiritual terms, it seems that instead of living focused on the beginning of our journey, we ought to live with the end in mind. God deserves more than just an entry prayer and shallow water dive. He doesn't want us to repent of our sins and then live on our own terms. When it comes to our faith, we often try to get the beginning right and then ride it out waiting for Heaven, doing as little as we can to get by. The point of being birthed into the Kingdom is to consistently pursue God's purposes with a whole heart, considering the beauty of His sacrifice for us and worshipping Him for all that He is. Being a Christ-follower means He deserves our best, every day, so that we may dwell in the house of the Lord all the days of our lives.

• THINK ABOUT IT •

How do you pursue God on a daily basis? Do you gaze on His beauty and seek Him in His temple every day?

Prayer

Heavenly Father, grant me continual opportunities to grow in knowing and serving You with my whole heart. May the end of my life be more fruitful than my beginning, that You can one day say to me, "Well done, good and faithful servant." In Jesus' name, amen.

JOB QUALIFICATIONS

In those days when the number of disciples was increasing, the Grecian Jews among them complained against the Hebraic Jews because their widows were being overlooked in the daily distribution of food. So the Twelve gathered all the disciples together and said, ". . . Brothers, choose seven men from among you who are known to be full of the Spirit and wisdom. We will turn this responsibility over to them. . . ."

ACTS 6:1-3

The early Church was growing quicker than its infrastructure, and the apostles realized they needed to expand their leadership team to meet their fellowship's practical needs. Their process reveals their priorities: choosing men who were "known to be full of the Spirit and wisdom." Perhaps you are wondering why you have not been given more responsibility in your own local church. If you are committed to fulfilling your purposes as a Christ-follower and serving Him well, you will need to seek the presence and power of the Holy Spirit. He will give you the wisdom and discernment you need to do the tasks God has chosen specifically for you, and opportunities to serve Him will follow.

• THINK ABOUT IT •

Do you actively and intentionally ask the Holy Spirit to fill you and empower you for greater service in God's Kingdom?

Prayer

Heavenly Father, serving You is a entrusted privilege, and I need the help of Your Holy Spirit—leading me and aligning my heart, attention, and words to Your wisdom. Help me always welcome and be filled to overflowing with Your Spirit. In Jesus' name, amen.

DAY 209

DAILY FAITH PRACTICE

Do not let anyone judge you by what you eat or drink, or with regard to a religious festival, a New Moon celebration or a Sabbath day. These are a shadow of the things that were to come; the reality, however, is found in Christ.

COLOSSIANS 2:16-17

Some contemporary Christians practice what they consider to be a more authentic faith, following Jewish dietary laws and celebrating Hebrew festivals and feasts. So what is our current responsibility in this regard? Paul, an observant Jewish man, called to take the gospel of Jesus Christ to the Gentiles, addresses this in his letter to the Colossians. The Jewish food laws and calendar are unmistakably part of our Christian heritage, but Paul clearly says we will not be judged by our observance of those things. The greater truth is those religious ordinances and activities were intended to point the Hebrews to what God was going to do in the Messiah. So the most important observance for Christ-followers is the daily acknowledgment that we believe Jesus of Nazareth is Christ, Lord, and King. We should celebrate the salvation that God accomplished for us, through Him, every day.

• THINK ABOUT IT •

What is your daily practice of acknowledging the lordship of Jesus and the salvation He accomplished for you?

Prayer

Heavenly Father, I want Paul's liberating counsel—refocusing me on Your character and Jesus' redemptive work on the cross—to be effectually evident in my life. May I consistently acknowledge Jesus as Christ, Lord, and King in all my ways. In Jesus' name, amen.

PROCLAIM FREEDOM

"He has sent me to proclaim freedom for the prisoners and recovery of sight for the blind, to release the oppressed. . . ."

LUKE 4:18

Physical bondage means to be locked up, shut in, chained—without liberty of movement or choice. Freedom is the opposite—to be unrestrained, unchained—liberty. As certainly as bondage and freedom have physical components, there is a spiritual component far more powerful than any confining locked door—spiritual forces that can exploit every appetite and desire, causing it to become a type of bondage. Many familiar things in life—food, money, possessions, sex, alcohol— are not inherently wicked or evil. But when misused, they can become compulsive and controlling with the help of spiritual forces working to shackle and prevent you from fulfilling God's purposes. But we are not without hope! Jesus came "to proclaim freedom for the prisoners. . . to release the oppressed." Let's neither be naïve about binding, destructive spiritual forces, nor underestimate God's power that is available to free us.

• THINK ABOUT IT •

Is there anything in your life that is not inherently evil but has become a point of bondage for you? Consider the power to live in freedom that God has already supplied for you.

Prayer

Heavenly Father, please reveal any binding thing holding me back from the spiritual freedom You paid dearly for me to possess. Thank You for Your deliverance freely, readily available through the sacrificial cross of Jesus Christ. In Jesus' name, amen.

A WIDE OPEN DOOR

In him [Jesus] and through faith in him we may approach God with freedom and confidence.

EPHESIANS 3:12

I was once introduced to a man whose disinterest in meeting me could not have been any more obvious—he might as well have turned his back on me! The significance of posture and body language has been studied and written about a lot, but most of us can instinctively tell if someone is interested or uninterested. That makes me think about what my posture and body language say about the way I approach God. Physically, we approach Him in many different ways: standing, sitting, kneeling, lying face down, lying in bed, driving a car. Our eyes may be open or closed—hopefully open if we're driving! Our hands may be clenched in grief or open in praise and supplication. These things may reflect the setting we are in or the situation we are praying about. But whatever your posture, and whatever the circumstance, we can approach God with freedom and confidence. Part of what Jesus did for us on the cross was to open wide the door to God. He is as near as your first word, and He will never turn His back on you.

• THINK ABOUT IT •

How do you approach God? With apprehension or fear? Or with freedom and confidence?

Prayer

Heavenly Father, thank You for revealing Your love through Jesus Christ and the freedom He offers. Help me confidently approach Your throne to experience the mercy and grace that allow me to boldly submit my requests to You in His name. In Jesus' name, amen.

DAY 212

VERY NEAR

What I am commanding you today is not too difficult for you or beyond your reach. It is not up in heaven, so that you have to ask, "Who will ascend into heaven to get it and proclaim it to us so we may obey it?" Nor is it beyond the sea, so that you have to ask, "Who will cross the sea to get it and proclaim it to us so we may obey it?" No, the word is very near you; it is in your mouth and in your heart so you may obey it.

DEUTERONOMY 30:11-14

Moses is preparing the Israelites for challenges awaiting them prior to entering the Promised Land: "There's hard work ahead, but you have what you need—the word—in your mouth and heart." It's easy to think, "Moses means the Bible, and when we memorize and put verses in our hearts they can come out of our mouths." Not an evil interpretation, but not one word of the Bible had been published when Moses made those statements. Moses was talking about the God-stories we each have lived, seen, and heard. Faith is not at a mountaintop, too high to climb. Nor is it across a vast ocean. The word of faith that you need is near you because God has spoken it into your life.

• THINK ABOUT IT •

During what seasons has it been obvious to you that God has given you the faith you need to live for Him in the world?

Prayer

Heavenly Father, thank You for the gift of faith. May it become the kind Moses had—faith that believes You can do anything and trusts You to make a difference in my world. May I reach out to You as I face the challenges before me. In Jesus' name, amen.

DAY 213

SO MUCH MORE

For in Christ all the fullness of the Deity lives in bodily form, and you have been given fullness in Christ, who is the head over every power and authority.

COLOSSIANS 2:9-10

We do ourselves a disservice when we talk about Jesus as having only a message of love. Love is a part of His message, certainly, but it's not the whole message. Sometimes in our desire to make Jesus a nice person we can relate to more easily, we diminish His power and His authority. But Jesus was "the fullness of the Deity . . . in bodily form." His life was an introduction to what God's Kingdom is like and what it means for us to be children of God and heirs of all that He promises. We don't fully understand this Kingdom yet, but Jesus showed us who we are in Him now and who we can become. I serve Him because He is God's Son and there is no one else like Him. When you read the Bible, ask God to give you a revelation of our Lord, Jesus of Nazareth. He is love, yes, but so much more.

• THINK ABOUT IT •

Great strength and gentleness often go together. What examples of those qualities can you recall from the life of Jesus?

Prayer

Heavenly Father, Jesus illustrated such love when He conquered Your enemy for my redemption. Please give me a full revelation of Jesus—His love and complete authority—that I might walk in the freedom available through His cross. In Jesus' name, amen.

SPHERE OF INFLUENCE

"They overcame him [Satan] by the blood of the Lamb and by the word of their testimony. . . ."

REVELATION 12:11

"How can I know what God wants me to do with my life?" This is a question I hear often, but sometimes we make it more difficult than it needs to be. There are a couple of things about our lives that are unique and important. One, each of us has a unique God-story, and this passage from Revelation shows just how powerful and important our God-stories are! What He has done for you is not up for debate or argument; it's simply your story. Second, God has given you a sphere of influence. There is a group of people around you who care about what you think and value. They'll be influenced by your perspective and your decisions. If you will take your God-story and make it known within your sphere of influence, God will begin to multiply the influence of your life. I know this is true because I have seen it happen over and over again.

• THINK ABOUT IT •

One of our most fundamental God-assignments is to use the influence He's given us to be ambassadors for Jesus. How are you using the influence He has given you?

Prayer

Heavenly Father, thank You for the ways You have helped, strengthened, and encouraged me. Use my life—my words, influence, and relationships—to let Your light shine forth in the darkness, bringing hope to those around me. In Jesus' name, amen.

DAY 215

CHOOSE JOY

A cheerful heart is good medicine, but a crushed spirit dries up the bones.

PROVERBS 17:22

Did you know we have emotional visitors? Some you are glad to see coming, and many you are glad to see departing. Disappointment and discouragement are two of those visitors who show up uninvited from time to time. Some of us have let them linger so long that they seem like old friends, but they are not our friends; they are adversaries, and we should not welcome them. Nor should we wait around and hope that they will eventually find their way to the door; we should take the initiative and kick them out. A cheerful heart is contagious, so instead of dwelling on disappointment and discouragement, let's find positive people who are willing to walk alongside us and encourage us on the journey. Let's focus on the blessings and provision God has shown us. Let's be grateful for our freedom to worship, to serve together, to lift up the name of Jesus in our homes and communities. Let's be cheerful. Let's choose joy!

• THINK ABOUT IT •

Have you allowed disappointment and discouragement to take up residence in your heart? If so, how can you see them through a proper spiritual perspective and make a conscious decision to choose joy?

Prayer

Heavenly Father, only You give real joy that satisfies my heart and mind. I welcome Your Holy Spirit afresh into my life today. Give me a cheerful heart and relationships with positive people that we might mutually encourage each other. In Jesus' name, amen.

NO ROCK THROWING

To those sanctified in Christ Jesus and called to be holy, together with all those everywhere who call on the name of our Lord Jesus Christ—their Lord and ours: Grace and peace to you from God our Father and the Lord Jesus Christ.

1 CORINTHIANS 1:2-3

The diverse expressions of the Church of Jesus Christ reflect many things: cultural surroundings, faith traditions, and personalities of previous and present congregants, along with their varied preferences in architecture, style, and forms of worship. Those factors are worthy of discussion, but they are very secondary concerns. We don't all have to read the same Bible translation or share the same color communion grape juice. We don't need to debate suits versus jeans, pews versus chairs. If we can hold divergent opinions with our brothers and sisters in Christ and still go to Heaven, let's extend a hand of fellowship instead of throwing a rock. We do not want to give our adversary the pleasure of seeing us caught up in distractions and missing opportunities to strengthen Jesus' Church and participate in the purposes of God.

• THINK ABOUT IT •

Do you speak positively about the other Bible-believing churches in your community? Do you pray for and encourage their people and their ministries?

Prayer

Heavenly Father, I am grateful to be part of Your Body of Christ and for all the churches filled with Christ-followers practicing their faith, perhaps differently than I. Unify us in purpose. Help me be a strength to Your Church. In Jesus' name, amen.

WISDOM AND REVELATION

I keep asking that the God of our Lord Jesus Christ, the glorious Father, may give you the Spirit of wisdom and revelation, so that you may know him better.

EPHESIANS 1:17

Our nation emerged from a unique set of circumstances. We began with a desire to be a Christian nation—not uniquely Christian in that everyone who lives here is required to be Christian, but a nation whose foundation was built on a Christian worldview. Fifty-two of the fifty-five signers of the Declaration of Independence were deeply committed, orthodox Christians. The other three believed in the Bible as divine truth, the God of Scripture, and His personal intervention. As we look across the span of American history, we see that almost all of our Presidents have claimed the Christian faith. Not every one of them has lived up to our faith's highest ideals, but neither are we without fault. Let us pray the Apostle Paul's words for our leaders, and for ourselves: "I keep asking that the God of our Lord Jesus Christ, the glorious Father, may give you the Spirit of wisdom and revelation, so that you may know him better."

• THINK ABOUT IT •

Our leaders need insight and understanding that only comes from God. Do you pray for our leaders as much as you complain about and criticize them?

Prayer

Heavenly Father, we have turned away from You in pride and rebellion. In mercy, forgive our sins and pour out a spirit of humility and repentance. Please give our leaders a Spirit of wisdom and revelation that they might honor You. In Jesus' name, amen.

CHOICE AND CONSEQUENCE

As Solomon grew old, his wives turned his heart after other gods, and his heart was not fully devoted to the LORD his God, as the heart of David his father had been.

1 KINGS 11:4

Solomon was best known for his great wisdom from God and his earlier success reigning as king. His later years were marked by a change in his attitude toward God and thus toward life. Scripture reveals one reason was his choice to make international treaties and alliances through marriage. That was common practice in the ancient Near East, but not one God initiated. Solomon married women from nations about which the Lord had told the Israelites, "You must not intermarry with them, because they will surely turn your hearts after their gods." Solomon acted against the wisdom God had given him and behaved foolishly, making choices contrary to God's direction. His actions had negative consequences for him personally and the nation as a whole. This principle is timeless: If we choose an ungodly path we will reap destruction, but if we choose a godly path we will reap blessing.

• THINK ABOUT IT •

Are there areas of your life where you have acted against the wisdom God has given you and reaped negative consequences? What is your plan for staying on a godly path in the future?

Prayer

Heavenly Father, seeking Your will is a priority. May temptations and distractions never weaken my commitment and devotion to You or accomplish the enemy's plan to take me off course. May Your name be honored through my choices. In Jesus' name, amen.

DAY 219

RELIGION VS. RELATIONSHIP

"Be on your guard against the yeast of the Pharisees and Sadducees." Then they understood that he was not telling them to guard against the yeast used in bread, but against the teaching of the Pharisees and Sadducees.

MATTHEW 16:11-12

The Pharisees and Sadducees were two sects of Judaism active during Jesus' lifetime. The Pharisees were laymen, believing God's revelation consisted of two parts: Torah (the first five books of the Old Testament) and the oral tradition that evolved and grew through interpretive writing of various rabbis. The Sadducees were priests in the Jerusalem Temple, the spiritual center of the nation. They were wealthy people of great political influence. Both groups were religious, but could not recognize the Messiah when He came because He did not fit their preconceived notions. We, too, can be outwardly religious and not believe in God. We can sit in church, carry a big Bible, and know every song, and yet have no relationship with Jesus. Let's examine our hearts to ensure our desire is not to put on a religious show, but to be a friend of Jesus.

• THINK ABOUT IT •

Are you sometimes tempted to focus on the outward expression of your religion rather than your personal relationship with Jesus? What can you do to keep your focus on Him?

Prayer

Heavenly Father, search my heart for any unclean thing. I trust Your Holy Spirit to discern my heart and reveal where I need to change. May I be quick to repent and obey, for I want to please You above all. In Jesus' name, amen.

FATHER KNOWS BEST

Many are the plans in a man's heart, but it is the LORD's purpose that prevails.

PROVERBS 19:21

Jesus' life was clearly influenced by His awareness of His Father's purposes for Him, and those purposes surely dominated His thinking. Do you imagine that in the context of your home and your business and your relationships that God has a purpose for you? There are times when God's plan is not easily known or embraced. But the Scripture is clear—it's asserted repeatedly—that God knows the end of the matter from the beginning, and that He has plans and purposes for each of us. Every one of us fights an internal battle against setting God aside and imagining ourselves to be the masters of our own fate. We think we surely know what is best for ourselves. As we mature as Jesus-followers, we will increasingly realize that it is to our great advantage to yield ourselves to an Almighty God and acknowledge that He is wise in ways that we are not and wants to bless us in ways we cannot imagine.

• THINK ABOUT IT •

What do you think about in the quiet places of your life? Do you tend to think about your wants and your desires, or do you put your mind to the purposes of God?

Prayer

Heavenly Father, Your agenda contains the highest purposes I will ever know. I repent of the times I have questioned Your plan and leaned into my own desires. May I seek Your direction above my own that I might bring You glory. In Jesus' name, amen.

CULTIVATE CONSISTENCY

The effective prayer of a righteous man can accomplish much.

JAMES 5:16 • NASB®

If there is an effective prayer that can accomplish much, by logic there are ineffective prayers that accomplish little. We don't want to spend our lives ineffectively, spinning our wheels spiritually, so an effective prayer life is something we want to work on. I can give you one key that will change everything: You need to read your Bible because the Word of God is the incubator for an effective prayer life. If you don't read your Bible, you really have no insight or authority. You don't have enough understanding of the character of God. You leave prayer in the realm of a mystery, something fuzzy and indistinct. If you'll take the time in a consistent way to put the Word of God in your heart, it will transform your prayer life, and you. I've seen this happen in the lives of thousands of people, so it is not a mystery to me any longer. Try it consistently for a season, and the outcome will be there—I promise you.

• THINK ABOUT IT •

Do you read God's Word consistently? How does this practice impact your prayer life?

Prayer

Heavenly Father, thank You for the authority of Your Word that sustains me and helps me pray according to Your will. I invite Your Holy Spirit to lead me as I meditate on Your Word and pray. Teach me to intercede effectively. In Jesus' name, amen.

A NAVIGATION GUIDE

So the LORD God banished him from the Garden of Eden to work the ground from which he had been taken.

GENESIS 3:23

Scripture consistently exposes the myth that life is easy. Of 929 chapters in the Old Testament, the first two describe God's loving acts of creation and care for the first people, Adam and Eve. In Genesis, chapter three, they doubt God's intentions for them and defy His instructions and are banished from intimate relationship with God. The remaining 926 chapters describe their descendants' struggles to stay close to God and earn His acceptance. The 260 chapters of the New Testament focus on Jesus Christ, God's loving and complete solution to our sin problem. Jesus faced persecution, rejection, and hatred—the leaders of His own faith wanted Him dead, and even those who saw His ministry firsthand struggled to understand and accept the new life that He offered. Not one of the people in the Bible had a life without challenges, and we will face challenges too. The Bible will not show us a path free of problems, but it will give us wisdom to know how to navigate life in a way that pleases God.

• THINK ABOUT IT •

Have you ever thought that a relationship with Jesus would keep you from problems? How does the Bible give you wisdom for living?

Prayer

Heavenly Father, life is hard, and I need Your help. I need the power that raised Jesus from the dead to be active in my life. Help me walk through challenges with the confidence that You will be my strength and a light to others. In Jesus' name, amen.

DAY 223

EXACT REPRESENTATION

The Son is the radiance of God's glory and the exact representation of his being, sustaining all things by his powerful word. After he had provided purification for sins, he sat down at the right hand of the Majesty in heaven.

HEBREWS 1:3

The Bible is a collection of sixty-six books written by many authors who lived during a span of over a thousand years. The first four books of the New Testament—Matthew, Mark, Luke, and John—are known as the Gospels. They are those writers' personal announcements of the good news about Jesus and the significance of His life. But the gospel is more than those four Bible books; the gospel is Jesus. Jesus didn't come to give us a message; Jesus IS the message. Jesus didn't come to give us a revelation; Jesus IS the revelation. Jesus is the exact representation of God the Father, and He is sitting at the right hand of His Father even now. So if you want to know God the Father—His attitudes, His thoughts, and His responses—get to know Jesus. That endeavor will be well worth the investment of your time.

• THINK ABOUT IT •

What does your knowledge of Jesus the Son tell you about God the Father?

Prayer

Heavenly Father, thank You that knowing Jesus is knowing You. He is both love and strength, fulfilling Your fatherly plan for mankind. I am filled with great hope just by knowing Your character and provision through Jesus' attributes. In Jesus' name, amen.

SEASONS OF CHALLENGE

Consider it pure joy, my brothers, whenever you face trials of many kinds, because you know that the testing of your faith develops perseverance.

JAMES 1:2-3

I cringe when people imply that being a Christ-follower means every day is a trip to a theme park and every meal is a dessert buffet. That is simply not the truth. Christ-followers lose their jobs, watch their investments nosedive, and get sick just like everyone else. Sometimes we are tempted to think that because there is turmoil or conflict in our lives that God has abandoned us. He hasn't. He is not angry with us or punishing us; this is just the nature of life in our fallen world. Thankfully, He has given us everything we need to live triumphantly and grow closer to Him through those seasons. If we have our minds directed toward the things of God, even in the challenging and uncomfortable places, we can walk through them with assurance, knowing that He is allowing us to develop perseverance and mature as Jesus-followers. With confidence say, "God, show me Your purpose in this"—and He will.

· THINK ABOUT IT ·

Maturing in Christ can be a painful process, but it is necessary if we are to fulfill what God has called us to do. Do you look for His purposes in the midst of your trials?

Prayer

Heavenly Father, in the midst of trials, help me remember to respond with joy that You count me worthy of the faith-test. May they increase faith and holiness in me. Your Word is truth, benefiting me when I believe in and yield to it. In Jesus' name, amen.

STOP AND LISTEN

Wisdom calls aloud in the street, she raises her voice in the public squares; at the head of the noisy streets she cries out, in the gateways of the city she makes her speech. . . .

PROVERBS 1:20-21

This passage gives a vivid description of wisdom as a woman who is crying aloud in the street, raising her voice and trying to be heard over the noise of a city. But people are covering their ears and turning their backs on her. This scene is unsettling. The God of the universe is telling us that He is literally crying out His perspective to us, but we are not interested. Have you ever seen children cover their ears and chant "La, la, la, la" to avoid hearing something? The adult version of that is to put our ear buds in and pretend that we are listening to something even when we are not! We are all a little guilty of doing that to the Lord, aren't we? "God, hear my prayers! Deliver me! Heal me! Bless me! Just don't expect me to listen to anything You have to say." In spite of our selfishness, the Lord is not avoiding us; He is seeking us and crying out to us so that we can know Him more intimately. What an amazing promise! What an amazing opportunity!

• THINK ABOUT IT •

When you approach the Lord, do you do more talking or listening?

Prayer

Heavenly Father, forgive me for when I have come to You in need or crisis, but not stopped to listen to Your opinion and answers. Help me come intentionally before You, listening with the intent to obey that I might know and honor You. In Jesus' name, amen.

REFLECT HIM

Serve wholeheartedly, as if you were serving the Lord, not men, because you know that the Lord will reward everyone for whatever good he does. . . .

EPHESIANS 6:7-8

Many of us think of our work as just a way to put food on the table and keep the electricity turned on. Work is that, certainly, but it is much more than that. God modeled work for us, and the way we go about our work and interact with our coworkers is an expression to the world of our relationship with Him. Do you work with integrity? Are you truthful and trustworthy? Do you arrive on time and give a full day's effort? Do you do what you say you will do? Do you encourage cooperation and unity? Do you value and respect your coworkers? Are you compassionate and concerned about them as people? Do you treat everyone fairly? Do you give credit where credit is due? Work is God's idea, so don't go about your workday as if you are working for someone else—you are working for God.

• THINK ABOUT IT •

God has given you a sphere of influence in the workplace, and the people there matter. What do your attitudes and behaviors in your workplace say to others about your relationship with God?

Prayer

Heavenly Father, thank You for the influence You have given me in many places. Help me keep in mind that I am working for You, wherever I am and whatever I am doing. Let me do it to the fullest to fulfill Your will for my life. In Jesus' name, amen.

SLIP OF THE TONGUE

"I tell you that men will have to give account on the day of judgment for every careless word they have spoken."

MATTHEW 12:36

My chainsaw is a wonderful tool, and I appreciate how quickly it can help me finish a task. But I'm always conscious that as much potential as it has for speed and efficiency, it also has enormous potential for harm and destruction. In a careless moment I can do something that can't be reversed, something that could change my future or someone else's. Words are tools that are even more powerful than a chainsaw, and sometimes we are reckless with them. In an unthinking moment we can say something that we can't unsay. We can say something that can change our future or someone else's. It is a sobering reality that our careless words are being duly noted and we will have to give an account for them on the day of judgment. Let's be careful that our words are not careless ones we will be reminded of on that day.

· THINK ABOUT IT ·

Are you sometimes careless with your words? How can you use your words to build up rather than destroy?

Prayer

Heavenly Father, keep my mouth from carelessly speaking worthless, harmful words with no regard for consequences. Give me an awareness of the spiritual consequences before I speak. Let the words of my mouth bring glory to Your name. In Jesus' name, amen.

FAMILY TIES

Israel loved Joseph more than any of his other sons, because he had been born to him in his old age; and he made a richly ornamented robe for him. When his brothers saw that their father loved him more than any of them, they hated him and could not speak a kind word to him.

GENESIS 37:3-4

Joseph was the eleventh of Jacob's twelve sons, born to two wives and two handmaidens. We can only imagine the dysfunction within this ancient clan as mothers and sons jockeyed for position. Jacob did not hide Joseph was his favorite, so when Joseph told two of his dreams depicting his family bowing down to him, his brothers' jealousy boiled over. Their emotions overruled judgment, and they plotted to kill him. Instead they sold Joseph into slavery, but through God's sovereignty he had one of the most famous political careers in the Bible. Joseph overcame great odds through the power and blessing of God. Just as Joseph's family did not define his future, neither do our families define our future. God is in control of your life, and He wants to do great things through you.

· THINK ABOUT IT ·

Have you allowed negative family experiences of the past to determine aspects of your present? How can you surrender those experiences to God and depend on Him for your future?

Prayer

Heavenly Father, forgive me for allowing negative family experiences to determine my life-perspectives. I submit afresh to Jesus' redemptive work on the cross. Help me to fully release my future to Your sovereign and loving rule. In Jesus' name, amen.

HE CAN

"If you can do anything, take pity on us and help us." "'If you can'?" said Jesus. "Everything is possible for him who believes." Immediately the boy's father exclaimed, "I do believe; help me overcome my unbelief!"

MARK 9:22-24

This is one of my favorite stories in the New Testament. A boy is possessed by an evil spirit that causes him to have violent convulsions. His father brings the boy to Jesus and says, "If you can do something, help him." I picture Jesus raising one eyebrow as He says, "If I can? If I can? All things are possible for him who believes." The father quickly assures Jesus that he believes. Sure he does—he loves his son and wants him relieved of this terrible condition. But then he realizes that he might have exaggerated to this teacher who some say is the Messiah, so he adds, "Help my unbelief!" Jesus helped his unbelief and helped his son. Never be afraid to acknowledge your doubts to God. He already knows them anyway, and He will gladly increase your faith.

• THINK ABOUT IT •

Have you ever said "If you can" to Jesus?

Prayer

Heavenly Father, at times I am weak, forgetful, and have belief in my mind but a degree of unbelief in my heart. Lord, help me in my unbelief. You are my Redeemer and Restorer, able to turn my doubt into belief for Your glory! In Jesus' name, amen.

A GOOD THING

I long to see you so that I may impart to you some spiritual gift to make you strong—that is, that you and I may be mutually encouraged by each other's faith.

ROMANS 1:11-12

Churches are such peaceful places when no one is in the building. The hassle factor goes up dramatically when we arrive, sneezing, coughing, dropping trash, cutting one another off in the parking lot. People outside the Church mistakenly think we gather in local congregations because we've "got it all together." Nothing could be less true. We're not in churches because we're perfect, but because we need help. Even Paul longed to see the congregation in Rome and be encouraged by their faith. That same encouragement and faith inspires hope for that in our family members, coworkers, and neighbors. The Church is a good thing and the most powerful transforming force available for a human life. We should extend an invitation to all people—struggling, broken, hurting people, even those who "have it all together." God loves people, and we, His Church, have to care about people and invite them in.

• THINK ABOUT IT •

Do you see the Church as a clubhouse for people who have it all together or a first-aid station for hurting people? How does this influence your relationship with your local congregation? How does this affect whom you will invite into your fellowship?

Prayer

Heavenly Father, Church is not a building, but people who believe in You and obey Your Word. The Body of Christ is a safe, hopeful place where I can learn to live a transformed life. May I strengthen Your Church, inviting others in. In Jesus' name, amen.

DAY 231

CONTEMPLATE MAJESTY

Let all the earth fear the Lord; let all the people of the world revere him. For he spoke, and it came to be; he commanded, and it stood firm.

PSALM 33:8-9

The Church would benefit greatly, individually and collectively, if we took the time to contemplate the majesty of our God. If we would routinely spend time with Him until we have a sense of the magnitude of who He is, it would completely reorient our priorities and change our lives. We would visit the hospital's newborn nursery and marvel at these new people, each one who is fearfully and wonderfully made in His image. We would visit a nursing home and see the unique dignity of old age. We would gaze up at the stars and contemplate the vastness of the creation He spoke into being. We would watch a spider construct a web and recognize the intricacy of His design. We would deposit a paycheck and thank Him for the abundance of His provision. We would gratefully tell our neighbors about the ways He has saved and sustained us. One day all the earth will revere the majesty of the Lord, but it can begin with us . . . now.

• THINK ABOUT IT •

How does your awareness of the majesty of God impact your life, spiritually and physically?

Prayer

Heavenly Father, I am in awe of You majesty, splendor, and perfection! Give me words that I may boldly and gratefully declare Your greatness and faithfulness demonstrated so clearly in Your creation and on the cross of Your Son. In Jesus' name, amen.

ORDINARY TO EXTRAORDINARY

*May the God of peace . . . equip you with everything good for doing his will,
and may he work in us what is pleasing to him, through Jesus Christ, to whom
be glory for ever and ever.*

HEBREWS 13:20-21

We like to think that when God told Noah to build an ark, Noah thought, "Yes! I get to use all my tools!" Or we imagine that when Jesus said to Peter, "Put that net down and follow me," Peter thought, "A new job—finally!" I don't really believe that. They were normal people, and I think it was just as hard for them to cooperate with God as it is for me. We sometimes project onto others an ease that we don't have in order to excuse our own reluctance. There are several reasons for that, but I think that many of us simply feel unqualified and unequipped to do the tasks God has set before us. The good news is that our God is faithful to give us everything we need to do His will. God has always equipped ordinary people to do extraordinary things, and you are no different. Ask Him to show you how you can serve Him, and He will give you every tool you need.

• THINK ABOUT IT •

When God equips us to do what we feel unqualified for, it is an opportunity for us to show that He lives in us and works through us. What has He called and equipped you to do?

Prayer

Heavenly Father, Your Word reveals how well You equip Your servants for their God-assignments. Show me how I can more effectively serve You, and help me trust You for every tool I will need. I am confident in Your faithfulness. In Jesus' name, amen.

ONE BLESSING AFTER ANOTHER

From the fullness of his grace we have all received one blessing after another.

JOHN 1:16

Grace is the undeserved, unearned, and unmerited blessing or good will of God expressed toward us. If it was deserved, or earned, or merit-based, it would not be grace. Grace is a reflection of God's character, and it is what makes the change in our lives possible. What has caused the blessings of God to come to us? Our kindness? Our moral integrity? No. The blessings of God have come to us because of God's goodness, not because of our own. God doesn't bless us because we've managed to keep eight of the Ten Commandments today. God blesses us because of His grace. Every good thing in our lives is because of the grace of God. As your relationship with Jesus deepens you are awakened to that reality and you increasingly realize that you are not just a self-made person. It is because of Him that we receive "one blessing after another."

· THINK ABOUT IT ·

Do you recognize the grace of God in your life? Do you express gratitude to Him for His good will and blessing toward you?

Prayer

Heavenly Father, open my eyes to recognize every demonstration of Your mercy and grace toward me, whether it comes through the ordinary or the extraordinary, so that I can worship You and thank You all the more. In Jesus' name, amen.

ON YOUR SIDE

He gives strength to the weary and increases the power of the weak. Even youths grow tired and weary, and young men stumble and fall; but those who hope in the LORD will renew their strength.

ISAIAH 40:29-31

I'm always amused by sports clichés. "We need to give 110%." "They left it all on the field." "They've got to bring their A-game today." The sentiment is the same: If you want to win, you need to give your best effort and not give up. That's true of our spiritual lives as well: We need to give our best effort, and we can't give up. The reality is we often feel we can't take another step, the obstacles are too many, and we're in the battle alone. Almighty God is on our side, however, and He empowers us to live in a way that honors Him and accomplishes His purposes. He takes our effort and adds His own to it, giving us His strength when we are weary, His power when we are weak, and His presence when we feel alone. Can you imagine the daily impact of this promise on our lives? Let's give Him our best effort and learn to call on Him when we feel weary, weak, and alone.

· THINK ABOUT IT ·

Do you attempt to face life's challenges under your own power, or do you ask the Lord to empower you? Do you live with the knowledge that He is on your side?

Prayer

Heavenly Father, forgive me when I have powered through on my own. May I consistently bring You my best efforts, knowing You will enable me. Help me increasingly know that You desire to strengthen and empower me for Your purposes. In Jesus' name, amen.

DAY 235

STRONGER FAITH REQUIRED

The Spirit clearly says that in later times some will abandon the faith and follow deceiving spirits and things taught by demons. Such teachings come through hypocritical liars, whose consciences have been seared as with a hot iron.

1 TIMOTHY 4:1-2

When I say a new spiritual season has come, I'm not suggesting a day you can point to and say, "That's the day when everything changed." Just as winter slowly turns to spring, there is ebb and flow over a period of time until one season yields to another. Even though a new spiritual season has arrived, we need to prepare ourselves to live in it. The first thing is recognizing the faith that was sufficient in the previous season is not adequate for the present season. Bold faith is required—authentic, deeply rooted faith that will hold firm under the attacks of "deceiving spirits and demons" delivered by "hypocritical liars." This faith begins with prayer and welcoming the Holy Spirit as we live for Jesus in daily simple things. Our faith will grow and deepen as we experience His faithfulness toward us. Let's live so that those around us will ask, "Where do you get your strength? How do you find such peace in this world?"

• THINK ABOUT IT •

What are you doing to prepare yourself spiritually for this new season?

Prayer

Heavenly Father, thank You for Your Holy Spirit who gives discernment and helps me guard my mind with vigilance. Help me be clear-minded and self-controlled, with firm and bold faith that watches expectantly for Your faithfulness. In Jesus' name, amen.

SPECIAL DELIVERY

All your words are true; all your righteous laws are eternal.

PSALM 119:160

One of the reasons why the Bible is such a remarkable book is that it is timeless. It was written centuries ago by about forty main contributors who lived in a variety of historical and social contexts. Yet when we open it up it speaks to us. The circumstances of my life and the challenges that I face are addressed there. The truths are timeless, but the ways we offer up the truth need to fit the seasons in which we live. Jesus said in Matthew 24 that before He comes back to earth, the message of His Kingdom will be preached in the whole world as a testimony to all the nations—and then the end will come. We have greater tools for the proclamation of the gospel today than at any time in human history, and we are using the digital world to communicate the gospel in a powerful way. Don't mock that person who reads Scripture on a brightly lit screen—praise God for His creative power!

• THINK ABOUT IT •

The truths of Almighty God don't change, but His delivery systems do. How has God used technology to advance His purposes in the earth?

Prayer

Heavenly Father, the truth of Your Word is timeless. Thank You for allowing me a place in Your plan "for such a time as this." Help me to creatively use tools You provide to share You with others in ways they can best receive. In Jesus' name, amen.

IN RIGHT STANDING

Christ is the end of the law for righteousness to everyone who believes.

ROMANS 10:4 • NASB®

We in Christian circles often read this verse selectively, stopping too soon and interpreting it as "Jesus was the end of the law." It actually says that Jesus was the end of the law "for righteousness." "Righteousness" is a big religious word that means the ability to stand in the presence of God without guilt, fear, or shame. Before Jesus showed people a better way, you had to abide by all the rules in order to stand before God with confidence—and there were a lot of rules! It was an all-or-nothing proposition; if you broke one rule, you were guilty of breaking every one. In today's terms, if you drove one mile over the speed limit or rolled through one stop sign, you'd lose your license and have to go back to driving school! Jesus didn't abolish the law, however; He fulfilled the law so that you and I might know God's grace. Our status, our ability to participate in the Kingdom of God is not because we have earned it or we deserve it or keep a set of rules. It is a gift Jesus purchased for us on the cross, the gift of His righteousness.

• THINK ABOUT IT •

How do you think Jesus' righteousness applies to your thoughts and your everyday activities?

Prayer

Heavenly Father, thank You for exchanging my sin for Your righteousness through the cross of Jesus Christ—something I could not do for myself. May Jesus' finished work of redemption direct and inspire all my thoughts and actions. In Jesus' name, amen.

SHARE THE STORY

The man from whom the demons had gone out begged to go with him, but Jesus sent him away, saying, "Return home and tell how much God has done for you." So the man went away and told all over town how much Jesus had done for him.

LUKE 8:38-39

If you want to see definite opinions, ask two people, who use two different computer technologies, what they use and why. You're going to hear about operating systems, hardware, applications, storage capacity, ease of use, cost, upgrades, and more. They are probably completely committed to their choice and feel very sorry for those uninformed people on the other side. They are entitled to either opinion and are probably not reluctant to share it. Why is it that when we come to Almighty God we're reluctant to say, "I have an opinion about the best way to be"? This man, who had been freed from the grip of demons, could not wait to tell everyone what Jesus had done for him. He wanted to stay with Jesus, but Jesus wanted him to go home and tell everyone that there is freedom and healing to be found in Him. This man had a Jesus-story to tell, and we do too.

• THINK ABOUT IT •

Your Jesus-story may not be as dramatic as this man's, but it is yours to own and share. Do you eagerly tell others what Jesus has done for you?

Prayer

Heavenly Father, prepare me to persevere, standing faithful with strength of character like those depicted in Scripture who unashamedly shared their God-stories. Help me effectively share my own God-story in a way that honors You. In Jesus' name, amen.

DAY 239

STREAMS IN THE DESERT

"See, I am doing a new thing! Now it springs up; do you not perceive it? I am making a way in the desert and streams in the wasteland."

ISAIAH 43:19

When we see a rhetorical "Do you not?" question like this in the Bible, the answer is typically, "No, we do not." There is no way in the desert, and there are no streams in the wasteland. That's why it's a wasteland; nobody goes there because we go where the streams are. Where there is water there is life and renewal and refreshment. But God says, "I will take the desert places and the wastelands and I will make them fruitful because I'm creative and innovative and I want to do that." We know the truth of that because God has taken the desert places of our lives and the wastelands we have created and brought life to them again. There are parts of our lives that people have spoken over and said, "I'm sorry. This is hopeless. There is no coming back from this." Yet God has brought hope into those desert places. That's our God.

• THINK ABOUT IT •

Have you been through desert places that God brought back to life? Tell someone what the Lord has done for you! Are you in one of those places now? Ask Him to make a way for you!

Prayer

Heavenly Father, I need renewal and restored hope. I know others who also need "springs in the desert." I humbly welcome all the restoration You desire that I might go forward with renewed power at work in me to help refresh others. In Jesus' name, amen.

THE ONLY WAY

Jesus answered, "I am the way and the truth and the life. No one comes to the Father except through me."

JOHN 14:6

God used Jesus' cousin, John the Baptist, to call a whole nation to repentance. John, who was a fulfillment of prophecy in his own right, had gained enough influence that he was arrested because the king was embarrassed by his call for righteousness. But even this famous preacher said, "Someone else is coming, and I'm not even worthy to untie His shoes." John was absolutely correct. Jesus is unique in the history of the world. There is no one like Him, and there never will be. There are no parallels to Jesus in other faith traditions. As our only pathway to God, He filled a place in the story of humanity that no one else can fulfill. You can't get to the Father through practicing yoga or reaching a heightened state of awareness. You can't get to the Father through good deeds or generosity or keeping a list of rules. Jesus said, "I am the way and the truth and the life." He is not one of the ways to God—He is the only way.

• THINK ABOUT IT •

In what ways is Jesus unique? Why does Jesus deserve our humility and complete devotion?

Prayer

Heavenly Father, Your Word declares there is no pathway of reconciliation to You except through Jesus Christ's sacrificial death on the cross and victorious resurrection. I humbly proclaim Him worthy to be Lord of my entire life. In Jesus' name, amen.

RELEASED FROM SLAVERY

When you were slaves to sin, you were free from the control of righteousness. What benefit did you reap at that time from the things you are now ashamed of? Those things result in death!

ROMANS 6:20-21

Life without Jesus is a horrific condition. The Bible tells us that a life without Jesus is a life enslaved to sin and death. Slavery is a word that carries a great deal of emotion, appropriately so. But we are more than our bodies; we each have a spirit, and that spirit can be enslaved just as if it were in chains. You can be educated, successful, and affluent and still be enslaved to sin. In the eyes of this world you may be recognized and celebrated; you may have achieved, attained, and become. But your physical body is on a countdown clock, and your spirit is eternal. When your body is finished, your spirit will step into eternity. If you are without Christ and still a slave to sin, everything you've done with your life will be judged as utterly useless and empty. This is the good news we have to offer of life in Christ—not to condemn or belittle others, but to offer them freedom from slavery.

· THINK ABOUT IT ·

Consider the constraints and limitations of a life of slavery. This is life without Christ. How does life with Christ compare to life without Christ?

Prayer

Heavenly Father, I was hopelessly bound to destructive selfishness before You revealed Your love, through Jesus, and saved me from slavery to sin. I have freely received Your righteousness. Please use my life to serve Your Kingdom. In Jesus' name, amen.

A STUBBORN DONKEY

The angel of the Lord asked him, "Why have you beaten your donkey these three times? I have come here to oppose you because your path is a reckless one before me. The donkey saw me and turned away from me these three times. If she had not turned away, I would certainly have killed you by now, but I would have spared her."

NUMBERS 22:32-33

The prophet Balaam owned perhaps the most famous donkey in history! A foreign king had offered Balaam a huge amount of money to curse the people of Israel, but God said, "Do not go with them. You must not curse these people, because they are blessed." Balaam returned to the king with the news, but the king upped his offer. God was angry at Balaam for even entertaining this wickedness, yet allowed him to go with the king's men. Balaam set out on his donkey, but God was so angry with Balaam's willingness to curse the Israelites that He sent an angel to kill him. Balaam was saved only when God opened the eyes of the donkey to see the angel with his sword drawn, and she would take Balaam no further. We would do well to remember God's desire to help His people is so great, His grace is so intense and pervasive, if need be, He'll work through a donkey.

• THINK ABOUT IT •

Have you ever been so willfully opposed to God's plan that He intervened in a completely unexpected way? What was the outcome?

Prayer

Heavenly Father, help me hear Your voice with a willingness to obey. If I fail to hear or recognize Your purposes, please intervene on my behalf as You did for Balaam. Thank You for the protection Jesus provided through the cross. In Jesus' name, amen.

CULTIVATING GOOD FRUIT

"I will ask the Father, and he will give you another Counselor to be with you forever—the Spirit of truth. The world cannot accept him, because it neither sees him nor knows him. But you know him, for he lives with you and will be in you."

JOHN 14:16-17

We choose many times every day either to cooperate with our sinful natures or to cooperate with the Spirit of God. We are all hard-wired toward ungodliness and don't need much coaching on dishonesty, rudeness, or selfish ungratefulness. We need the help of the Holy Spirit to allow His fruits to emerge and grow in our lives. "Love, joy, peace, patience, kindness, goodness, faithfulness, gentleness, and self-control" (Galatians 5:22-23) are not accidental. These reflections of godly character are attributes He offers to us but does not force on us; we must seek and cultivate them purposefully. This is not beyond our reach, however, because "He lives with you and will be in you." The best indicator I know of spiritual maturity is evidence of the fruit of the Spirit, because it will not happen without the intentional pursuit of godliness.

• THINK ABOUT IT •

You and I choose every day, in choices big and small, whether or not we will allow our sinful natures to control us. Who is in control of your life: you, or the Holy Spirit?

Prayer

Heavenly Father, I want and need to increasingly know You. Thank You for answering my need through Your Holy Spirit, who is forever with me. Help me cultivate the fruit of Your Spirit in my life so that I can honor and serve You. In Jesus' name, amen.

GO TELL

Then Peter, filled with the Holy Spirit, said to them: "Rulers and elders of the people! If we are being called to account today for an act of kindness shown to a cripple and are asked how he was healed, then know this, you and all the people of Israel: It is by the name of Jesus Christ of Nazareth, whom you crucified but whom God raised from the dead, that this man stands before you healed."

ACTS 4:8-10

Jesus came to the earth to commission people, and the book of Acts tells us what His closest friends did after He left. If all you know of Peter, James, and John is from the Gospels, you'll lose hope. They fumbled and messed up time after time. While the Gospels tell us what they were, the book of Acts tells us what they are after being filled with God's Holy Spirit and empowered for service. They are like superheroes—healing the sick, opening blind eyes, and raising the dead. We are really not much different from those early disciples. We have learned about Jesus, trusted in His work on the cross, and can have the power of His Holy Spirit to carry on that same assignment of telling about Him in our generation.

• THINK ABOUT IT •

Do you consider Jesus' assignment to "go and tell" to be one He gave to "someone else" or one He personally gave to you? Have you asked God to empower you with His Holy Spirit?

Prayer

Heavenly Father, You chose me—imperfect and broken—to be transformed into Your image, that I might walk in trust and not fear. I ask You to empower me more fully with my Helper, Your Holy Spirit, for all You desire for my life. In Jesus' name, amen.

DAY 245

IMPORTANT TO GOD

A certain man of Zorah, named Manoah, from the clan of the Danites, had a wife who was sterile and remained childless. The angel of the LORD appeared to her and said, "You are sterile and childless, but you are going to conceive and have a son. . . . He will begin the deliverance of Israel from the hands of the Philistines."

JUDGES 13:2-3, 5

The son that the angel announced would be born to Manoah and his wife would be the famous Samson. Samson had some great victories and some tremendous failures, but he would become one of Israel's leaders whom God would use to deliver His people from their enemies. Before Samson was even conceived, God had a plan for his life. Did you know that God has a plan for you too? There is a crushing weight of messaging saying to us, "Only famous people are important. You are insignificant and will live and die without making much of a difference." But the Bible says that before the foundations of the earth were laid, God knew and imagined you with a purpose in His eternal Kingdom. Remember that no matter what the world says, or what your life-circumstances seem to be, you are important to God.

• THINK ABOUT IT •

Have there been people or circumstances in your life that have made you feel unimportant? Compare those opinions with God's opinion of you.

Prayer

Heavenly Father, when I have been confronted with challenges, even of my own making, You have never abandoned me. Instead, You helped me see that I still have a hope and a future of significance with You, sharing in Your purposes. Thank You! In Jesus' name, amen.

AN EXCITING MESSAGE

"I am the Alpha and the Omega," says the Lord God, "who is, and who was, and who is to come, the Almighty."

REVELATION 1:8

Many people hold the idea that there could be no God involved in the earth. This absolutely contradicts the message of Scripture. God did not create the world and then step out of the story. The Bible is filled with instance after instance where God is engaged in the activities of humans to effect His desired outcome. During Noah's day, God judged the people of the earth so severely that only a few survived to tell the story and begin again. The people had no imagination of such a possibility, mocking Noah as he built the ark. Scripture tells us there is more judgment to come. This is the message of Revelation: God will step into history again and make all things new. This is not a frightening message; it is an exciting message. Until then we have a message for the world: There is a God, you matter to Him, and He has a plan for your life. If you cooperate with Him and serve Him, He will change your life for the better.

• THINK ABOUT IT •

Jesus said that at the end of the age it will be just like it was in the days of Noah. People will mock those who believe in God, and they will have no imagination that judgment is imminent. How do you see this happening in the world today?

Prayer

Heavenly Father, You are the Designer of my past, present, and future—You know the beginning from the end. I will trust You whether life is fair and blessed or dark and pain filled. Help me always cooperate with and honor You. In Jesus' name, amen.

DAY 247

A GODLY HEART TRANSPLANT

"I will give you a new heart and put a new spirit in you; I will remove from you your heart of stone and give you a heart of flesh."

EZEKIEL 36:26

If your physical heart isn't working as it was intended to, it limits every part of your life because it affects every part of your body. If your spiritual heart is not healthy, it diminishes every aspect of your life as well. We were all born with hard hearts. We are by nature stubborn and rebellious. Bit by bit, every time we tolerate ungodliness it leaves us a bit more diminished and our hearts a little harder. God has a remedy for that. He said, "I can give you a new heart—a heart that's not hardened by sin." What a wonderful promise! It's as true as the promise of the new birth! You may be thinking you've lived a lot of years and made a lot of bad choices, but God is not intimidated by that. There is no part of your life or mine that has surprised God, and He has a new heart just waiting for you. Won't you receive it today?

• THINK ABOUT IT •

Have you received a heart transplant from God? How has it changed your life? If not, won't you ask Him for a new heart today?

Prayer

Heavenly Father, through the cross, You have given me a new heart and a new spirit. I yield my life to You, submitting to Your will to be more like You. Reveal the truth I need to know so that I may do the work You have called me to do. In Jesus' name, amen.

ALL IN THIS TOGETHER

May the God who gives endurance and encouragement give you a spirit of unity among yourselves as you follow Christ Jesus, so that with one heart and mouth you may glorify the God and Father of our Lord Jesus Christ.

ROMANS 15:5-6

What does it mean to be a people of God? The evangelical Christian perspective emphasizes our personal faith, our personal rights and privileges as children of God, and our personal reward—Heaven. We tend to focus on individual discipleship to grow our personal faith and do what God wants us to do. We talk about churches in terms of existing to meet the needs of me and my family. There is nothing wrong with that, but it is incomplete if we don't talk also about the faith and welfare of the community of believers. The question for us is, if everyone in the church sacrificed their time and talents and treasure and served others with the enthusiasm that we do, would it be a place where we would want to worship and bring our families? The Church isn't just a place for consumers. The Church is us—sacrificing and serving together.

• THINK ABOUT IT •

If everyone gave with the generosity that you give, would yours be a church you would choose to worship in? If everyone served the way you do, would it be a place you would bring your family?

Prayer

Heavenly Father, thank You for placing me in a community of caring believers who help me in my spiritual journey. In gratitude, allow me opportunities to demonstrate my love and commitment to You through standing with and serving Your people. In Jesus' name, amen.

DAY 249

OUR GENERATION

[Jesus] told them, "This is what is written: The Christ will suffer and rise from the dead on the third day, and repentance and forgiveness of sins will be preached in his name to all nations, beginning at Jerusalem. You are witnesses of these things."

LUKE 24:46-48

It's fashionable in the Christian community to be angry at the Jewish people, saying they failed to recognize the coming of the Messiah. They didn't all fail. Jesus' friends gathered at the foot of the cross, brokenhearted. They were so aligned with Him that they thought with certainty they would soon be executed themselves. When Jesus was resurrected He gave them an assignment, and they spent their lives in the pursuit of that assignment. It's bad history to say that the Jewish people missed Jesus. Some of them did, but others of them were responsible for the spread of the gospel of Jesus Christ and the establishment of the early Church. In this season God is delivering His message through the Church, which is comprised of people from every nation, race, and language. We have just as much an assignment for the redemptive purposes of God in the earth as the Jewish people did in delivering us a Messiah.

• THINK ABOUT IT •

We, as part of the Church, are God's messengers in this generation. How do you think we are doing with that assignment?

Prayer

Heavenly Father, You have entrusted me to be one of Your messengers to my generation. Help me stay in step with You daily and not miss the opportunities You put before me. Give me love for and compassionate boldness toward all those You desire to influence. In Jesus' name, amen.

MORE THAN FORGIVEN

As high as the heavens are above the earth, so great is his love for those who fear him; as far as the east is from the west, so far has he removed our transgressions from us.

PSALM 103:11-12

It is hard to comprehend how thoroughly Jesus paid for our sins. This Old Testament passage describes our distance from our sins in geographical terms—as far away as we could possibly be. The New Testament says God does not count our sins against us. Christ-followers are more than forgiven; the Bible says we are made new. I think we imagine forgiveness to be like a wrecked car: God hammers out the dents and gives us a new coat of paint. The reality is we are like a new car just rolled off the assembly line: brand new and without blemish. Now we are not always immediately delivered from the consequences of our sins. Sometimes we have to live out the consequences of those choices. When God forgives us, however, He wipes the slate clean. I imagine Him looking at us like He doesn't know what we are talking about if we should ask Him about those things in the past. This is an indescribable gift from our Almighty God.

• THINK ABOUT IT •

Even though God is omniscient, and knows everything, He chooses not to remember our sins. In your relationships, do you remember offenses against you, or do you choose not to remember them?

Prayer

Heavenly Father, thank You for putting my sins far away from You through the cross. Help me vigilantly guard my mind; I seek to honor You with all that enters it. May I also forgive others and then choose not to bring their offenses to mind. In Jesus' name, amen.

BETTER OUTCOMES

Let us not become weary in doing good, for at the proper time we will reap a harvest if we do not give up.

GALATIANS 6:9

Sometimes people say to me, "Pastor, being a good person must be easier for professional Christians like you." Really? If they only knew! In our area, our church has become known for magnets with the message "Jesus Is Lord" printed on them. Thousands of cars in our area have them. Frankly, it was hard for me to put that magnet on my car because it influences how I drive. Now I have to think twice before I keep you from merging in traffic. But that magnet reminds me that Jesus is Lord—my Lord. I want to make Him happy, so please, come on over and get ahead of me. If I keep practicing that generous and kind behavior, I'm trusting that one day my feelings will catch up. No, it's not always easy being a good person; but that's what Jesus wants me to do, so I give it my best effort. My experience has shown that pleasing Him really does bring better outcomes: more contentment, more fulfillment, and more joy.

• THINK ABOUT IT •

You can try to be a good person without following Jesus, but you cannot follow Jesus without trying to be a good person. What do your actions say to the world about your relationship with Jesus?

Prayer

Heavenly Father, thank You for the privilege of being Your ambassador in the earth. May my words and deeds represent You well. Thank You for inviting me to invest my strength and resources in pursuit of Your agenda, bringing eternal value to my life and others. In Jesus' name, amen.

DOORS OF OPPORTUNITY

If the Spirit of him who raised Jesus from the dead is living in you, he who raised Christ from the dead will also give life to your mortal bodies through his Spirit, who lives in you.

ROMANS 8:11

Many people hesitate to take a step of faith toward Jesus because they know they do not have the willpower or strength of character to overcome their old selves. When we become brand new in Christ, however, there is a new power at work within us to give us a fresh start, and it is nothing less than the Spirit of the Living God. This is a tremendous blessing because life tends to narrow our options the further we go into it. Many factors contribute to this— where we were born, our family systems, the educational opportunities that were available to us, etc. But the Bible says the same Spirit that raised Jesus from the dead dwells in you and me. No matter what pain we have endured or what limitations we have had to overcome, God lifts the ceiling on our future and opens doors of possibility we never dreamed of.

· THINK ABOUT IT ·

How has following Jesus helped you overcome limitations? How has He opened new doors of possibility and opportunity?

Prayer

Heavenly Father, You give me hope for my future. Help me yield to the power of Your Holy Spirit, to navigate the paths You open before me. I trust You to fulfill Your promises to me, Lord, because You are faithful in all things. In Jesus' name, amen.

DAY 253

FOCUSED PERSEVERANCE

Abram said, "Sovereign LORD, what can you give me since I remain childless and the one who will inherit my estate is Eliezer of Damascus?" He took him outside and said, "Look up at the heavens and count the stars—if indeed you can count them." Then he said to him, "So shall your offspring be."

GENESIS 15:2, 5

It's easy to become discouraged if we take a step of faith and don't see an immediate response. The Bible links faith and perseverance, and the only way I know to learn perseverance is to persevere. God told Abraham that He would make from him a mighty nation and his descendants would be as numerous as the stars in the sky, yet Abraham went forty years before that promise would be fulfilled. God sent Samuel to anoint David king of Israel, yet David lived as a fugitive for twenty years because Israel's king did not want to give up the throne. The fulfillment of God's purposes in our lives is not always immediate. I readily follow the Lord on the days when it's easy, and I still choose to follow the Lord on the days when it's not so easy. The Bible assures us that we will be rewarded in due time if we persevere, so let's wait on the Lord and not give up.

· THINK ABOUT IT ·

Have there been times when you have had to show perseverance in waiting on the Lord? How has He rewarded your faithfulness?

Prayer

Heavenly Father, Your mercy has been shown through all generations. I am filled with hope because of the promises in Scripture. Give me grace to persevere as I wait to see Your promises fulfilled. May my perseverance be marked by joyful obedience to You. In Jesus' name, amen.

A LIFE-CHANGING ASSIGNMENT

He said to another man, "Follow me." But the man replied, "Lord, first let me go and bury my father." Jesus said to him, "Let the dead bury their own dead, but you go and proclaim the kingdom of God." Still another said, "I will follow you, Lord; but first let me go back and say good-by to my family." Jesus replied, "No one who puts his hand to the plow and looks back is fit for service in the kingdom of God."

LUKE 9:59-62

It seems incredible that anyone could receive a personal invitation from the Son of God and turn away. But they had other plans and goals, and they wanted their discipleship to be on their terms. There was a group of people who embraced the assignment, however, and their lives were forever changed. They spent less than three years with Jesus, yet the impact on them was so significant that they were willing to live the rest of their lives telling people about Him and even die for Him. Something remarkable and absolutely life-changing happened to them, and I believe something remarkable and absolutely life-changing will happen to any person who chooses to follow Jesus.

• THINK ABOUT IT •

What do you remember about Jesus' invitation to you to follow Him? How would your life have been diminished if you had not followed Him?

Prayer

Heavenly Father, I chose and still choose to serve You and give You first place in my life. I am grateful You created me for a purpose in Your Kingdom. Help me follow You daily, that I might fulfill Your plans. You alone satisfy my soul. In Jesus' name, amen.

DAY 255

ORDINARY PEOPLE – EXTRAORDINARY PATH

"You of little faith, why are you so afraid?" Then he got up and rebuked the winds and the waves, and it was completely calm. The men were amazed and asked, "What kind of man is this? Even the winds and the waves obey him!"

MATTHEW 8:26-27

Jesus lived with an awareness of a power that we struggle to imagine. He spoke to the winds and the waves, and they grew still. He spoke to demons, and they obeyed. He commanded the dead to rise, and they rose. He told the lame to walk, and they walked. He told the blind to see, and they saw. Jesus was constantly inviting His followers to witness and participate in situations that were beyond their understanding and their comfort level and saying, "Believe in Me. Trust Me. Watch and see what I can do." We need to understand that Jesus is inviting us to lead a different kind of life in our world. We are no different than those first disciples. He is inviting us, as He invited them, not to be attendees or observers but to believe in Him fully and trust His power to act in us and through us. Jesus' power is still changing lives today, just as it did then.

• THINK ABOUT IT •

Have you ever seen God's power at work to accomplish something that was unexplainable in human terms? How did that impact your understanding of what He is able to do in your life?

Prayer

Heavenly Father, Your Holy Spirit gives me the power to live, breathe, and accomplish all You have entrusted to me. Thank You that the power that raised Jesus Christ from the grave also raises me above my fear and weaknesses. In Jesus' name, amen.

A PERSONAL INITIATIVE

Paul entered the synagogue and spoke boldly there for three months, arguing persuasively about the kingdom of God. But some of them became obstinate; they refused to believe and publicly maligned the Way. So Paul left them. He took the disciples with him and had discussions daily in the lecture hall of Tyrannus. This went on for two years, so that all the Jews and Greeks who lived in the province of Asia heard the word of the Lord.

ACTS 19:8-10

The spread of the gospel by the early disciples was an incredible feat, even by modern standards. The missionary journeys of Paul show that his plans were carried out very methodically and intentionally, always led by the Holy Spirit, in this case until "all the Jews and Greeks who lived in the province of Asia heard the word of the Lord." We should be just as intentional about reaching people for Christ. Every local congregation has the assignment of telling the people in its area about Jesus, preaching and teaching and training people to tell their Jesus-stories. It's not just up to one congregation—there are others telling the story too—but that's why we are here.

• THINK ABOUT IT •

Do you take the assignment to spread the gospel of Jesus Christ personally? How can you be more intentional in effectively sharing the freedom available through the cross with family, friends, and coworkers?

Prayer

Heavenly Father, I want to be more than just a consumer of Your love and acceptance. Teach me how to share the truth of the cross with others that they also might see and know You. Help me reach others for Your Kingdom and Your glory. In Jesus' name, amen.

DAY 257

JUST ENOUGH

"Two things I ask of you, LORD; do not refuse me before I die: Keep falsehood and lies far from me; give me neither poverty nor riches, but give me only my daily bread. Otherwise, I may have too much and disown you and say, 'Who is the LORD?'"

PROVERBS 30:7-9

Most of us, if we are completely honest, would have to admit that we have tried to find fulfillment in life apart from Christ. Maybe it was a degree, a job, a larger house, a neighborhood, a vehicle, or even a friendship or club membership that we thought would benefit our ambitions. We gave time and energy and effort to those things only to discover that we were not quite fulfilled. The Bible says apart from Jesus, apart from a God-perspective on life, we are enslaved to desires that are not aligned with the purposes of God. The author of this "inspired utterance" from Proverbs wisely asked the Lord for just enough—but not too much—so that he would not lose sight of the Lord. That thinking is in stark contrast to the expectations of our culture, but it makes perfect sense for a person whose priority is a proper relationship with the Lord.

• THINK ABOUT IT •

How have you tried to find fulfillment in life apart from Christ? What was the result of that? What did you learn about yourself, and about the Lord?

Prayer

Heavenly Father, Your grace is sufficient for me. Your purposes and faithfulness fulfill my life. May I never lose sight of Your plans that have transformed my heart and soul. May I live to serve my Lord and Savior. In Jesus' name, amen.

SOBER JUDGMENT

Do not think of yourself more highly than you ought, but rather think of yourself with sober judgment, in accordance with the measure of faith God has given you.

ROMANS 12:3

Humility is a quality that requires us to examine ourselves with honesty. Humility doesn't say, "I'm the best thing going, and I can do it all." Neither does it say, "I'm worthless, and I can't do anything." God says you are fearfully and wonderfully made and there's nobody quite like you. You've been given gifts and talents for this season to make a difference for God, but that doesn't mean you have every gift and talent. I was not given the tools to play in the NBA. I was just about a foot too short and several steps too slow and way too bound by gravity. It would be easy to be upset about what we don't have, but humility is appreciating and understanding how to use the gifts and talents we do have. Humility isn't forfeiting opportunity. Humility is the pathway to opportunity, because the Bible says God will promote the humble. It goes against the grain of what the world teaches, but humility is a good thing.

• THINK ABOUT IT •

What place does humility have in your life? Do you think of yourself with sober judgment, asking the Lord to use the gifts and talents He has given you for His purposes?

Prayer

Heavenly Father, You declared my value through the sacrifice of Your Son, Jesus, on the cross for me. You have given me new life and purpose, promising to conform me into the image of Jesus. Help me to embrace and walk in the humility Jesus modeled. In Jesus' name, amen.

DILIGENTLY FAITHFUL

We want each of you to show this same diligence to the very end, in order to make your hope sure. We do not want you to become lazy, but to imitate those who through faith and patience inherit what has been promised.

HEBREWS 6:11-12

One of the greatest challenges for Christians is to be intentionally and consistently faithful across every aspect of our lives. It is much easier to limit God to certain times and places! It's like my exercise routine when I go to my gym and exert enough to burn calories. First, I drive around the parking lot to find a spot close to the door, do my thirty minutes of cardio, and then hurry back to the office so I can sit down again—oh, I might stop by the donut shop on the way. Just as optimizing our health doesn't happen in a few minutes a day in one location, optimizing our faith doesn't happen just on Sunday mornings sitting in church. It's a decision we make twenty-four hours a day, wherever we are. God has given us everything we need to live faithfully. We are reminded in Hebrews that we have to choose diligence over laziness in order to let Jesus be Lord of our lives 24/7.

• THINK ABOUT IT •

Do you have a church façade that you don't use in other places? Or does the faith you show and speak about when you are in church permeate all the areas of your life?

Prayer

Heavenly Father, I need the fruit of Your Holy Spirit to develop and ripen in my life. I cannot effectively fulfill Your plans without that growth. Help me embrace and practice the diligence necessary to be abundantly fruitful in Your sight. In Jesus' name, amen.

SAVED, NOT SUPERIOR

"Come now, let us reason together," says the LORD. "Though your sins are like scarlet, they shall be as white as snow; though they are red as crimson, they shall be like wool."

ISAIAH 1:18

Isaiah issued this prophecy to the Jewish people, a very religious group. Yet God said to them, "Your lives are stained by sin." God's people are not perfect. We are not better than other people because we are Christ-followers; we are simply people who have been redeemed from an empty way of life. God says to His people, "Sin is staining your lives, but if you will come to Me, you can be clean. The stain will be washed away. You'll not only be forgiven, you'll be transformed. I can redeem you from that place to an entirely different place." That is our story. We are not just rule keepers or moralists. We are not here to debate whether our ethics are superior to someone else's ethics. God has done something for us and in us that is so remarkable that it would be selfish to keep it to ourselves. We are not here to pretend that we are better than everybody else. We are here to say, "I have found a resolution to the challenges that left me broken. I have found hope for my life."

• THINK ABOUT IT •

Consider what God has done in your life to rescue and redeem you. How can you share that story with others?

Prayer

Heavenly Father, You made a new future for me when I trusted in Jesus' work on the cross. Please help me yield to Your perspective. Open my eyes to recognize my opportunities to share my God-story with others in loving boldness. In Jesus' name, amen.

DAY 261

THE TRUE PATH

The devil took him to a very high mountain and showed him all the kingdoms of the world and their splendor. "All this I will give you," he said, "if you will bow down and worship me." Jesus said to him, "Away from me, Satan! For it is written: 'Worship the Lord your God, and serve him only.'"

MATTHEW 4:8-10

The temptation of sin—whether in the first garden, in a desert wilderness, or in your daily routine—is Satan's attempt to get you to yield to his ideas and turn your back on God. He will assure you that his plan is best and will make you happy, but he cannot deliver on his promises. His way may initially seem to be fulfilling what it promised; but if you walk that path very far, it becomes bitter and destructive. In contrast, when you choose godliness and holiness and you cooperate with God, He leads you on a path that is transformational and brings you to a place of contentment and joy. Satan is the great imitator, so let's ask the Holy Spirit for the wisdom to see his true nature and the strength to turn away from him.

• THINK ABOUT IT •

Have there been times when you followed Satan's deceptive path toward fulfillment? What was the result? What did you learn about his true nature?

Prayer

Heavenly Father, whatever temptations to sin come my way, help me quickly seek out and cooperate with Your Word. Thank You for the Holy Spirit who gives me discernment to know Your voice and not be fooled by the deceptions of evil. In Jesus' name, amen.

HELP CARRY THE BURDEN

Carry each other's burdens, and in this way you will fulfill the law of Christ.

GALATIANS 6:2

Sometimes we find ourselves fumbling for words when we want to encourage someone who is facing adversity or hardship or tragedy. Whether our friend is facing a job loss, an illness, or a relationship that is deteriorating, the things that come to mind can sometimes sound pretty hollow in light of the gravity of the situation. I've found that we often tend to overthink what our response should be when we want to show the love of Christ to our friends in these situations. Prayer is always an appropriate response, of course; but sometimes we need to give them assurance that we are not going away, that we are willing to help carry the burden. If you know someone who is in a hard place, just let them know that you are there for them. You don't have to find clever words to make it better. Just say, "You matter to me, and it's a privilege for me to stand with you right now. God is with you. We are not going to quit; we are going to keep our eyes on Him and make it through this."

• THINK ABOUT IT •

Have you been in a situation where a friend came alongside you and helped you carry a burden? Have you helped carry a burden for someone else?

Prayer

Heavenly Father, thank You for when You have encouraged and strengthened me through Your fellowship of believers. Use me to encourage and strengthen them that we might help each other "run our race" well for Your glory. In Jesus' name, amen.

DAY 263

INFINITE AND SOVEREIGN

Oh, the depth of the riches of the wisdom and knowledge of God! How unsearchable his judgments, and his paths beyond tracing out! "Who has known the mind of the Lord? Or who has been his counselor?" . . . For from him and through him and to him are all things.

ROMANS 11:33-34, 36

I am at peace with not totally understanding God. I am a finite creature worshipping an infinite God, and by definition, I will not be able to fully explain Him. In the plainest of language, God is smarter than I am. I am not complacent or lazy; I study and apply myself in a very systematic and intentional way. But I know that if I learn something new about God every day for a thousand years, there still will be more to learn on the next day. If we could fully explain God and everything He does, why would we want to worship Him? If we could master God, why would we need to yield to Him? I have a profound respect and reverence for God. I want to know His Word, and I want to cooperate with Him as fully as I can. "For from him and through him and to him are all things." Amen!

• THINK ABOUT IT •

Some people have a great deal of head knowledge about God but do not give Him much room in their hearts. Others place so much emphasis on emotion that they do not try to study and learn about Him. Could either of those things be said about you?

Prayer

Heavenly Father, though I neither fully know nor understand You, You fully know me. So I choose to trust You, knowing all things are in Your hand. Help me to know Your character through Your Word and cooperate with Your Holy Spirit. In Jesus' name, amen.

DAY 264

TWO SIMPLE PRAYERS

Then they cried out to the LORD in their trouble, and he brought them out of their distress.

PSALM 107:28

No matter how dark the place we are coming from, the power of God and the light of His love are sufficient to set us free. If you are struggling with bondage to anything that is addictive in your life, give it to the Lord in repentance: "God, I'm sorry. I've been wrong. No excuses. No justification. Forgive me. I want to go a new way. In Jesus' name, amen." He will help you. Something supernatural is released when you repent. Now I invite you to pray a prayer of renunciation: "God, I renounce any unholy or unclean thing that I have given access to my thoughts and my behaviors. I renounce it and thank You that through the power of Jesus' blood I am clean, forgiven, delivered, redeemed. In Jesus' name, amen." Tuck those two prayers into your portfolio for yourself either today or for some point in the future, or for someone who comes across your path. We are not powerless before the things that challenge our lives.

• THINK ABOUT IT •

God is able to set you free from anything that would ensnare you and keep you from experiencing His best. What is your mental picture of the power of God that is available to deliver you?

Prayer

Heavenly Father, please forgive and cleanse me through the blood of Jesus for these sins: _____. Take back the ground evil gained through my willful rebellion. I submit my body as an instrument of righteousness to glorify You. In Jesus' name, amen.

DAY 265

HOLD YOUR HORSES

On one occasion, while he was eating with them, he gave them this command: "Do not leave Jerusalem, but wait for the gift my Father promised, which you have heard me speak about. For John baptized with water, but in a few days you will be baptized with the Holy Spirit."

ACTS 1:4-5

My dad was an equine vet, and the thoroughbred race horses he treated were bred and trained to do one thing: Go! There is an electric atmosphere on race day as these powerful animals that have been focused on that one moment burst through the open gate. That's the image I have of Jesus' followers at this meal. These folks have spent three years with Jesus. They have heard His public presentations, and they have been coached privately. They have seen blind eyes opened and the dead raised and thousands fed. They watched Jesus die on a cross, and they have been with Him for forty days since He came back to life. They are uniquely prepared to tell the world about Jesus; but He instructs them to wait on the Holy Spirit, who will fill them with power and reveal God's plans to them.

· THINK ABOUT IT ·

Have there been times when you have sincerely tried to carry out a God-assignment, but in your timing and under your own power? What did you learn from stepping out on your own?

Prayer

Heavenly Father, my times are in Your hands, and Your timing is perfect. Only by Your Spirit can I fulfill Your assignments. Help me keep in step with Your Spirit, obedient not only in the "what," but also the "when" and the "how." In Jesus' name, amen.

A LIFELONG NECESSITY

Then Jesus declared, "I am the bread of life. He who comes to me will never go hungry, and he who believes in me will never be thirsty."

JOHN 6:35

Most of us have been coached from our earliest days on how to behave in polite society; and if you grew up in the South, you've got a whole extra layer. But if we get hungry enough or thirsty enough, all of those good manners will disappear pretty quickly. Hunger and thirst are powerful motivators, so when Jesus uses them as an example, He's suggesting something that is a driving force within us. The other aspect of being hungry and thirsty is that no matter how much of your favorite meal you have just consumed, you will want another meal in a few hours. Our spiritual lives are a lot like that. We have a mistaken idea that after our initiation into the Kingdom, we're good to go. But when Jesus invites us to come to Him to satisfy our hunger and thirst, He's talking about something that is a lifelong necessity. We cannot be satisfied with a one-time encounter with Jesus. He is the source of our spiritual nourishment, and a relationship with Him is absolutely necessary for our well-being.

• THINK ABOUT IT •

Have you tried to get by with a one-time encounter with Jesus? Or do you recognize Him as a daily necessity for your well-being?

Prayer

Heavenly Father, make me hungry for Your Word and truth, and thirsty for Your righteousness. My belief is in You, and I desire to know You more. I long for Jesus' triumphant return. Let my faith in You be a light for those in the darkness. In Jesus' name, amen.

DAY 267

INTEGRITY MATTERS

The integrity of the upright guides them, but the unfaithful are destroyed by their duplicity.

PROVERBS 11:3

Integrity is bringing alignment between what you say you believe and who you really are. Integrity is bringing alignment between who you are in church and who you are with your friends. Integrity is bringing alignment between what you say at home versus at work. To the degree that your life is out of alignment, you forfeit integrity—and integrity matters. I encourage you to coach integrity into your children. Help them to understand we don't win at all costs or look for every advantage. Show them what it looks like to live by God's values and let those values be consistent in your heart. Why? God will bring opportunities to us that we did not manipulate into our lives. The world won't understand it, because you're accepting a set of values that they haven't yet accepted. That is the message you can share: "I've wrestled with this and taken advantage of anyone to get ahead. But after becoming a Christ-follower I've increasingly tried to live with integrity; it's amazing how it's changed my life."

• THINK ABOUT IT •

In your personal and professional life, do you practice complete integrity? Are you comfortable being the same person at church, at home, at school, at work, and with your friends?

Prayer

Heavenly Father, help me be faithful to what I say I believe. Teach me to be a person of integrity as I do business and as I worship You. Let my yes be yes and my no be no. I accept Your perspective and values with a grateful attitude. In Jesus' name, amen.

MISSED INVITATIONS

"O Jerusalem, Jerusalem, you who kill the prophets and stone those sent to you, how often I have longed to gather your children together, as a hen gathers her chicks under her wings, but you were not willing."

MATTHEW 23:37

If I could take you on a tour of Jerusalem, I'd begin on the Mount of Olives, looking across the Kidron Valley toward the Old City. This is the "money shot" you see on the covers of travel guides, with the city sprawled before you and the gold dome of the Temple Mount dominating your view. About halfway down the Mount of Olives is a little chapel called Dominus Flevit, which commemorates the place where Jesus wept over the city of Jerusalem (Luke 19:41-44). He wept because the people didn't recognize the invitation that God had put before them; and because they failed to recognize it, there would be significant negative consequences for them. It's one of my favorite places in the city, and it always reminds me to say to the Lord, "I don't want to miss Your invitations for me."

• THINK ABOUT IT •

Have there been times when you have missed the invitations the Lord has placed before you? What were the circumstances? What did you learn through those experiences?

Prayer

Heavenly Father, open my mind and heart to see and recognize Your invitations wherever I am today. May Your Holy Spirit help me cooperate with Your opportunities in all wisdom and courage that I might bring You glory. In Jesus' name, amen.

DAY 269

ENSLAVED

We know that the law is spiritual; but I am unspiritual, sold as a slave to sin.

ROMANS 7:14

In the first century slavery was widespread in the Roman Empire, which conquered various people groups and took those they considered valuable in some way and sold them in slave markets to the highest bidder. This inhumane process would have been very vivid to the believers of that day, and it is the mental image that Paul is evoking here when he says we were sold as slaves to sin. The modern Church has been reluctant to acknowledge the power of sin or even the existence of sin. Who has the right to say a behavior is wrong, after all? I would answer that by saying simply that the Creator of Heaven and earth has identified behaviors that will destroy you. That's what sin is. When the Bible says the consequence of sin is death, it's not God being punitive; God told you the outcome of that behavior at the beginning and then pleads with us, "Don't do that." Let's recognize the reality of sin and be grateful that our Lord and Savior, Jesus Christ, paid the price for our freedom.

• THINK ABOUT IT •

Consider the degrading process of being sold in a slave market and being held in bondage. Think about the nature of enslavement to sin and how God has redeemed you from that way of life.

Prayer

Heavenly Father, without receiving Jesus' sacrificially redemptive work on the cross, I remain a slave to sin. Thank You for the ability to repent, receive Your forgiveness, be delivered from sin's bondage, and walk in Your freedom. In Jesus' name, amen.

UNVARNISHED TRUTH

As for me, I will always have hope; I will praise you more and more. My mouth will tell of your righteousness, of your salvation all day long. . . .

PSALM 71:14-15

We do not choose to follow Jesus because we have life all worked out—no challenges, no problems, no hurdles, no difficulties. We follow Jesus because He gives us hope that we can change and strength to help us rise above life's difficulties. Rather than lead our lives bent over by shame and guilt and condemnation, we have found freedom and forgiveness. Some of us have sanitized our life before Christ to the point that we cannot acknowledge what it was like to be without Him. Without that honest reflection on our sin and the transformation He has worked in us, we have no Jesus-story to tell. I would not encourage you to glorify the sinful state of your life before Christ, but neither would I encourage you to deny the transformation He has brought to you. When you are truthful with yourself and others about what He has done for you, you open the door for Him to continue working in your life, and you give yourself opportunities to tell about how gracious your God is.

• THINK ABOUT IT •

Are you honest with yourself about what God has done for you? Do you acknowledge the ways He has transformed your life?

Prayer

Heavenly Father, thank You for Your abundant grace, forgiveness, and freedom. Help me share my unvarnished God-story, that others may see and know the riches of Your sacrificial kindness and Your great power for those who would believe. In Jesus' name, amen.

NO CHALLENGE TOO GREAT

"'He who has an ear, let him hear what the Spirit says to the churches. To him who overcomes, I will grant to eat of the tree of life which is in the Paradise of God.'"

REVELATION 2:7 • NASB®

The book of Revelation opens with individual messages to seven churches. Each one is given an analysis of its current situation and then the resolution that is required. For every group of believers the answer is the same: Overcome! Then we read about the end of the age, which culminates with the glorious return of our King, Jesus. Finally, the promise of Revelation is restated: The one who overcomes is the one who will be blessed. All that talk of overcoming means we can count on facing obstacles, difficulties, and disappointments. I have interacted with enough people to know that we all face them; if you think others' lives are always easy, you just don't know their stories. But the good news is that Almighty God has given you the strength you need to overcome any obstacle in your path. If you'll put your faith in Him and welcome His Spirit into your life, there is no challenge that you cannot rise above.

• THINK ABOUT IT •

To receive the fullness of what God intends for us, we need to be prepared to overcome. Do you welcome the Holy Spirit into your life to help you with life's daily challenges?

Prayer

Heavenly Father, Your Word and Spirit give me strength to overcome and persevere through the persistent life-challenges. I depend on You and welcome Your Holy Spirit that I might overcome and walk in the fullness of Your purposes. In Jesus' name, amen.

GOD LOVES YOU

"I know every bird in the mountains, and the creatures of the field are mine."

PSALM 50:11

One of the mind-boggling characteristics about God is that He knows everything. The big word for that is "omniscient." This verse says that God knows every bird, and I don't think it means He knows their species. I think He knows every bird in existence individually. We might think that one robin looks like every other robin, but He can tell them apart and knows them every one. If He knows every bird, we can also assume that He knows every ant, every hippopotamus, and every pesky mosquito. How can this be? I don't know, and that's OK. The Bible says that God knows when we sit and when we rise, He knows our thoughts, and He is familiar with all of our ways (Psalm 139:2-3). God is not unaware or disinterested in the tiniest details of our lives. He knows who we are, what we are interested in, and what concerns us. We matter to Him.

• THINK ABOUT IT •

Does realizing that God knows everything about you intimidate you, frighten you, or comfort you? Why?

Prayer

Heavenly Father, You know everything, and that brings me great comfort. I, on the other hand, know very little about this world, even less about the world to come. Help me to rely totally upon You and trust You fully with my life. In Jesus' name, amen.

GRACE FREELY GIVEN

To the praise of his glorious grace, which he has freely given us in the One he loves.

EPHESIANS 1:6

We are a nation of achievers. Most of us have parents and grandparents who worked hard in order that their children and grandchildren would have a better life and more opportunities than they did. It's the American way. I think that's why many of us struggle with the idea of grace. We think that anything worth having must require hard work and sacrifice on our part. But the grace of God is just the opposite: It is the supernatural intervention of God on our behalf, freely given because God loves us. We can't work hard enough to earn grace because it is beyond any ability we have. We can't be good enough to deserve it because we are incapable of being that good. Grace isn't about you or me. It's about God and His great love for us. It's about Jesus sacrificing Himself on the cross so that you and I can have a glorious future in time and in eternity.

• THINK ABOUT IT •

God's desire is for us to be a part of His Kingdom. Have you accepted the gift of His loving grace that purchased salvation for you?

Prayer

Heavenly Father, thank You for Your abundant gift of grace and the redemption and freedom it lovingly purchased for me. May I consistently yield to You as my great treasure. You are my Shepherd, and I lack no good thing if I have You. In Jesus' name, amen.

THREE SIMPLE WORDS

"Come, follow me," Jesus said, "and I will make you fishers of men."

MARK 1:17

We often hear people expound upon the last part of this verse—what it means to be "fishers of men"—but we don't hear as much about Jesus' invitation to "Come, follow me." Perhaps that's because this is such a straightforward request. It is impossible to confuse the meaning of it, yet even as Jesus-followers many of us spend our lives holding back until we determine just how completely we will obey. We tell ourselves we are waiting to find the "right church" before we commit to worshipping and serving and growing together. Then we begin judging: Parking—6. The lot was paved, but it was quite a walk. Music—4. Too loud. Preaching—5. Long-winded. Read from the wrong version of the Bible. Better keep looking! Many of us spend our entire lives evaluating presentations instead of humbly following Jesus, getting connected to a body of believers, and allowing Him to change us for the better as we serve Him. His invitation for initiating transformation in your life is simple: "Come. Follow me."

• THINK ABOUT IT •

Are you connected and committed to a local congregation where you can worship and serve and grow in faith with other Jesus-followers?

Prayer

Heavenly Father, thank You for my church and the truth it teaches from Your Word. I want to be concerned for the spiritual lives of others and help them be more fully devoted to You. May I follow You in humble obedience to Your invitation. In Jesus' name, amen.

DAY 275

DANGER AHEAD

Many of those who believed now came and openly confessed their evil deeds. A number who had practiced sorcery brought their scrolls together and burned them publicly. When they calculated the value of the scrolls, the total came to fifty thousand drachmas. In this way the word of the Lord spread widely and grew in power.

ACTS 19:18-20

A drachma was worth about a day's wage, so the destruction of these scrolls reflected the income from fifty thousand days—a significant financial sacrifice for any community. Can you imagine the city-wide impact when that amount of evil material was destroyed? The outcome of the teaching, repentance, and removal of wickedness was that "the word of the Lord spread widely and grew in power." I would encourage you in the strongest possible terms to avoid anything to do with the occult—Ouija boards, fortune telling, psychics, and the like— because they are evil and directly opposed to the purposes of God. We can only imagine how our communities would be blessed if people would turn away from those practices and turn toward God.

• THINK ABOUT IT •

Are you in the habit of reading your horoscope or having your palm read or consulting a psychic? If so, repent of those things and trust your future to the Lord. He will bless you beyond what you can imagine!

Prayer

Heavenly Father, I confess any idols I have ever put before You, such as _____. I repent and renounce any occult practices or false religions in which I have ever participated, willingly or not, such as _____. Thank You for freedom through the blood of Jesus. In His name, amen.

STILL ELIGIBLE

"The cry of the Israelites has reached me, and I have seen the way the Egyptians are oppressing them. So now, go. I am sending you to Pharaoh to bring my people the Israelites out of Egypt."

EXODUS 3:9-10

Moses was one of the most remarkable men in all of history. The child of slaves rescued by a princess and brought up in Pharaoh's palace with all the education and opportunity that afforded him, he was uniquely positioned to deliver his own people from bondage. But in a moment of rage he murdered a man and forfeited everything. He fled, his life's purpose seemingly destroyed by his own actions. There seemed to be no way back. He wandered in the desert, chasing sheep for forty years. Don't you think that was hard to live with? Don't you imagine he was consumed with regret that he had failed his God? Then one day a bush caught on fire and God said, "Come here, Moses. I've got a job for you. You're going to get my people out of Egypt and take them to the Promised Land." Nothing we can do puts us beyond God's redemption. Nothing we can do disqualifies us from being used to further God's purposes in the earth.

• THINK ABOUT IT •

Was there ever a time when you felt you had failed God so completely that you could never participate in His purposes again? How did He rescue you and use you?

Prayer

Heavenly Father, thank You for redeeming me, even in the midst of my rebellion towards You. Your love shown through Jesus' sacrifice is undeniable. Thank You for forgiving, rescuing, and restoring my soul for Your highest purposes. In Jesus' name, amen.

DAY 277

DELIVERED FROM DESPAIR

Then he said to Thomas, "Put your finger here; see my hands. Reach out your hand and put it into my side. Stop doubting and believe." Thomas said to him, "My Lord and my God!"

JOHN 20:27-28

Jesus' disciple, Thomas, will always be known for his doubt. He had followed Jesus faithfully, seen all the miracles, and watched His friend die on a cross. For some reason, Thomas was not present on the evening of the resurrection when Jesus appeared to the others and showed them the physical marks of His crucifixion. When they told Thomas what had happened, he said, "The only way I will believe again is if I can see His scars for myself!" Thomas only asked for the same proof the others had seen. History calls Thomas a doubter, but what I hear is the same depth of despair they all had wrestled with. Jesus didn't criticize Thomas, but simply showed him His scars and said, "Stop doubting and believe." We, like Thomas, can be faithful followers of Jesus and still find ourselves wrestling with doubt and discouragement. When that happens, take your questions to Jesus, and He will help you increase your faith.

• THINK ABOUT IT •

Do you sometimes find it hard to put aside your skepticism and believe that Jesus wants to help you increase your faith? Consider all the times He has delivered you from despair, then thank Him for His faithfulness to you.

Prayer

Heavenly Father, when I take You at Your Word, doubt flees and despair retreats. Forgive me for my divided heart: partly listening to my circumstances, partly listening to Your Word. Give me singleness of heart and action. In my belief, help my unbelief! In Jesus' name, amen.

EXPERTISE NOT REQUIRED

A Jew named Apollos, a native of Alexandria, came to Ephesus. He was a learned man, with a thorough knowledge of the Scriptures. He had been instructed in the way of the Lord, and he spoke with great fervor and taught about Jesus accurately, though he knew only the baptism of John. He began to speak boldly in the synagogue. When Priscilla and Aquila heard him, they invited him to their home and explained to him the way of God more adequately.

ACTS 18:24-26

One of the things I find most interesting about Apollos is that he did not hesitate to tell others the story of Jesus even as he was learning more about it himself. Sometimes we think we should wait to talk about our faith until we have it all figured out. If we do that we'll never tell our Jesus-stories because we will be learning about God for the rest of our lives. Let us be faithful to tell others what He has done for us, serving Him even as we continue to learn about Him.

• THINK ABOUT IT •

Are you envious of those who have an incredible testimony of life transformation after accepting Jesus as Savior? Do not be ashamed of your testimony! Jesus works in every life differently, but the miracle of His saving grace is the same for all of us.

Prayer

Heavenly Father, I am a beginner when it comes to many spiritual things, but I do know that Your Word can be trusted. You have a plan for me through Jesus' redemptive work on the cross and I can share that life-changing truth with others. In Jesus' name, amen.

EMPTY FAITH

We know also that the Son of God has come and has given us understanding, so that we may know him who is true. And we are in him who is true—even in his Son Jesus Christ. He is the true God and eternal life.

1 JOHN 5:20

I believe that Jesus was conceived supernaturally by the Holy Spirit and born to Mary in a stable in Bethlehem. He grew to adulthood in Nazareth and ministered publicly for about three years. His teaching threatened the religious establishment, and they orchestrated His arrest with the help of the Roman government. He died on a Roman cross outside Jerusalem's walls, and His friends buried Him in a borrowed tomb. After three days God said, "Enough!" and rolled the stone away. Jesus walked out alive and ascended to Heaven after forty days. He will return to earth one day to judge the living and the dead. If I believe all those things but fail to implement what Jesus taught about loving my neighbor and using my time and resources to serve Him, my faith is empty. Don't let your knowledge of Jesus be just an exercise in memorizing facts. Let Him change your heart. Let Him be Lord of your life.

• THINK ABOUT IT •

Is your knowledge of Jesus mainly about historical facts? Or have you allowed His example and His power to transform your life?

Prayer

Heavenly Father, knowing You and being known by You has changed my life. I know You are at work in me both to will and to work according to Your good purposes. Help me walk in those good works that You have prepared in advance for me to walk in. In Jesus' name, amen.

A GRATEFUL RESPONSE

"I have no need of a bull from your stall or of goats from your pens, for every animal of the forest is mine, and the cattle on a thousand hills. . . . If I were hungry I would not tell you, for the world is mine, and all that is in it."

PSALM 50:9-10, 12

I think that most of us, somewhere along the way, became convinced that God needed us. I remember when I began to sense God was inviting me toward ministry. In my heart I thought, "God must be pretty excited about me joining the team!" I look back now and realize the liability He was taking on! We approach the stewardship of our resources the same way. We think that God needs our tithes and our offerings or His work won't get done. It's laughable when we think that through. He is the Creator of the universe and everything in it—how could He possibly need anything from me? The answer is that He doesn't. God wants us to recognize the wonder of the salvation He offers and acknowledge the fullness of His provision for us and then respond to Him in gratitude.

• THINK ABOUT IT •

Do you approach the stewardship of your life and your resources with a heart of gratitude? Think of all God has done for you. What is the appropriate response?

Prayer

Heavenly Father, You have provided me with everything I need for life and godliness. You are generous toward me so that I too can be generous. Thank You for Your faithful provision for me. I ask for wisdom to steward Your provision wisely. In Jesus' name, amen.

FOR ONE, FOR ALL

Just as each of us has one body with many members, and these members do not all have the same function, so in Christ we who are many form one body, and each member belongs to all the others.

ROMANS 12:4-5

There are many obvious differences between the Christian faith and the Jewish faith, but one that is not so obvious is this: To many Christians, being the people of God is about making a personal profession of faith and then doing your own thing. To the Jewish people, being the people of God is about the spiritual health of the community and living for a cause greater than yourself. Which perspective is correct? I believe there is significant truth in both perspectives. It is true that each of us must make a personal decision about the lordship of Jesus followed by many personal decisions regarding how we live our lives and how we practice our faith. But it is equally true that we are part of a larger whole, and we have responsibilities to the community of faith. So when people ask me if our faith should be a personal thing or a community thing, my answer is "Yes!"

• THINK ABOUT IT •

Do you view your faith as personal, or corporate, or both? How do you live this out?

Prayer

Heavenly Father, You have given me influence that I might reflect Your love and truth. Forgive me for when I have not owned my responsibility to fellow believers. Help me starve selfishness and nurture my faith, personal and corporate. In Jesus' name, amen.

GOD'S RULE BOOK

Solid food is for the mature, who by constant use have trained themselves to distinguish good from evil.

HEBREWS 5:14

It should not be too hard to distinguish good from evil, but culturally we are blurring the lines between them. If you watch baseball, pay attention to how the precisely lined batter's box changes over the first innings. Hitters step into the box and begin to move the dirt around with their feet. Soon it's hard to see where the chalk lines are. We're living in a season where people are blurring the lines; a lot of people are moving dirt around with their feet. As a culture we somehow feel imposed upon just by seeing ten moral boundaries given official sanction, and we've stood by as the Ten Commandments are removed from public places. A prayer for good sportsmanship and protection before a high school sporting event may cost someone a job. The only way for us to keep God's perspective on right and wrong is through training ourselves by the constant use of His Word. It will not give a specific answer to every question, but the moral principles that run through it from beginning to end will give us guidance for how to live in this generation.

• THINK ABOUT IT •

What is your guide for determining right from wrong? Do you hold every decision up to the light of God's Word?

Prayer

Heavenly Father, help me recognize Your perspective in Your Word and obey it across the span of my life. Thank You for others who hold me accountable to Your boundaries. Use my life to make a difference in this generation. In Jesus' name, amen.

CHILD OF GOD

How great is the love the Father has lavished on us, that we should be called children of God! And that is what we are!

1 JOHN 3:1

It is a sad fact that many of us feel unlovable. Some of us have suffered the abuse of parents or a spouse, and we have been conditioned to believe that there is little about us that is worthy of love. Many of us have bought into the world's definition of beauty and significance and know we will never measure up. Others of us are quiet and shy and think we could not possibly be as lovable as those who are more outgoing and friendly. Some of us have made choices that have hurt and perhaps harmed others, and we are convinced that we will never again deserve love. The good news is that God loves you. If a voice in your head is trying to convince you that you are not worthy of His love or that you are beyond His love, that is a lie planted there by the enemy. Rest assured that God created you as a completely unique and lovable person, and you are precious to Him. Our response is to love Him in return.

• THINK ABOUT IT •

Do you ever feel unlovable? Scripture says that God loves us, so what other voice or voices are telling you otherwise? What should your response to them be?

Prayer

Heavenly Father, Your love, expressed in Scripture and poured out upon my life, is humbling. Your Word is filled with the promises and purposes You have for my life. Help me walk so closely to You that other voices cannot redirect my path. In Jesus' name, amen.

HOPE RESTORED

The LORD is close to the brokenhearted and saves those who are crushed in spirit. A righteous man may have many troubles, but the LORD delivers him from them all.

PSALM 34:18-19

A significant part of Jesus' ministry after His resurrection was to His closest friends. They were in great need of hope and encouragement. I tell you that because I want you to know that it is possible to be a Christ-follower with some experience, doing the best you know to live for the Lord, and still find yourself in some really dark places. I want you to know that you haven't missed God. The psalmist said God is close to the brokenhearted, not angry with them, or punishing them, or judging them. If you are in one of those dark places, know that you matter to the Lord. Remember that He loves you and will deliver you in His time. Don't bear this season alone. Spend time with other godly people and just listen to the joy they have for the Lord. It's contagious, and it will refresh you like a steady rain on parched ground.

• THINK ABOUT IT •

Remember a time when you were crushed in spirit. How did the Lord bring you through that season?

Prayer

Heavenly Father, I lift up to You those in my life who need Your healing and whose hearts are hopeless and broken. I have seen You restore my hope and give purpose back to my life. Help me share what You have done for me with those who suffer. In Jesus' name, amen.

DAY 285

BETTER THAN NEW

Then a man named Jairus, a ruler of the synagogue, came and fell at Jesus' feet, pleading with him to come to his house because his only daughter, a girl of about twelve, was dying.

LUKE 8:41-42

I was once visiting multiple people in the hospital, and as I went from room to room, it seemed like every situation was worse. In some cases the doctors didn't have many answers. I prayed for each patient and tried to encourage their families, but I didn't have any answers either. I left frustrated, both with God and an elevator that seemed to stop on every floor. Soon I was surrounded by people in white coats. It occurred to me that none of these well-educated professionals seemed embarrassed by not having all the answers; they were doing the best they knew to do. Every one of those I visited that day got better, and some had seemed like hopeless cases. It isn't fruitful to sit in the seat of the skeptic. Don't be afraid to say you don't know. Don't hesitate to invite the Lord into difficult situations. Don't be afraid to pray for people. God moves in remarkable ways, and healing is not about us. Healing is about God glorifying Himself by showing His mercy and power.

• THINK ABOUT IT •

Do you ever hesitate to invite God into hard situations for fear that He will not act and your faith in Him will be seen as empty?

Prayer

Heavenly Father, thank You for Your restoration and healing, that You bring possibility to the impossible. Help me remember this when everything seems hopeless, and fearlessly invite You to make a difference in hard circumstances. In Jesus' name, amen.

OUTSIDE THE WALLS

The foolishness of God is wiser than man's wisdom, and the weakness of God is stronger than man's strength.

1 CORINTHIANS 1:25

God is our only true source of wisdom and strength. Many of us live in affluence and opportunity unknown to most of the world, but others of us face violence and uncertainty every day. The question looming over us is this: "What will the Church do?" The quality of life in many of our communities seems to be diminishing, but we must realize that solutions to those problems are not determined by governments; they are directly attached to the health and vitality of the Church. Why? Because the Church is in the business of helping sinful humans become more like Jesus. If we are going to live in peace and unity, see violence diminished and well-being increased, it will not be because government has come up with a new program or built more prisons; it will be because the Church is increasingly about the Lord's business. Let's ask God to forgive us for the casual way we have approached Him about expanding His Kingdom. Let's ask Him how we can be a part of His purposes and then watch to see what He will do.

· THINK ABOUT IT ·

Truth be told, do you expect agencies to be our peacekeepers? Are you willing to accept more fully God's assignment to be an agent of His peace? What would that look like for you day to day?

Prayer

Heavenly Father, thank You for Your assignment of helping others find hope and encouragement. The Church is a safe place in a corrupt world, but we want to take Your message of hope and healing outside our walls. Assignment accepted! In Jesus' name, amen.

FAITHFUL TEACHER

Again Jesus said, "Peace be with you! As the Father has sent me, I am sending you." And with that he breathed on them and said, "Receive the Holy Spirit."

JOHN 20:21-22

It is after Jesus' resurrection, and He has appeared to His disciples to prove that what was foretold has indeed happened. In all of history, this group of people had the best training to be Jesus' representatives. They had spent three years with Him. They had seen Him walk on water and cast out demons and heal the sick and raise the dead. They had heard His public teaching and then had the opportunity to ask Him questions in private. Yet these years of intense teaching and training were not enough, and Jesus knew that they would need ongoing help after He was gone. He gave them the life-changing gift of the Holy Spirit, the same Spirit that is available to us every day. Do not be discouraged if you do not understand all that you would like to about the teachings of Scripture. Ask the Holy Spirit to help you and guide you, and He will.

• THINK ABOUT IT •

Do you put your Bible down in frustration when you encounter a difficult teaching, or do you ask the Holy Spirit to give you greater understanding?

Prayer

Heavenly Father, thank You for the gift of Your Holy Spirit and the promise of His help to learn and understand and obey Your Word. Help me listen to You more diligently each day as You speak to me through Scripture. In Jesus' name, amen.

A CHANGE OF CLOTHES

The Lord has anointed me to . . . bestow on them a crown of beauty instead of ashes, the oil of gladness instead of mourning, and a garment of praise instead of a spirit of despair. They will be called oaks of righteousness, a planting of the LORD for the display of his splendor.

ISAIAH 61:1, 3

Despair is not just an emotion, but a lingering spirit of despondency and hopelessness. Circumstances can bring sadness to your life, and it's normal to feel that for a season. But when you choose to allow despair to settle over you like a garment, it can overcome you, trapping you inside it. Isaiah says we have a choice to make: We can dwell in a spirit of despair, or we can choose to wear a garment of praise and give voice to the grace and goodness and mercy of God. Choose to praise Him even when your heart is broken. Honor Him even when others show you dishonor. Thank Him for watching over your life and leading you through the valleys. Finally, tell others what He has done for you. Your Jesus-story will "display His splendor" and increase your faith, and others will want to know more about the God you trust and serve.

• THINK ABOUT IT •

Have you ever allowed despondency and hopelessness to settle over you like a heavy robe? How did you replace them with a garment of praise?

Prayer

Heavenly Father, despair is not my friend. I will not embrace it, but will choose to worship You even in brokenheartedness. When You lead me through the valley, help me to yield to Your Spirit to use me and prepare me for better days. In Jesus' name, amen.

EVERY EFFORT

Make every effort to live in peace with all men and to be holy; without holiness no one will see the Lord.

HEBREWS 12:14

We are to make every effort to live in peace and be holy. Not a half-hearted effort or an occasional effort—every effort. That means whatever the cost, whatever the inconvenience it may cause, whatever changes we must make, we are to do everything within our ability to live in peace with one another and be holy. We don't keep the law to be holy; we keep our hearts pure to be holy. We put a bridle on our tongues. We put some fences around our emotions. We choose godliness when there are many voices tempting us to ungodliness. We set apart time to spend with God and in His Word. Why? Because without holiness no one will see the Lord. Every one of us struggles with holiness—that's a part of our humanity—but God will help you with this. Ask Him to help you reflect His character more fully at home, at work, and with your friends. This is His desire for you, and He will gladly show you what to do.

• THINK ABOUT IT •

Would the people who spend time with you regularly say that you are able to guard your tongue and rein in your emotions? Do they see you striving toward holiness?

Prayer

Heavenly Father, You are a holy God. May I hunger and thirst for Your righteousness. My tongue is the hardest part of my body to control, and I ask for Your help to tame it and submit it to You anew that I might effectively serve You. In Jesus' name, amen.

FIRST PRIORITY

Whatever happens, conduct yourselves in a manner worthy of the gospel of Christ.

PHILIPPIANS 1:27

Do you ever stop to consider what people will say about you after you die? If the people who live with you, work with you, and interact with you were gathered at your graveside, what stories would they tell? What would they identify as the focus of your life? Would they laugh about your unwavering loyalty to a sports team? Would they comment on your love for your vehicle? Would they mention your tenaciousness in business? Would they bring up the time and money you spend on your hobbies? We all have different interests, but before all of those we want to be known as people whose first priority in life is to honor God. I would challenge you to shape your priorities so that you will be known as a person who seeks the Lord. Be known as a friend who not only promises to pray, but actually stops and prays. Be a generous coworker and boss. Be a devoted family member. Love others because God first loved you. Tell them all about the great God you serve.

• THINK ABOUT IT •

If they were asked today, what would your family and friends identify as your life's first priority?

Prayer

Heavenly Father, in the midst of every opportunity, I desire to give You the first priority and place in my life. Reveal where I have not done that, and forgive me for putting You in the backseat. May I be known for always putting You first. In Jesus' name, amen.

DAY 291

NO MIDDLE GROUND

I am not ashamed of the gospel, because it is the power of God for the salvation of everyone who believes: first for the Jew, and then for the Gentile.

ROMANS 1:16

When Paul writes to the church at Rome and says, "I am not ashamed of the gospel," you can be certain it's because he is addressing a group of people who are finding themselves publicly ashamed of the gospel. Two millennia later, I have to say we're not that different. There is enormous cultural pressure to be ashamed of the gospel. The good news—the gospel—about Jesus of Nazareth, that He died on a cross to exhaust the curse of sin and set us free from slavery, is good news for every person, whether they choose to believe it or not. Either Jesus is who He said He is and deserves the allegiance of our whole heart, or He's a liar and a farce. There is no middle ground on this. I believe in Jesus. I believe He is who He says He is. And I'm not ashamed of that.

· THINK ABOUT IT ·

How do you respond when you hear someone deny Jesus' claim to be the Son of God and the Savior of the world?

Prayer

Heavenly Father, forgive me for any hesitancy to give an account for the hope within me. I am not ashamed of You and want to be Your representative. Help me be courageously ready to seize every opportunity to advance Your gospel. In Jesus' name, amen.

BOTH AND

Not to us, O LORD, not to us but to your name be the glory, because of your love and faithfulness.

PSALM 115:1

The topic of the fruit of the Spirit and the gifts of the Spirit can be polarizing among Christians. One group says, "I want the gifts of the Spirit (i.e. healing, prophecy, working of miracles)." Another group says, "I'm more interested in the fruits of the Spirit (i.e. love, joy, peace, patience, kindness, goodness, faithfulness, gentleness, and self-control)." Some of us view those two categories as if they are "either/or" instead of "both/and." The truth is we need the fruit of the Spirit in order to mature in our character so that God can entrust us more frequently with the gifting of the Spirit. So rather than making an either/or choice, we should say, "I want to cooperate more fully with the Spirit of God." The most important thing to remember is that the gifts of the Spirit and the fruit of the Spirit are to be treasured and approached with great humility because they have one purpose: to glorify God.

• THINK ABOUT IT •

Have you learned through teaching or tradition that either the gifting or the fruit of the Spirit is more important than the other? How can you cooperate more fully with the Spirit of God today?

Prayer

Heavenly Father, thank You for conforming me to the image of Jesus Christ. I need both the fruit of Your Spirit and Your gifts in order to more fully reflect Your character. Help me yield to Your Holy Spirit for both these to emerge in my life. In Jesus' name, amen.

PRAISE DEFEATS DOUBT

"Now have come the salvation and the power and the kingdom of our God, and the authority of his Messiah. For the accuser of our brothers and sisters, who accuses them before our God day and night, has been hurled down."

REVELATION 12:10

One of Satan's titles is the "accuser of the brethren." External accusations are easy to identify—the enemies, adversaries, the inappropriate things. The greater challenges are accusations within me: "What gives you the right to tell anybody anything?" "Why would you pray for anyone? The last person you prayed for had to go to the hospital." "Do you really believe God loves you?" "Do you really think the Bible will change your life?" So I have to decide what I'm going to listen to and what my response will be. I've learned to stop and thank the Lord for who He is—for His love, protection, and provision—that He is greater than all the spirits in the world. I thank Him the "accuser" is powerless over me and he does not win in the end. God wants to help you overcome the enemy's whispered doubts, so let your response of praise be louder than the voices in your head.

• THINK ABOUT IT •

The Creator of Heaven and earth is on your side, and the Spirit of the Living God dwells within you. How does this knowledge help you face the doubts the enemy puts in your mind?

Prayer

Heavenly Father, thank You for grace to discern and authority to resist the "accuser." Help me be ready to exalt Your truth to fight my doubts and insecurities. Praise You for Your goodness and faithfulness—You are my strong Deliverer! In Jesus' name, amen.

POWERFUL LOVE

I will always remind you of these things, even though you know them and are firmly established in the truth you now have.

2 PETER 1:12

It isn't the mysterious, unknowable spiritual things that change us. It's the simple but profound truths of Scripture that we can know, understand, and deeply sink our roots into that change our lives. Peter, writing to a group of believers, tells them he will keep reminding them of things they already know because they are worth remembering again. One foundational truth I want you to remember is that Jesus loves you. Sometimes life-events make us wonder if God still loves us: How could this be happening if He does? But I want to remind you that no matter what your circumstances are, He does love you and He will help you make it through whatever you are facing. This little chorus brings me comfort when I find myself doubting: "Jesus loves me—this I know, for the Bible tells me so; little ones to Him belong—they are weak, but He is strong. Yes, Jesus loves me! Yes, Jesus loves me! Yes, Jesus loves me! The Bible tells me so."

• THINK ABOUT IT •

Is Jesus' love for you at the center of your awareness, or have you allowed it to drift to the edges? Does His love for you affect your daily thoughts and actions?

Prayer

Heavenly Father, help me to continually remember and recount Your steadfast love and faithfulness as I face each day. When doubt arises, may I trust in the simple truths expressed in Your Word to guide me toward hope and forgiveness. In Jesus' name, amen.

DAY 295

BOLD PRAYER

"When you pray, do not be like the hypocrites, for they love to pray standing in the synagogues and on the street corners to be seen by men. . . . But when you pray, go into your room, close the door and pray to your Father, who is unseen. Then your Father, who sees what is done in secret, will reward you."

MATTHEW 6:5-6

Sometimes people say to me, "Pastor, Jesus said you should pray in your closet." Jesus was certainly an advocate for private prayer, but this passage is warning us to avoid being like the outwardly religious people, using prayer just to draw attention to themselves. If we only pray in private, however, we fail to demonstrate our dependence on God and the power we believe prayer has. Jesus prayed publicly, as did Peter and John, that people might see what prayer could accomplish, and whole communities were changed. If the Church fails to pray, we will fail our assignment and will not complete what God has called us to. If we can become comfortable praying in public—simple, sincere prayers—then those around us will understand prayer is part of the fabric of our lives. They will see God at work and wonder how He can change their lives too.

• THINK ABOUT IT •

Do you really believe that prayer is a powerful tool in your spiritual toolkit? Do you pray aloud with your family and friends in order to show the importance you place on prayer?

Prayer

Heavenly Father, teach me to come boldly to You in prayer with the help of Your Holy Spirit. Help me become increasingly at ease talking to and petitioning You—both privately and publicly—that many hearts and lives might be changed. In Jesus' name, amen.

CHOOSE CONTENTMENT

Whoever loves money never has money enough; whoever loves wealth is never satisfied with his income.

ECCLESIASTES 5:10

Contentment has been an issue for people since almost the beginning of our story. The problem began in Genesis 3—we only made it through two chapters before we wanted more than the beautiful life that God had provided. Discontentment is part of our fallen human nature, but for some of us it seems to rule our lives. Discontentment is like a corrosive acid that will eat through your soul. It will rob you of joy and pleasure and happiness. Some of the saddest people I know are those who think if they could just get all the money they need their souls would be at peace and they would finally be content. But that is simply not true; money will not, cannot, make us content. We hear of wealthy people who take their own lives and wonder why. They seem to have every material blessing, but they are still so unhappy that life seems meaningless. Contentment will not come to us through possessions. Contentment is a decision, a choice we make every day to be satisfied with God's provision for our lives.

· THINK ABOUT IT ·

Do you struggle with discontentment? Begin writing down all the ways the Lord has blessed you, and thank Him for what He has done.

Prayer

Heavenly Father, Your provision is a gift in my life—spiritually and materially—covering all I need. Forgive me for when I have either taken Your blessings for granted or been discontent. May I always find my satisfaction in You. In Jesus' name, amen.

OUT OF ALIGNMENT

"When you stand praying, if you hold anything against anyone, forgive him, so that your Father in heaven may forgive you your sins."

MARK 11:25

Prayer can certainly change our circumstances or the people around us. But prayer is also about initiating a change in us. Prayer facilitates alignment between ourselves and God, and sometimes the alignment is about obedience. Prayer isn't always just about changing the immediate things. Sometimes we have to pray about the things that are behind us as well. Our lives so often are defined by what has happened in the past, and Jesus tells us here that we have to let those things go. When you forgive someone, it not only releases them, it unleashes spiritual forces on your behalf. As we open the dialogue with God, and we listen to Him, and we make room in our lives for the work of the Holy Spirit, most typically we are the ones who are transformed. We forgive because we have been forgiven, and we forgive because it releases God's favor in our lives.

• THINK ABOUT IT •

Do you struggle to forgive a person or people who have hurt you in the past? Give your hurts to God and allow Him to free you from the bondage of unforgiveness.

Prayer

Heavenly Father, as You have graciously forgiven me, I also forgive _____ for offense. Please bless them. I choose to cancel their debt to me right now because You cancelled mine when You forgave me. Thank You for setting me free. In Jesus' name, amen.

PROFOUND PEACE

"I have told you these things, so that in me you may have peace. In this world you will have trouble. But take heart! I have overcome the world."

JOHN 16:33

Fear seems to be gripping our world in an unprecedented way. We are afraid of an ever-changing list of foods and ask for nutrition information for a fast-food hamburger. We are afraid of weather and have our phones set to alert us when the forecast calls for wind or rain. We post a photo of our supper on social media and panic when not enough "friends" say they "like" it. Some fears are more serious than others, but it is true that fear—both real and imagined—is very real in our society. Thankfully, there is no fear that cannot be overcome with the peace that Jesus gives us. His life was filled with situations that would cause real fear in the bravest of us, but He was never afraid. His life was marked by criticism and rejection, but He demonstrated a calm assurance that God was always with Him. If Jesus said we don't have to be afraid, we don't have to be. If Jesus gives me His peace, that's good enough for me.

· THINK ABOUT IT ·

No matter what happened to Him, Jesus was never frightened or intimidated. How do you use the peace He offers to conquer fear in your life?

Prayer

Heavenly Father, thank You that in this troubled world You provide peace, security, and abundant life through the cross of Jesus Christ. May Your Holy Spirit counsel me daily in Your peace. When I am afraid, I will trust in You. In Jesus' name, amen.

DAY 299

OPEN DOORS

"I know your deeds. See, I have placed before you an open door that no one can shut. I know that you have little strength, yet you have kept my word and have not denied my name."

REVELATION 3:8

The book of Revelation opens with letters to seven specific churches, and this one is to the group of believers in Philadelphia, located in modern Turkey. To every church Jesus says, "I know your circumstances. I know what's going on." In this particular case, He commends them for their faithfulness and tells them He has placed before them an open door that no one can shut . . . in spite of their weakness. This is so encouraging to me. He doesn't say, "You have great strength, so I have given you an open door to a great opportunity." He says, "I know you are exhausted, so I have given you a door that no one can keep you from walking through." Don't ever think that God is not watching over you. He is interested and invested in your life. Sometimes when we are faithful but still feel weakened by the challenges of life, we feel abandoned by God—but that is not the case. God loves you, and He wants to open doors of opportunity for you.

· THINK ABOUT IT ·

Do you feel that you can fully trust God with your future? Think about all the times He has been faithful to you, and remember them when your faith is small.

Prayer

Heavenly Father, You open doors of opportunity for me, and by Your grace I will go through them. When I feel like I have no strength to go forward, help me remember Your faithfulness and that You are holding the door open for me. In Jesus' name, amen.

INTRINSIC VALUE

So God created man in his own image, in the image of God he created him; male and female he created them.

GENESIS 1:27

The opening chapters of the Bible introduce us to God as the Creator of all things. At the culmination of His creative process, He made human beings in His own image. What does this mean for us? Being the image-bearers of Almighty God separates humans from every other created being and gives dignity to each one of us—the unborn, the newborn, the elderly, the weakest, the strongest, the least intelligent, the most intelligent, the least productive, the most productive. We usually celebrate people who have qualities we appreciate, and we tend to overlook the people whose qualities we don't think have much merit. Every person is made unique by Almighty God, however, and if you'll make it your personal life-assignment to discover what makes each person special, it will bring you joy and change your relationships. People will matter to you in a whole new way.

• THINK ABOUT IT •

Every human being has an intrinsic value in the sight of God. Do you judge people as the world judges, or do you try to recognize the unique gifts of every person?

Prayer

Heavenly Father, You place a high value on every person—we are made in Your image. Forgive me when my affinities increased or lessened my favor toward others. Help me honor You by diligently looking for Your qualities in each person. In Jesus' name, amen.

DAY 301

POWER TO CHANGE

"Stretch out your hand to heal and perform miraculous signs and wonders through the name of your holy servant Jesus."

ACTS 4:30

Peter had healed a lame man in the name of Jesus in Acts 3. The man evidently had been begging in the same spot for a while and was a familiar sight near the Temple gate. His healing caused such a commotion in the city that the religious leaders took notice. The apostles' teaching about Jesus landed them in jail, but many people had already heard their message and believed He was the Messiah. When Peter and John were released and returned to the other believers, they prayed this earnest prayer for God to do mighty things in their midst. Instead of being content just to study and talk about God, we should pray this kind of prayer for ourselves. Before we gather for any kind of ministry opportunity or convene a small group, let's ask the Lord to do a miracle in our midst. Let's ask Him to demonstrate His power in ways that will change people's lives.

• THINK ABOUT IT •

Do you truly want to see God at work around you? Do you pray expectantly, looking for Him to unleash His power in order to change people's lives?

Prayer

Heavenly Father, nothing is too hard for You. Help me believe You will respond in great power to the needs I present—both privately and publicly. May Your miraculous answers to prayer cultivate greater faith in You. In His name I pray, amen.

YOU BELONG

You're no longer strangers or outsiders. You belong here, with as much right to the name Christian as anyone.

EPHESIANS 2:19 • THE MESSAGE©

Have you ever had the humiliating experience of being chosen last, or not being chosen at all? Perhaps you were at the end of the bench, with a starting lineup who could do it all. Perhaps you were the one who practiced jumping and twisting and tumbling and memorized every cheer but still didn't make the cut. Perhaps what seems like a parade of prospective spouses has marched in and out of your life. Perhaps you can't seem to break into the inner circle of decision-makers in your office. It is good to know that in spite of how anyone feels about us, God loves us, values us, and has chosen us. He will never put us on the bench or relegate us to the second team or say we are not worthy of His attention. He has blessed us with a unique mix of personality, gifts, and talents for us to use as we honor Him and advance His Kingdom purposes. "You belong here!" the Bible says.

• THINK ABOUT IT •

Do you see yourself as God sees you: His child, uniquely created, whom He loves and cherishes?

Prayer

Heavenly Father, thank You for choosing me in Your infinite love and making a place for me in Your Kingdom, giving me a sense of true worth. You and You alone are able to keep me from falling. Your love brings great value to my life. In Jesus' name, amen.

DAY 303

GOD'S PERFECT TIMING

On the day the LORD gave the Amorites over to Israel, Joshua said to the LORD in the presence of Israel: "O sun, stand still over Gibeon, O moon, over the Valley of Aijalon." So the sun stood still, and the moon stopped, till the nation avenged itself on its enemies.

JOSHUA 10:12-13

One frustration for many people is a struggle to understand God's timing. Is it possible that we are too focused on our perspective of time and would benefit from being more focused on God's perspective of time? If you are unhappy or anxious with God over the timeline of your life or events that have not happened in the timing you thought best, think about this Israelite victory over the Amorites. The Israelites were winning the battle, but the sun would set before the victory was assured. So God stopped the sun and the moon in their usual course and extended the day! We get so wrapped up in days, weeks, and years that we begin to think that God can't, or won't, act to accomplish His purposes. He doesn't get anxious about time, nor is He limited by our concepts of time. Say to the Lord, "I trust You. I would rather look into Your face than at my calendar."

• THINK ABOUT IT •

Have there been seasons of your life when God's timing was not what you would have chosen? What did you learn about God and about yourself in those situations?

Prayer

Heavenly Father, Your Word reveals nothing is too difficult for You, and at the appointed time, You will reveal what I need to know. I trust You with my life in time and eternity and find my peace in the King of kings and the Lord of lords. In Jesus' name, amen.

SHARED FREEDOM

Therefore there is now no condemnation for those who are in Christ Jesus. For the law of the Spirit of life in Christ Jesus has set you free from the law of sin and of death.

ROMANS 8:1-2 • NASB®

We read over this verse pretty quickly, seeing "No condemnation!" and then not really hearing the rest. But what condemnation are we freed from, and who is still condemned? Life without Christ, it says, is life ruled by "the law of sin and of death." This brings mental pictures of bondage . . . sadness and limited freedom in this life and torment in the next. It is easy for us to be happy and secure in our own salvation but not be too concerned about those who have not accepted Jesus as Savior and Lord. The reality is that they are enslaved in this life and will be in the next unless they repent of their sins and turn to Him. Let's not be content with our own salvation but unconcerned with the lives of others. Let's keeping telling others what Jesus has done for us and how He can change their lives too.

• THINK ABOUT IT •

Are you prepared to share your Jesus-story? What has Jesus done for you that others might be able to relate to?

Prayer

Heavenly Father, I rejoice in the freedom You have brought into my life through the cross of Jesus Christ. Give me a deep desire and the confidence to share Your plan for salvation and freedom with others who are still in bondage. In Jesus' name, amen.

TREASURES IN HEAVEN

Then he said to them, "Watch out! Be on your guard against all kinds of greed; a man's life does not consist in the abundance of his possessions."

LUKE 12:15

Many of us spend our time and energies as if our lives consisted of how much we own. Online shopping has increased this tendency greatly; we can now buy nearly anything with a few clicks from the comfort of our easy chairs. The result is that our packed cabinets and closets overflow into storage bins that are stacked in our attics and storage units. Our prized possessions sit there gathering dust and crumbling from age until we die and pass them on to our children and grandchildren, who shake their heads as they pack up their "inheritance" and drop it off at a thrift store . . . or the dump. We all need to own things, of course, and I'm not opposed to nice things; but Jesus tells us to "Watch out!" and be careful that our things don't begin to define our lives. Jesus says our focus should be on accumulating the things that will matter in the life to come—"treasures in heaven"—so let's focus on those things instead of amassing "treasures on earth" (Matthew 6:19-21).

• THINK ABOUT IT •

Take a look around your house. How much of your time and energy is spent on accumulating things that have no eternal value?

Prayer

Heavenly Father, thank You for inviting me to invest my strength and resources in pursuit of Your agenda in my generation. Help me give priority to this rather than to earthly treasure, that I might bring glory to Jesus as Messiah and Lord. In Jesus' name, amen.

THE BEGINNING AND ENDING

When they reached the place God had told him about, Abraham built an altar there and arranged the wood on it. He bound his son Isaac and laid him on the altar, on top of the wood. Then he reached out his hand and took the knife to slay his son.

GENESIS 22:9-10

When God told Abraham to offer his son Isaac as a sacrifice to Him, He knew what Abraham would do. This story is about Abraham coming to understand what was in his own heart. It is about Abraham choosing to yield to God, giving Him the most precious thing he had. We say "The Lord will provide" pretty casually, but Hebrews 11:17-19 says that Abraham believed that if he sacrificed his son that God would raise him back to life again. Such confidence in the Lord was built in Abraham over a long period of time. I think about the difference in Abraham as he was walking up the hill and then down the hill. On the way up he must have been lost in his own thoughts, wondering how God's plan would unfold even as Isaac walked beside him. On the way down he must have felt immeasurable joy, with his son still beside him and knowing that he had honored the Lord.

• THINK ABOUT IT •

Just as God knew the end from the beginning in Abraham's life, He knows the end from the beginning in every circumstance we face. Determine to trust Him completely, and honor Him in all you do.

Prayer

Heavenly Father, You have saved me from destruction and given me abundant life and wholeness. Serving You daily brings transformation to my life. May I never stray from Your precepts, walking always in the faithfulness of Abraham, David, and Joseph. In Jesus' name, amen.

THE ONLY SOURCE

For our struggle is not against flesh and blood, but against the rulers, against the authorities, against the powers of this dark world and against the spiritual forces of evil in the heavenly realms.

EPHESIANS 6:12

You may have noticed subtle influences of Eastern religions on our lives. Some people engage in them unwittingly for the purpose of relaxation or exercise. Others buy a statue of a god or goddess to sit in a flower bed. Our culture is so saturated with political correctness that even Jesus-followers hesitate to say those religions are false and their practices dabble with "powers of this dark world." When we talk about "spiritual forces of evil," Christians are a little naïve; we imagine that intent is necessary to have consequences. That is simply untrue; intent is not necessary to have a consequence. If you've been involved in even a casual way, don't defend it or justify it. Just say to the Lord, "I'm sorry. I renounce any unclean thing that could have impacted my life through that behavior. Forgive me."

• THINK ABOUT IT •

Are you aware of the dark spiritual forces at work in false religions? Are you ready to say—anywhere, anytime, to anyone—that Jesus is the Son of God, and belief in Him is the only way to peace in this life and for eternity?

Prayer

Heavenly Father, please bring to my mind any and everything that I have done knowingly or unknowingly that involves false religious teachings or practices. I want to experience Your freedom by renouncing any and all false guidance. In Jesus' name, amen.

20/20 HINDSIGHT

And we know that in all things God works for the good of those who love him, who have been called according to his purpose.

ROMANS 8:28

Have you ever been around a child whose parents never said no? You hoped it was a short visit, didn't you? I did not grow up with that kind of parents. They did not orchestrate my life based on what they thought was going to bring me the greatest joy; they had another agenda, and it was focused on my future. God has a parenting plan too, and He cares more about what we are becoming than what will make us happy in every moment. When you feel like God is either not opening doors of opportunity for you or He is closing doors that you have forced open, know that He is doing that for your own good. Sometimes we are able to see why God directs our paths in the way He does, but many times we will not be able to understand His plan. Our knowledge and understanding is limited to what we can see and hear, but His plan has eternity in view "for the good of those who love him, who have been called according to his purpose."

• THINK ABOUT IT •

Has there been a time when you could not understand God's purpose in the moment but could see it in the rearview mirror of time? What did you learn about God's desires for you in that situation?

Prayer

Heavenly Father, I love You and thank You for making all things work for my good. Give me strength to look to You as I look expectantly to that day when You will be revealed in all of Your glory. I trust You with all of my life. In Jesus' name, amen.

WISDOM BY ASSOCIATION

The heart of the discerning acquires knowledge; the ears of the wise seek it out.

PROVERBS 18:15

Over the course of my walk with Jesus, I have benefited greatly from spending time with people who have been following Him longer than I have. There are some things about being a Christ-follower that are difficult to understand and put into practice, and I want to benefit from the accumulated knowledge and experience of the generations that have gone before me. We assume that we will acquire other knowledge and skills that way, but in spiritual matters we think, "I'm not going to take anybody else's word for it. I'm going to figure this out for myself." Imagine if you learned chemistry that way: "I'm not going to read the textbook or hear any lectures. I'm going to do all new experiments and discover new compounds and build my own periodic table." That doesn't make much sense, does it? I'm going to be discerning and surround myself with other people who have the benefit of personal experience with Jesus, people who can help me avoid some pitfalls and steer me on the right path.

• THINK ABOUT IT •

Do you seek out and associate with people who have been following Jesus longer than you have, and then ask them to share their God-experiences with you?

Prayer

Heavenly Father, I have been encouraged, instructed, and blessed by those who know and serve You. Thank You, Lord, for their generosity in freely sharing their faith-stories with me. Together, may we continue to honor You. In Jesus' name, amen.

NOT OVERWHELMED

Let us then approach the throne of grace with confidence, so that we may receive mercy and find grace to help us in our time of need.

HEBREWS 4:16

If you are connected to a group of Jesus-followers who are committed to sharing their lives with one another, you have heard prayer requests that will threaten to overwhelm you. Each of us has burdens that sometimes feel as if they might be too much to bear. Job loss, financial setbacks, prodigal children, illness, broken marriages, depression, addictions, pressures at school and at work—the list goes on. It is such a relief to me to know that God has not abandoned us and that we can approach Him with confidence. He has given us a great High Priest who pleads for us and the Holy Spirit who intercedes for us even when we don't know how we should pray. God is attuned to the cries of the hurting in a way that no human can ever be. He hears our prayers with the ears of a loving Father who has promised His presence and comfort through life's circumstances. No matter how deep the valley of trouble seems, take your burdens to Him, knowing that you will "receive mercy and find grace."

• THINK ABOUT IT •

Are you sometimes overwhelmed by the problems facing you and those you care about? How can you begin to give your concerns to the Lord?

Prayer

Heavenly Father, thank You for allowing and encouraging me to come boldly before You with my requests. I give my burdens and concerns about _____ to You. You are strong, loving, and faithful. All glory, honor, and praise belong to You. In Jesus' name, amen.

DAY 311

DEFINING GRACE

When Jesus rose early on the first day of the week, he appeared first to Mary Magdalene, out of whom he had driven seven demons.

MARK 16:9

How would you like it if every time your name was mentioned the darkest chapter of your life was given as your byline? There were other things Mark could have said to describe Mary Magdalene: She was from the village of Migdal, or Magdala, which was near Jesus' ministry base, Capernaum. She had followed Jesus for three years and had been present for His crucifixion and burial. But when Mark mentions that Mary Magdalene was the first one to see Jesus after His resurrection, he immediately adds that Jesus had driven seven demons out of her. Mark chose to remind us that the most important thing that we need to know about Mary Magdalene was that Jesus had delivered her from evil and given her freedom from what had possessed her. When Jesus brings freedom to your life it defines you and becomes an unmistakable part of your future. He has done something miraculous for every one of us, and we should be glad to make that an important part of our life story.

• THINK ABOUT IT •

When you think about the things that define your life and what you want people to know about you, is your relationship with Jesus at the top of the list?

Prayer

Heavenly Father, in spite of my past ungodliness, You reveal Your love and forgiveness to me day after day. May Your grace teach me to say no to ungodliness and yes to the things You place before me. Lord, You are my strength and Redeemer. In Jesus' name, amen.

GRUMBLY OR GRATEFUL

It is good to give thanks to the Lord and to sing praises to Your name, O Most High; to declare Your lovingkindness in the morning and Your faithfulness by night.

PSALM 92:1-2 • NASB®

If I am not careful, I can just go through the routine of another day without stopping to fully recognize the provision, the people, and the opportunities that God has poured so generously into my life. Will you join me in intentionally cultivating an attitude of thankfulness? From morning to night, let's thank the Lord with greater enthusiasm than we grumble. Let's look for God in our circumstances and ask what we can learn about Him in the midst of them, even if we don't always understand His plan. Let's thank Him for our very lives. Let's thank Him for the opportunities He has given us. Let's thank Him for the forgiveness He shows when we do less than our best for Him, and for the second and third chances He gives us. When we are tempted to grumble, let's look around and find reasons to be grateful instead.

• THINK ABOUT IT •

Is your attitude toward God more grumbly or grateful? Think about all the things you have to be grateful for, and give Him the thanksgiving and praise He is due.

Prayer

Heavenly Father, I have been ungrateful when all was well and grumbled and fretted in adversity. Forgive me, Lord. I choose today to thank You for protecting and guiding me. May I not take Your grace for granted. I will praise You day and night, for You are worthy. In Jesus' name, amen.

DAY 313

IT'S ALL IN THE BOOK

Do not conform any longer to the pattern of this world, but be transformed by the renewing of your mind. Then you will be able to test and approve what God's will is—his good, pleasing and perfect will.

ROMANS 12:2

We rightly do all kinds of things to protect ourselves. We try to eat nutritious food, exercise, wear our seat belts, brush our teeth and floss, use sunscreen. But we fail to do one of the things that offers the most protection when we don't read our Bibles regularly in order to renew our minds. What you or someone else thinks the Bible might say could possibly do you some good; but in order to protect yourself from manipulation and deception, you need to know what it says for yourself. You will not know your Bible adequately if your only interaction with it is listening to preachers—we're not that good! You need to read it to learn about the character of God and the salvation offered only through His Son, Jesus of Nazareth. This knowledge and awareness will allow you to live differently than "the pattern of this world," and you will flourish as you become more like Christ and understand His will and purposes for your life.

• THINK ABOUT IT •

Is reading and thinking about God's Word part of your daily routine? If so, how has it changed your life? If not, won't you consider making it a priority?

Prayer

Heavenly Father, open my mind to understand Your Word, which reveals Your character and Your ways. I want to be more like You and choose to submit my heart and mind to You to transform them for useful service in Your Kingdom. In Jesus' name, amen.

JUST SAY YES

By faith Abraham, when called to go to a place he would later receive as his inheritance, obeyed and went, even though he did not know where he was going.

HEBREWS 11:8

In Genesis 12 we meet a man by the name of Abram. God said to Abram, "If you will leave your family and everything you know behind and go to a place that I will show you, I will make your descendants a mighty nation. And I'll make you a blessing to everyone, now and in the future." Imagine if you went home today and there was an angel sitting on the front step who said, "I want to make you a blessing to everyone on the planet." Most days, I'm happy if I can be a blessing to the people in my house! Do you know what Abram did? He rented a trailer, loaded his stuff, told the GPS to follow God, and off he went. You and I, millennia later, are still being blessed because that man said yes to God's invitation. Just as certainly as there was an invitation for Abram, there are invitations for you and me. Say yes to God when He invites you into His plan; His opportunities will change the future for you and many others.

• THINK ABOUT IT •

Have you ever said yes to God's invitations that reached into a future you could not imagine? What were the results?

Prayer

Heavenly Father, I desire faith like Abraham's to believe Your promises for my life. Today I offer myself as a living sacrifice. May Your invitations be more real to me than those of the world. I choose to live for the glory of the King. In Jesus' name, amen.

TEACHING ASSIGNMENT

Fix these words of mine in your hearts and minds. . . . Teach them to your children, talking about them when you sit at home and when you walk along the road, when you lie down and when you get up.

DEUTERONOMY 11:18-19

I think that parents often underestimate the influence they have over their children and overestimate the window of time they have to influence them. Parenting is one of the most significant expressions of leadership in your life, but it's a very temporary season. You get just a handful of years. After that, you become a co-traveler with them, and your influence changes dramatically. Parenting seems to be physically challenging during the earliest years and emotionally challenging as the years pass. In spite of that, parents have been given the assignment to teach and shepherd their children in the ways of the Lord—and you will give an account for it. I don't mean that you should expect to raise perfect children; that cross is not yours to bear. But teach your children the Scriptures and tell them what God has done for you. Let them see that following Jesus is the most important thing in your life.

· THINK ABOUT IT ·

Would your children and grandchildren, or other children you influence, say that following Jesus is the most important thing in your life?

Prayer

Heavenly Father, I want the children in my sphere of influence to know You and live for You. May they each have a personal experience with You and call upon Jesus as their Savior and Lord, able to trust You in the storms of life. In Jesus' name, amen.

AN EARTH-SHAKING CHOICE

"Go into all the world and preach the good news to all creation."

MARK 16:15

Jesus' three years of ministry with the disciples had been almost entirely focused on the Jewish people who lived within a small geographical area. He sent the disciples ahead of Him into the villages and towns of Israel, and they avoided the areas where Romans lived. "I was sent only to the lost sheep of Israel," He said in Matthew 15:24. Now, in His first conversation with the disciples after His resurrection, He says, "Stop being doubters. Go into all the world!" Those men and women, who were His closest friends and followers, embraced the initiative, even though "going global" in the first century meant more than sending a few emails—it required a lot of steps of the feet. They packed up and went, taking Jesus' message beyond all of the ethnic and social boundaries they had known—and by doing so they shook the world.

• THINK ABOUT IT •

Following Jesus will take greater courage and conviction than anything you have ever done. How has following Jesus changed your life?

Prayer

Heavenly Father, thank You for sending people around the world to share Your good news. Help me to be an ambassador for You. I choose to be a person of truth and love who can bring the message of the cross to the world around me. In Jesus' name, amen.

INTENTIONAL PRAYER

Jesus went out to a mountainside to pray, and spent the night praying to God. When morning came, he called his disciples to him and chose twelve of them, whom he also designated apostles.

LUKE 6:12-13

Jesus was preparing to make a decision that would greatly affect His ministry and the course of the Church. Before He chose twelve apostles from the larger group of His followers, He went off alone and spent an entire night in prayer. "But this was Jesus," we think, God's Son, who had experienced His Father's Kingdom in its fullness. This was the Messiah who had turned water to wine, brought the dead to life, and quieted the wind and the waves. Still, He felt the need to spend several hours seeking His Father's will in the matter. If God's own Son relied on prayer so deeply and gave so much attention to His prayer life, I think we should follow His example. Let's give the Lord more than our last fading thoughts of the day; let's make prayer a priority in our lives.

• THINK ABOUT IT •

A fruitful prayer life requires intentionality or it will be lost in the busyness of our days. What is your plan for spending time with the Lord?

Prayer

Heavenly Father, thank You for hearing my prayers and for Your Holy Spirit who teaches us how to intercede for one another. I am overwhelmed You would want to have a personal conversation with me. Forgive me for taking this gift for granted. In Jesus' name, amen.

OUR SAFE SPACE

When I felt secure, I said, "I will never be shaken."

PSALM 30:6

It is true that what we say often reflects what we are feeling, but I also know it to be true that our feelings will follow what we say. This is actually a matter of choice; we often allow our feelings to dictate our words, and that is not always helpful. Each of us is bombarded with negative thoughts about ourselves—we are worthless, unlovable, incapable, and incompetent—because we have an enemy who wants us to feel insecure about who we are in Christ. If we allow those negative feelings to dictate the way we think of ourselves and drive all of our responses to life, we remain very vulnerable to his schemes. If we will begin to remind ourselves of the security and identity we have in Christ—we are worthy, loved, capable, and competent—our feelings can be transformed, and we will rest on a sure foundation that can never be shaken.

• THINK ABOUT IT •

Do you typically allow negative feelings to dictate your responses to life, or do you respond based on your identity in Christ?

Prayer

Heavenly Father, my security is in You. I submit my heart and mind to my Savior and Lord to seek You with all my heart. The world is shaking all around me, but You are always steady. You are my firm foundation, rock, and safe place. In Jesus' name, amen.

DAY 319

STRONG AND COURAGEOUS

In the temple courts he found people selling cattle, sheep and doves, and others sitting at tables exchanging money. So he made a whip out of cords, and drove all from the temple area, both sheep and cattle; he scattered the coins of the money changers and overturned their tables. To those who sold doves he said, "Get these out of here! How dare you turn my Father's house into a market!"

JOHN 2:14-16

The Bible gives us no description of Jesus' appearance. As a Middle Easterner of that day, He would have had dark hair and a dark complexion. We know that His earthly father, Joseph, was a carpenter by trade, so we can assume that Jesus probably was accustomed to doing manual labor. He was a man of great compassion and love, but there was strength in Him that we sometimes miss. When He spoke to people who were opposed to the Kingdom of God—including these who had turned the Temple into a marketplace—He was angry and showed it. The image of Him driving people and animals out with a whip is powerful. Jesus was a strong and courageous man in every sense of those words. Don't ever allow anyone to convince you that He was weak. Don't ever apologize for following Him.

• THINK ABOUT IT •

When you hear Jesus' name, what is the first image of Him that comes to mind? Do you think that image is accurate?

Prayer

Heavenly Father, You sent Your Son to earth to live and die for me, experiencing total rejection on my behalf. He, without sin, paid the price for my sin on the cross. I am in awe of Jesus' strength, and I worship Him for all He endured for me. In Jesus' name, amen.

IT'S THE LITTLE THINGS

Therefore, as God's chosen people, holy and dearly loved, clothe yourselves with compassion, kindness, humility, gentleness and patience.

COLOSSIANS 3:12

Sometimes a person will ask me what they should be doing as a faithful follower of Jesus. I don't know a specific answer to that question for every person, but I do know that God wants each of us to be faithful to Him in the little things. Faithfulness does sometimes mean supersized projects and extravagant plans and international initiatives. But most often faithfulness is lived out in the assignments of our day—in our home, in our office, at school, at the gym, and on the interstate. We should conduct ourselves in all of those situations with "compassion, kindness, humility, gentleness and patience" that show the world we are different because Jesus is Lord of our lives. Show Him your faithfulness in these seemingly small, daily situations, and He will bless you for it.

• THINK ABOUT IT •

Do you respond to the daily situations of life in a way that reflects your relationship with Jesus and gives glory to Him?

Prayer

Heavenly Father, today is a new day with new opportunities, and I pray I will make the most of it. Open my eyes to see the ways I can demonstrate Your compassion, kindness, humility, gentleness, and patience today. In Jesus' name, amen.

FREELY GIVEN

Riches do not endure forever, and a crown is not secure for all generations.

PROVERBS 27:24

Why is it so important for us to invest our financial resources in the things of God? God certainly doesn't need anything we have. Any monetary gift we can offer will not put the heavenly economy over the top. The angels are not clipping coupons in order to make it to the end of the month. They haven't called a special meeting to decide what to do if tithes and offerings don't meet the annual budget. God's view of money is completely different than ours. He has no need of it, but He gives us the privilege of having a part in His Kingdom purposes so that we can show Him our love and gratitude. He in turn demonstrates His provision for us in this life and then rewards us in eternity. "Riches do not endure forever," the writer says. This truth contradicts our human inclinations toward greed and selfishness, so ask the Lord to help you see His perspective with more clarity and then live it on a daily basis.

• THINK ABOUT IT •

We will never have enough money if we have not yielded what money we do have to the Lord. Does the way you use your money reflect God's attitude toward it?

Prayer

Heavenly Father, You have blessed me abundantly. May I remember it all comes from You, not from my own power or strength. As You have freely given to me, help me freely give to others. I am grateful for what I have, and ask You to bless it to its best purpose. In Jesus' name, amen.

A FOCUSED HEART

"To the angel of the church in Laodicea write . . . I know your deeds, that you are neither cold nor hot. I wish you were either one or the other! So, because you are lukewarm—neither hot nor cold—I am about to spit you out of my mouth."

REVELATION 3:14-16

The message to the Laodiceans is unsettling: "You're not really hot or cold. You're not really in or out. You're willing to say Jesus is Lord, but you worship a lot of other things. Your hearts are distracted and unfocused. Go away from me." If I had to look for a passage that is descriptive of the contemporary American church, it would be hard to find one that is more appropriate than this one. With our abundance and our freedoms, we have become complacent about the Lord. As a result, we are witnessing a precipitous decline of Christian influence. That's not on the doorstep of the ungodly or the government. That falls on the doorstep of the Church, and the Church is us. Let us—each of us—determine in our hearts to devote ourselves to the purposes of God so that He will never say to us, "Go away from me."

• THINK ABOUT IT •

Is your heart focused on the Lord, or do you allow other things to distract you from His purposes? Are you living so as to make a difference in our world?

Prayer

Heavenly Father, each day brings unexpected challenges that distract my attention. Help me keep my eyes set on You. Renew my zeal for Your Kingdom purposes. May the words of my mouth please You and my thoughts be aligned with Your Word. In Jesus' name, amen.

INVESTMENT OPPORTUNITIES

Another disciple said to him, "Lord, first let me go and bury my father." But Jesus told him, "Follow me, and let the dead bury their own dead."

MATTHEW 8:21-22

Some Bibles title this section of Scripture, "The Cost of Following Jesus," but I'd rather title it, "The Invitation to Invest Our Lives with Jesus." Following Jesus doesn't feel like a cost, an expense that will diminish our resources; it feels like an investment, a way to use our resources that will bring a great return. Jesus invited this man, who was already known as a disciple, to leave what he was doing and follow Him. The nameless man could not see beyond his current circumstances, and he declined Jesus' invitation. We too may already be disciples, but Jesus is still offering us invitations toward new levels of commitment, new experiences, and new opportunities. Let's not be complacent and content with the status quo. Let's celebrate what Jesus has done through us in the past, but let's also be ready to follow Him and look forward with great expectation toward what He will do in the future.

• THINK ABOUT IT •

Following the Lord means we consistently make a commitment to honor Him with our lives. Do you commit your days to Him, with the expectation of being used in great ways?

Prayer

Heavenly Father, wherever You need me to go, and whatever You want me to do, I will be willing. I will need Your help. I know You are faithful, and You always provide a way for me. I trust You. Your thoughts are higher than mine. In Jesus' name, amen.

AUTHENTIC FAITH

He has shown you, O man, what is good. And what does the LORD require of you? To act justly and to love mercy and to walk humbly with your God.

MICAH 6:8

The messaging coming from the Church these days is a bit confusing. We want to show love to a world that doesn't know God, but we don't want to sound self-righteous or condemning. We want to be able to say, "The grace and mercy of God make it possible for you to be clean, and following Jesus will lead you to greater happiness and contentment." This makes our privilege of leading holy lives very important. We cannot have a "designer faith" based on our personal preferences and temptations, excusing our weaknesses but standing in judgment of others. An authentic and loving life will be easier when we filter our thoughts, words, and actions through this verse: Am I acting justly? Am I showing mercy? Am I living humbly? Am I honoring God?

• THINK ABOUT IT •

Do your thoughts, words, and actions reflect the love and mercy of Christ to the world—without judgment or condemnation?

Prayer

Heavenly Father, the world is increasingly antagonistic to those who hold onto Your values. In the midst of strife and turmoil, let my love not grow cold. Remind me to trust in Jesus, act justly, love mercy, and walk humbly with my Lord and Savior. In Jesus' name, amen.

ILLUMINATING INFLUENCE

"You are the light of the world. A city on a hill cannot be hidden. Neither do people light a lamp and put it under a bowl. Instead they put it on its stand, and it gives light to everyone in the house. In the same way, let your light shine before men, that they may see your good deeds and praise your Father in heaven."

MATTHEW 5:14-16

There are shelves of books written about leadership—how to attain a leadership position, how to be an effective leader, and how to lead people who don't want to be led. Real leadership is not about a title or a position, however. We all know people with both, and other people could care less. Leadership is about using the influence of your life for good, and the challenge for the Church in the world is to use the influence of our lives to further the cause of Christ. Jesus says here that Christian influence—our influence—is "the light of the world." When we allow others to see the "good deeds" we do in the name of Jesus, they will know that our God is worthy of praise. The light of Christ in the world is the only thing that will heal the wounds of hurting people, and we are called to show it gladly.

• THINK ABOUT IT •

Does your life show Jesus to the world? If not, how might you begin to reflect the glory of what He has done for you?

Prayer

Heavenly Father, I want to reflect the love of Christ to all who have never seen it nor felt its warmth. I am a thankful servant who is glad You sent someone to show me the light of Christ. Help me to go and do the same. In Jesus' name, amen.

RIPPLE EFFECT

Be imitators of me, just as I also am of Christ.

1 CORINTHIANS 11:1 • NASB®

There is historical evidence to show that cultures can be renewed, even those that have been the most corrupt or inflexible. But if we are to change our world, we first have to shake off the notion that Christianity is merely a personal experience that only affects our private lives. Some would tell us that no one should dictate our behavior as long as no one gets hurt. We rather conveniently forget that every private decision contributes to the moral and cultural climate in which we live. The consequences ripple out across our personal lives, then our family's lives, then our communities and the broader society. Paul is pleading with his readers to follow his example and imitate Christ. If we commit to yield ourselves to Him daily and model our thoughts and behaviors after Jesus' thoughts and behaviors, we will be worthy of imitation and bring radical transformation to the world.

• THINK ABOUT IT •

The cross is a place of execution where we take our desires and yield them to God's perspective. Do you consciously submit your daily decisions to God?

Prayer

Heavenly Father, I want to imitate Christ. Holy Spirit, reveal where I need to change. I repent for my church mask that concealed a heart more interested in worldly things. May I be radically transformed into the image of Your Son. In Jesus' name, amen.

A MAP FOR TROUBLED TIMES

The law of the LORD is perfect, reviving the soul. The statutes of the LORD are trustworthy, making wise the simple.

PSALM 19:7

Today's messaging says that while the Bible may be an important work of cultural and literary significance, it is ludicrous to believe it is the Word of God. If you dare to say you believe the Bible is the inspired and authoritative Word of an Almighty God, a "perfect" and "trustworthy" guide for life, a whole myriad of voices will say you are lacking intellectually. I believe the Bible is inspired by the Creator of Heaven and earth, and it gives us guidelines and boundaries for faith and practice. I believe it is worth an investment of our time and energy to know it. There are words in it I can't pronounce and parts of it that remain a mystery to me. I work hard to live up to the part I can understand—just learning to love my neighbor as much as I love myself keeps me busy! Don't let the world convince you that God's Word is not important. The seasons ahead will be difficult for those of us who follow Jesus, and the Bible will be the map that will help us navigate those troubled times.

• THINK ABOUT IT •

Are there voices in your world that minimize or criticize the Bible? Have you allowed them to influence the way you think about God's Word?

Prayer

Heavenly Father, Your Word gives me hope, builds my faith, and prepares me for each day, helping me see where I need to stand and the kind of person I need to become. Your Word also reveals You are a healing and forgiving God—thank You! In Jesus' name, amen.

ACCEPTED BY THE KING

A man with leprosy came and knelt before him and said, "Lord, if you are willing, you can make me clean." Jesus reached out his hand and touched the man. "I am willing," he said. "Be clean!" Immediately he was cured of his leprosy.

MATTHEW 8:2-3

Leprosy sufferers were considered unclean and were forced to live apart from the community, announcing their presence loudly so people would not accidentally make contact with them. To live with leprosy was not only physically challenging; it forced people into a very isolated and lonely existence. This man showed great trust in Jesus. Not only was he willing to risk rejection; He knew that if Jesus was willing to heal him, He had the power to do it. Jesus responded with a brief but beautiful statement: "I am willing." Then He reached out to touch a man who probably had not experienced human touch in a long time, and the man was immediately healed. If you feel you are living in physical or emotional isolation, know that Jesus is there for you. No matter what has touched your life to make you feel separate, He will welcome you with open arms.

• THINK ABOUT IT •

Isolation can lead to a feeling of being unaccepted and rejected, but in Christ we are invited into the Kingdom of God. Have you accepted His invitation to be a part of His family?

Prayer

Heavenly Father, You were willing to heal the leper, and You are willing to heal and restore broken lives—renewing and making them whole. In Your family I find belonging and healing, and together we will praise You with gladness for all You have done. In Jesus' name, amen.

DAY 329

A WALK-IN CLINIC

Jesus answered them, "It is not the healthy who need a doctor, but the sick. I have not come to call the righteous, but sinners to repentance."

LUKE 5:31-32

Some people seem to think of a church as a museum where you go to admire perfect specimens of Christians—beautifully pristine and untouched by the world. I think of a church as more of a walk-in clinic—a redeeming place where hurting people come together before Almighty God to invite His help in finding restoration and wholeness. We may be bruised or even bloodied from the challenges life has thrown at us, or even as the result of our own mistakes. But we press on together and learn about repenting and trusting Almighty God to bind our wounds and help us get through. Don't ever stop inviting people who don't know Jesus to church. Don't ever hesitate to admit your mistakes and brokenness to yourself and others, because we imperfect people are the ones Jesus came for. When we see the Lord at work in us and in the people around us, it strengthens our faith and gives us hope for the future.

• THINK ABOUT IT •

Have you ever waited to "clean yourself up" or "get your act together" before you asked the Lord for help? What does this verse say about that attitude?

Prayer

Heavenly Father, we are damaged and broken in many different ways. You know each one of our stories. In Your marvelous mercy You know how to reach us. I come to You just as I am. Give me ears to hear You when You call on me. May I never become deaf to Your voice. In Jesus' name, amen.

SWING FOR THE FENCE

Peter knocked at the outer entrance, and a servant girl named Rhoda came to answer the door. When she recognized Peter's voice, she was so overjoyed she ran back without opening it and exclaimed, "Peter is at the door!" "You're out of your mind," they told her.

ACTS 12:13-15

Gathered inside this room were a group of people who had been praying for several days that Peter would be released from prison. So what was their response when someone said Peter was free and standing at the door? "You're out of your mind!" There is no confusion about cause and effect in this account. These highly committed people of faith had been praying together with unity of heart and mind for a specific thing, so why were they so surprised when it happened? It is not arrogant or demanding or presumptuous to ask God to do something big. As a matter of fact, that is exactly what He wants us to do. And when He answers those prayers, don't say, "You're kidding!" Say "Yay, God!"

• THINK ABOUT IT •

Do you limit your prayers to small things that seem reasonable by human standards? Or do you "aim for the fences" and ask Him to do what seems impossible?

Prayer

Heavenly Father, it is easy to forget that You can do anything. There are no limits for You except for boundaries created by my own unbelief. Help me to grow in faith so that I can see You doing the impossible in my generation. In Jesus' name, amen.

REFINING WORK

Jesus called the crowd to him and said, "Listen and understand. What goes into a man's mouth does not make him 'unclean,' but what comes out of his mouth, that is what makes him 'unclean.'"

MATTHEW 15:10-11

Some faith traditions have their own ideas of which foods are "clean" or "unclean"—acceptable or unacceptable. Here Jesus is challenging a set of rules that establish righteousness from the outside in. We shake our heads at a rule that would keep someone from eating bacon, but we all feel some degree of self-righteousness. We think we are better than others because we go to church, and we are shocked to see people there who don't meet our standards. Self-righteousness is a limiting factor on our lives, but on the other end of the spectrum is the notion that God would never frown on anything we say or do that makes us happy. While God is not opposed to our happiness, it is not His primary agenda for our lives. He will evaluate each of us based on His standards of holiness and righteousness, and the challenge is for us to be open to the Holy Spirit's refining work so that we will be ready for that day.

• THINK ABOUT IT •

Jesus said that what is in your heart is more important than what you wear or what you eat. Do you ever judge yourself or others based on external things?

Prayer

Heavenly Father, forgive me for considering myself better than others because of what I do or don't do. Please cleanse me from self-righteousness. Christ in me can overcome the spirit of the world. Thank You for Your loving conviction. In Jesus' name, amen.

IF YOU BELIEVE

The fool says in his heart, "There is no God" . . . The LORD looks down from heaven on the sons of men to see if there are any who understand, any who seek God.

PSALM 14:1-2

It is unfashionable today to say there is one holy, Almighty God. Haven't we become a little more educated, more enlightened about other world religions? Why would we encumber ourselves by imagining there is one God deserving our complete love and loyalty? If you assert there is a God who created the heavens and the earth, that you believe Jesus of Nazareth is His Son who died on a cross and was raised to life again, that the Holy Spirit empowers us today, there will be a chorus of people who will say you are living in the past. This is not new. When the Psalms were written centuries ago, there was a group of people who were saying, "There is no God." The Bible says it's foolish to live as if there is no God, and that God is looking down from Heaven to find those who are seeking Him. Do not sit in the seat of the skeptic about the reality of Almighty God. To deny Him is foolishness; to acknowledge Him and live for Him will bring His blessings to your life.

• THINK ABOUT IT •

Are you ever with people who mock your belief in God? How do you prepare for that and respond?

Prayer

Heavenly Father, I want to be useful to You in Your Kingdom. You have revealed Yourself to me and required that I put my trust in You and the work of Jesus on the cross. Help me never fail to proclaim You are the one true God. In Jesus' name, amen.

FIRST PRIORITY

Martha was distracted by all the preparations that had to be made. She came to him and asked, "Lord, don't you care that my sister has left me to do the work by myself? Tell her to help me!" "Martha, Martha," the Lord answered, "you are worried and upset about many things, but only one thing is needed. Mary has chosen what is better, and it will not be taken away from her."

LUKE 10:40-42

Jesus and His disciples were at the home of Mary and Martha. Mary was sitting, listening to Jesus, while Martha was stressing over meal preparation. Finally Martha said to Jesus, "Mary is just sitting there! Tell her to help me!" I would expect Jesus to say, "Bless your heart, Martha. You've been so gracious to welcome us on short notice. We'll all come and help you." Instead He said, "Mary has made a better choice than you, and you should be acting more like her." Martha had seemingly good reason to be upset, but she got a gentle reprimand for her heart's condition. It is sobering we could be in proximity to God's Son but miss the blessing because we are consumed with mundane things. When life's busyness presses us from every direction, let's be careful to keep Him central in our priorities.

• THINK ABOUT IT •

We can rationalize just about any attitude or behavior, so we need God's help to discern the condition of our hearts. How do you keep Him as your first priority?

Prayer

Heavenly Father, teach me when to be still and listen, and when to work and prepare. I need Your discernment and help as I endeavor to serve You. Allow my life to be occupied by serving You in Your Church, among Your people. In Jesus' name, amen.

GOD'S FAITHFUL PROMISE

"'For I will take you out of the nations; I will gather you from all the countries and bring you back into your own land. . . . You will live in the land I gave your forefathers; you will be my people, and I will be your God.'"

EZEKIEL 36:24, 28

This centuries old prophecy about the Jewish people is just as relevant to the world today. The Romans destroyed Jerusalem in 70 A.D., and for two thousand years the Jewish people were scattered throughout the world. It defies logic that they survived and maintained their identity, but they did. In 1948 the modern nation of Israel was born, going beyond anything like it. Other nations have been created, but they didn't reflect the gathering of a unique people to their ancient homeland. The whole map of the Middle East had emerged between World Wars I and II, when politicians drew lines on the map as the spoils of war. They didn't take into account the tribal alliances or the ethnicities of the people, and most of those nations are currently disintegrating. But the nation of Israel is different. God said, "I give that land to Abraham and his descendants forever." When the Jewish people began to return from over one hundred nations, it was an amazing expression of the power of God to keep His promises.

• THINK ABOUT IT •

When have you seen God defy human logic and power in order to keep His promises?

Prayer

Heavenly Father, Your faithfulness has been displayed to all generations by You keeping Your scriptural promises. You are the author and completer of my faith. Believing in and cooperating with Your promises, I worship You alone. In Jesus' name, amen.

DAY 335

LIVE THE MESSAGE

Even if you should suffer for what is right, you are blessed. "Do not fear what they fear; do not be frightened."

1 PETER 3:14

Do you ever feel that in some places in your life you are alone as a Jesus-follower? Perhaps you are the only person in your family who has chosen Him as Savior, and times together feel awkward and strained. Perhaps your office environment is hostile to expressions of faith, and you find it difficult to share your true self with your coworkers. Although we do not face persecution as believers do in some parts of the world, it is possible in twenty-first century America that you have been discriminated against for your Christian faith. Once we step outside the walls of our church buildings, we are different from the world around us—and it is that very difference that bears witness to the change Jesus has brought in our lives. Do not be afraid to tell others what He has done for you, wherever you are. This is what we are called to do, and God has promised to bless us for it.

• THINK ABOUT IT •

Are there places in your life where you feel awkward about sharing your faith in Jesus? What are some gentle ways you can express what He has done for you?

Prayer

Heavenly Father, even in the midst of persecution, You are God! Therefore, I will share Your truth to those around me who are searching. Help me to forgive those who reject You, and seek Your forgiveness when I fear and lose hope. In Jesus' name, amen.

WORSHIP THE LORD

Praise the Lord, all nations; Laud Him, all peoples! For His lovingkindness is great toward us, and the truth of the Lord is everlasting. Praise the Lord!

PSALM 117:1-2 • NASB®

The so-called worship wars have been going on for a while now, but we'll settle them right here. Which is the right way to worship: Contemporary worship? Yes! Traditional worship? Yes! Liturgical worship? Yes! If the folks leading worship are wearing jeans and T-shirts, worship the Lord. If they are wearing robes, worship the Lord. If they have a kazoo band, worship the Lord. If they have a pipe organ, worship the Lord. If you're singing words on a screen, worship the Lord. If you're holding a hymn book, worship the Lord. If the song was written in 1918, worship the Lord. If it was written in 2018, worship the Lord. These things all pale in comparison to the glory of our God. Don't allow yourself to be distracted from the privilege of approaching Him and thanking Him for all He is and all He has done. Ask the Holy Spirit to keep your heart focused on the object of worship—our Almighty God—rather than the style of worship.

• THINK ABOUT IT •

Do you ever allow worship styles to distract you from worshipping the Lord?

Prayer

Heavenly Father, I will praise You in every circumstance, good or bad, because You are worthy. You chose and changed me to be useful, giving me purpose for Your specific purpose. May I maintain my focus on You alone in every act of worship. In Jesus' name, amen.

REFLECTED GRACE

Don't repay evil for evil. Don't retaliate with insults when people insult you. Instead, pay them back with a blessing. That is what God has called you to do, and he will grant you his blessing.

1 PETER 3:9 • NLT®

Adults have an enormously significant role to play in the lives of their young family members. Little people will rarely get much long-term benefit from a lecture; but they are mirrors of our everyday attitudes, words, and behaviors. In a very practical way, we are teaching and training and forming a generation by what we say and do. Families today are often blended and realigned, and relationships among extended families can be strained. It is our human inclination to "retaliate with insults" when people speak ill of you. Even across the hurt of separation or divorce and the struggles they bring, we have the responsibility to "take the high road" and let our children see us treat each other with dignity and respect. Demonstrate to them that every person was created by God and is valuable to Him. Show them that we can forgive because we have been forgiven. Show them that you can be gracious because God has been gracious to you.

• THINK ABOUT IT •

Do your words and actions reflect the forgiveness and grace that God has shown to you?

Prayer

Heavenly Father, let me be such a person of truth and faith that others will recognize I value and serve You. You have blessed beyond measure. Help me pay forward Your blessings, putting others first before my own agenda. In Jesus' name, amen.

DAY 338

LET HOPE RISE UP

The city does not need the sun or the moon to shine on it, for the glory of God gives it light, and the Lamb is its lamp. The nations will walk by its light, and the kings of the earth will bring their splendor into it.

REVELATION 21:23-24

Most of the time we are so focused on our earthly lives that we don't stop to contemplate the glories of Heaven. There is much about Heaven that we don't know, but Revelation 21 gives a physical description that overwhelms my imagination. It describes a city of massive dimensions, walls covered with precious stones, gates of pearls, and streets of gold. There will be no sun or moon because the glory of God will light it continually. Nothing impure will be allowed in it, and the only inhabitants will be those whose names are written in the book of life. The atmosphere will be one of joy, praise, and worship. This is our reward in eternity if we will honor Him in this life. When you are feeling discouraged by the cares and concerns of the day, remember that our days under the sun are but a moment compared to the infinite ages we will spend with our Lord in His glorious Heaven.

• THINK ABOUT IT •

What is your perception of Heaven? Read Revelation 21, and give thanks for the home prepared for you.

Prayer

Heavenly Father, increase hope within me as days become darker, and remind me You are going to give us a new earth and a new Jerusalem. I want to be fully invested in Your plans and Kingdom. Prepare me for my home with You in eternity. In Jesus' name, amen.

FOCUS ON THE FUNDAMENTALS

This is my comfort in my affliction, That Your word has revived me.

PSALM 119:50 • NASB®

The famous NFL coach Vince Lombardi is remembered for his memorable motivational statements. One of my favorites is his reminder to the Green Bay Packers on the first day of training camp: "Gentlemen, this is a football." These were professionals who had played the sport for many years, but Lombardi knew that the key to victory was mastering the fundamentals so that they were second nature during a game— and his record proved that he was right. I have found that the best way to master the fundamentals of Christianity is to cultivate a desire to know more about God and read my Bible. In challenging seasons it is enormously comforting and helpful to me to remember what God has said in His Word—about Himself, about me, about my days in the earth, and about my future. Let's not forget the fundamental value of God's message to comfort and revive us as we are on life's journey: "Friends, this is a Bible!"

• THINK ABOUT IT •

Is your Bible a vital and necessary part of your daily routine? Do you have God's Word in your heart so that you can lean on it in times of trouble?

Prayer

Heavenly Father, thank You for the Bible and its message of hope and restoration. It is a comfort and a strength during times of testing and crisis—revealing the future, while giving direction for the days in which we live. In Jesus' name, amen.

SPIRITUAL DIET

Live as children of light (for the fruit of the light consists in all goodness, righteousness and truth) and find out what pleases the Lord. Have nothing to do with the fruitless deeds of darkness. . . .

EPHESIANS 5:8-11

Physical health and spiritual health have some parallels. You can choose a diet with no nutritional value; you can eat it today, and get up tomorrow in good health. But if you keep eating that diet, it will one day wreak havoc on you. You won't know when the tipping point is coming, and it will not be easy to reverse the effects. The same is true spiritually. If you choose a lifestyle that is not God's best for you, you may be able to hide or excuse it for a while. But make no mistake: You will face the consequences at some point. You've heard the saying, "An ounce of prevention is worth a pound of cure," and that applies to our spiritual selves too. "Find out what pleases the Lord" and keep those things at the center of your desires. Seek "goodness, righteousness, and truth." Soon those things will create happiness, and you will see God's blessings pouring over your life.

• THINK ABOUT IT •

Are there attitudes and behaviors in your life that you know are unpleasing to the Lord? Confess those to Him right now, and ask the Holy Spirit to give you the desire to please Him in everything you do.

Prayer

Heavenly Father, thank You for the assignment to be a child of light. Your challenge motivates me to walk steadfastly toward You, and Your Holy Spirit empowers me to accomplish Your purposes. Please continue to teach me Your Word that I might know You and please You in all I do. In Jesus' name, amen.

HAM HOCKS AND TRADITIONS

Test everything. Hold on to the good.

1 THESSALONIANS 5:21

There is a story about the generations of women who had a tradition of cutting off the end of a ham before cooking it. The youngest asked why, and as the question moved through her extended family, the answer was the same: "I do it because that's what my mother did." Finally the question reached the elderly mother who had begun the practice, and her answer surprised them: "I cut off the end so it would fit in my pan!" I am not opposed to traditions—sometimes they bind us together in meaningful ways. But traditions can sometimes be meaningless practices that hold us in bondage, and we need the wisdom of God and the help of the Holy Spirit to make the distinction between what is necessary and what is not. Rather than hold fast to a practice or an idea that was handed to you, say to the Lord, "Show me Your truth, and then let that become alive in me."

• THINK ABOUT IT •

Are there practices or ideas that have been passed down in your family or in your church? Have you ever wondered why and explored their purpose or meaning?

Prayer

Heavenly Father, thank You for unifying traditions that honor You. Others are more like strongholds passed down through generations. Help me know the difference, abolish any not pleasing to You, and create new godly traditions that bring You honor. In Jesus' name, amen.

MAINTENANCE PLAN

I prayed to the LORD my God and confessed: "O Lord, the great and awesome God, who keeps his covenant of love with all who love him and obey his commands. . . ."

DANIEL 9:4

Confession and repentance are not singular experiences but vital parts of a healthy spiritual life. Our aim is not just to be "born again" but to maintain consistently a heart-allegiance to Jesus Christ, our Lord. Daniel was a man continually seeking to deepen his relationship with the Lord; this passage reveals his heartfelt sincerity. I often pray something similar to remind myself of who God is, and who I am in relationship to Him. Won't you pray it with me today? "Almighty God, I am a sinner, and I need a Savior. I believe Jesus is Your Son, that He died on a cross for my sin and You raised Him to life again. Through the blood of Jesus, I am justified, sanctified, and set apart to God. Through the blood of Jesus, I have been redeemed from the hand of the enemy. Jesus, be Lord of my life. Forgive me of my sins. I thank You I belong to the family of God. I am a child of the King, and His Holy Spirit lives within me. May I bring glory to Your name. In the precious name of Jesus, amen."

• THINK ABOUT IT •

Do you make confession and repentance a regular part of your conversations with the Lord?

Prayer

Heavenly Father, thank You for Jesus' sacrifice on the cross, granting me reconciliation to You. Thank You for the gift of repentance and Your readiness to hear my confession and offer me Your forgiveness, healing, and hope for the future. In Jesus' name, amen.

DAY 343

DESIGNED TO WORK

Greet Tryphena and Tryphosa, those women who work hard in the Lord. Greet my dear friend Persis, another woman who has worked very hard in the Lord.

ROMANS 16:12

Tryphena, and Tryphosa, and Persis. These three women made The Book not because of their demonstration of a spiritual gift, or because of some miracle that was attached to their lives, but because of their hard work. Could it be that we have somehow not grasped the significance of our work? Could it be that we have misunderstood and come to think of it as intrusive, or burdensome, or limiting? Work isn't something we endure until we get to do something more important. Work is not a punishment that is put upon us to keep us from a more leisurely way to live. We are designed by our Creator with the capacity for work—both physically and mentally—and work is one of the ways we honor God. My parents thought work was a positive thing, and one of their goals was to teach me to work. I didn't always appreciate it at the time, but that lesson has been a blessing in my life.

• THINK ABOUT IT •

Do you work "with all your heart, as working for the Lord" (Colossians 3:23)?

Prayer

Heavenly Father, thank You for those who have modeled good work habits, teaching me the value of finishing a job, no matter how difficult. Thank You for giving me a sound mind and strength to work and diligently serve You all my days. In Jesus' name, amen.

HARD SEASONS

There is a time for everything, and a season for every activity under the heavens . . . a time to weep and a time to laugh, a time to mourn and a time to dance. . . .

ECCLESIASTES 3:1, 4

The Bible says there is a time and season for everything. This passage is speaking about more than just emotional responses to specific situations; it is about understanding the season we are in and knowing how to react to it. If Jesus had shown what we would consider appropriate emotional responses, He would have been bitter and angry when He faced people who opposed Him and wanted Him dead. But that wasn't His response at all. He continued patiently telling people, even those who hated Him the most, "Trust in Me. I was born for this. I am here for this. My response to your hatred will change lives and change the course of history." Even in this season—when Jesus' message and the change He can bring is openly mocked—keep loving people. Keep telling them that we will all go through seasons of mourning and weeping, but Jesus can change their lives too.

• THINK ABOUT IT •

Consider some of the hard seasons of life you have been through. How has God shown Himself to be faithful during those times?

Prayer

Heavenly Father, seasons of the year add texture to my life, as do seasons of the heart. I learn from these and mature in ways that prepare me to encourage others. May I always maintain Your perspective and learn from each experience. In Jesus' name, amen.

EXPONENTIAL REWARD

"Everyone who has left houses or brothers or sisters or father or mother or children or fields for my sake will receive a hundred times as much and will inherit eternal life. But many who are first will be last, and many who are last will be first."

MATTHEW 19:29-30

Once again, Jesus had been patiently explaining to His listeners the difference between God's perspective and ours. When Peter blurted out what the others were probably thinking—"We've left everything behind to follow You! What's in it for us?"—Jesus explained again that choosing Him as Lord of your life will not diminish you. In fact, the opposite is true: Jesus said that you will receive an exponential reward for whatever you turn away from in turning more fully toward Him. There will be some rearranging of people in His Kingdom as well, as those who have pushed their way to the front will be asked to trade places with those in the back. Jesus' teaching contradicts what our culture tells us about what our priorities should be, and the principles are just as true today as they were in Jesus' day. The more we make His priorities our own, the more we will be able to serve Him with joy and abandon.

• THINK ABOUT IT •

What is the deepest longing of your heart? Do you have a desire to honor the Lord above all else?

Prayer

Heavenly Father, thankfully, what I release, You return in abundant ways. I am honored You entrust me with wonderful opportunities to serve You and help others. May I continually abide in You, washed in the blood of Jesus, Your Son. In Jesus' name, amen.

INVESTMENT INVITATION

Above all else, guard your heart, for it is the wellspring of life.

PROVERBS 4:23

We put quite a bit of effort into protecting ourselves from various things. We wear sunscreen to protect against skin cancer. We lock our houses against intruders. We protect our personal data with passwords and firewalls. We protect investments that we hope will provide for us in the future. We wear seatbelts. Certainly all those things are good and necessary, but the Bible says we should give even more attention to guarding our hearts . . . "above all else," actually. Why? Because what happens to us is a small matter compared to what happens within us, and everything in our lives flows from our inward state—the condition of our hearts. We guard our hearts intentionally by doing things such as seeking understanding of the Lord and His purposes for us; using discernment when choosing friends; and being a Spirit-filled consumer of television, movies, and music. The condition of your heart will determine the course of your life both in time and eternity, so guard it with great care.

• THINK ABOUT IT •

Do you spend as much effort guarding your heart as you do protecting your possessions?

Prayer

Heavenly Father, reveal to me where I need extra caution regarding my heart that I might be a reflection of You and Your transformation. May I stay diligently focused on living a holy life through You. I choose You afresh today. In Jesus' name, amen.

DAY 347

SECURITY CONSCIOUS

A man ran up to him and fell on his knees before him. "Good teacher," he asked, "what must I do to inherit eternal life?" . . . "You know the commandments: 'Do not murder, do not commit adultery, do not steal, do not give false testimony, do not defraud, honor your father and mother.'" "Teacher," he declared, "all these I have kept since I was a boy." Jesus looked at him and loved him.

MARK 10:17-21

When this man told Jesus with all sincerity that he had kept the commandments since he was a boy, He looked at him and loved him, then extended the same invitation He had given to others: "Liquidate your assets, give the proceeds to the poor, and follow me." The man thought about what was required, decided his investment portfolio was too strong, and took a pass on an invitation that would have changed his life. We have the benefit of hindsight, but in doing so he turned down the opportunity to see Jesus walk on the water, open blind eyes, and call the dead to life. Forget for a moment the gift of eternity; it would have changed His life in time completely. Let's stay aware of God's invitations and be prepared to say yes when they come.

• THINK ABOUT IT •

How do your days on earth reflect your relationship with Jesus? How are you using your life as an investment in eternity?

Prayer

Heavenly Father, help me sacrificially say yes to every invitation You extend. Nothing is free, and I need help reminding myself that it is important to decide ahead of time what my answer must be. Thank You for helping me invest in Your eternity! In Jesus' name, amen.

DECONTAMINATION

"Come now, let us reason together," says the LORD. *"Though your sins are like scarlet, they shall be as white as snow; though they are red as crimson, they shall be like wool."*

ISAIAH 1:18

We live in a world where it is very easy to make a mess of things. Perhaps you have allowed yourself to drift far from God and doubt there is a way back to Him. Perhaps you have become dishonest in your business transactions and fear being discovered. Perhaps you have allowed the plague of pornography to take root in your life and jeopardize your relationships. Perhaps it seemed easier to tell a lie than the truth, and one lie has snowballed into a thousand lies. All of us are tempted to sin in many ways, but we do not have to be controlled by sin. The good news is that even if you've made a mess of things, God is able to wash you clean and make your heart "as white as snow." You may still face earthly consequences of your behavior; but He will help you through that as He forgives you, restores you, and shows you the power of the Holy Spirit to transform your life.

• THINK ABOUT IT •

Has there been a time when you made a mess of things and God washed you clean and made your heart "as white as snow"?

Prayer

Heavenly Father, I am so thankful that You chose me, even in my rebellion against You. My heart was dark from sin and my mind was closed with doubt, but You broke through to save me. Restore my hope daily and fill me with Your Holy Spirit. In Jesus' name, amen.

FORGIVENESS WINS

Consider him who endured such opposition from sinful men, so that you will not grow weary and lose heart.

HEBREWS 12:3

Jesus is a wonderful example of how to face opposition without losing heart. During His three years of public ministry, He faced more hostility than most of us will encounter in a lifetime. At His crucifixion, He had been betrayed, falsely accused, condemned to death, and beaten beyond recognition. Then He was nailed to a cross, where He would slowly suffocate to death—naked, thirsty, and surrounded by His enemies. Through all of that injustice and physical suffering, He was not defeated. If that had been me on the cross, with the power of God at my disposal, I think the story would have been different. I would've looked down at the centurion and reduced him to a puddle as an example for the other Romans in the crowd. I would've spun the High Priest up into a tornado and given the rest of the Sanhedrin something to think about. But not Jesus. What did He say? "Father, forgive them."

• THINK ABOUT IT •

Do you seek retribution against those who have opposed you or treated you unjustly? Or do you pray, "Father, forgive them"?

Prayer

Heavenly Father, give me perseverance to pursue You in adversity. I need Your power to break the chains of unforgiveness and bitterness. The battle is first won in my mind and will. I choose, therefore, to forgive everyone of everything. In Jesus' name, amen.

FAITH REFINED

For you, O God, tested us; you refined us like silver. You brought us into prison and laid burdens on our backs. You let men ride over our heads; we went through fire and water, but you brought us to a place of abundance.

PSALM 66:10-12

God cares about us enough that He will give us spiritual check-ups so that we can be healthier spiritually. In testing us, God puts us in places that can be as uncomfortable as a refiner's fire—not to leave us there, not because He enjoys our torment, but to expose our character so that we can see what we are made of and make adjustments. His reward for us at the end of that process is "a place of abundance." God the Father even allowed His Son to be tempted, and we all benefit from that same refining process. As we see His plan and purposes for us with greater clarity, we will want to serve Him with greater abandon. When our faith is proved genuine, it will result in praise and glory and honor at the time when Jesus is revealed. That will be a wonderful day!

• THINK ABOUT IT •

What times of testing can you identify in your life? How did the Lord refine your character through those times? What did you learn about Him?

Prayer

Heavenly Father, I recognize opportunities every day to choose Your ways, and I have been radically changed by choosing You. Knowing You has removed so many limitations in my life. I praise You for the freedom to live a life of eternal significance. In Jesus' name, amen.

DAY 351

ETERNAL GLORY

We do not lose heart. Though outwardly we are wasting away, yet inwardly we are being renewed day by day. For our light and momentary troubles are achieving for us an eternal glory that far outweighs them all.

2 CORINTHIANS 4:16-17

We've all watched people we care about suffer and sometimes die prematurely. We've seen things that seem unfair because we live in a world where sin is still very much present and we don't have full knowledge and understanding. It has taken a lot of life lessons for me to get to this place, but it no longer embarrasses me to say I don't know why these things happen. Nor do I "lose heart." We are complex beings—body, soul, and spirit—and simple answers often are not apparent. I've stopped demanding them. I don't have to defend God. He is sovereign, and I can tell you His intent is for us to be well and holy. I trust Him to produce in us "an eternal weight of glory far beyond all comparison." There are some things I don't know yet; but I do know God, and I'll invite Him into every circumstance.

• THINK ABOUT IT •

How have you seen God at work in the midst of suffering? What did you learn about trusting Him?

Prayer

Heavenly Father, on days weighed down by difficulty, You are a prayer away from my call. Your faithful presence in the midst of pain brings encouragement I desperately need. Thank You for continually inviting me to trust You more fully. In Jesus' name, amen.

INTEGRITY, RIGHTEOUSNESS, AND TRUTH

O LORD, who may abide in Your tent? Who may dwell on Your holy hill? He who walks with integrity, and works righteousness, and speaks truth in his heart.

PSALM 15:1-2 • NASB®

Since we need to walk with integrity in order to dwell with the Lord, we need to know what that means. Integrity means alignment between what you believe and what you do—if that's wrapped in the insulation of a worldview that's derived from Scripture. If you believe something evil and then do something evil, you are not a person of integrity. But if you start with a worldview that's informed by Scripture, with God's perspective, and then you bring alignment between what you believe and what you do, you're a person of integrity. Truth is the glue that facilitates that. We live in a season when integrity and truthfulness are diminishing because our culture doesn't attach much value to them anymore. Getting ahead by manipulating the truth is considered good business in many circles, but I call that bad character. Be a person of truth and integrity. It matters in God's economy, and it matters in our world.

• THINK ABOUT IT •

Do you ever bend the truth to suit your needs, or do you strive to live with integrity in everything you do?

Prayer

Heavenly Father, above all, I desire to be a person of integrity. Teach me about being a person of integrity and truth. I choose today to confess my inconsistency. May my life be used to bring others to know Your love and saving plan. In Jesus' name, amen.

DAY 353

DEFINED BY JESUS

There came a man who was sent from God; his name was John. He came as a witness to testify concerning that light, so that through him all men might believe. He himself was not the light; he came only as a witness to the light.

JOHN 1:6-8

John the Baptist was Jesus' contemporary. His story, however, was foretold in the Old Testament, and the angel Gabriel announced John's forthcoming birth to his father, Zechariah. God's hand was uniquely on him, and he was even mistaken by some as the Messiah. John was quick to correct them, announcing the Messiah was yet to be publicly revealed. His entire life, especially his adult ministry, was defined by his relationship to Jesus. Our purposes in the earth may not seem as dramatic as John's, but we also are "sent from God" and should continually pursue what He has for us. We also should nurture our children with the expectation that God will use them in a mighty way. May it be said of us and our families that our lives are defined not by the things of this world, but by our relationship with Jesus.

• THINK ABOUT IT •

What does it mean today to live a life defined by Jesus? Would you consider your life to be defined by your relationship with Him?

Prayer

Heavenly Father, thank You for revealing the truth of Your extravagant love, poured out at the cross. Thank You for sending Your best in Your Son Jesus, who died for me. May I always bring my best as I come to worship and serve You. In Jesus' name, amen.

DAY 354

ABRAHAM BELIEVED

These are the names of the sons of Israel who went to Egypt with Jacob, each with his family: Reuben, Simeon, Levi and Judah; Issachar, Zebulun and Benjamin; Dan and Naphtali; Gad and Asher. The descendants of Jacob numbered seventy in all. . . . the Israelites were fruitful and multiplied greatly and became exceedingly numerous, so that the land was filled with them.

EXODUS 1:1-7

God's covenant with Abraham, woven through the book of Genesis, is beautifully reaffirmed in this opening passage of Exodus. God had promised to bless Abraham by making his descendants a great nation, providing a homeland for them, and blessing all the peoples of the earth through them. In these verses we read the names of Abraham's great-grandsons, and we're told that at this point in time there were seventy descendants in all. Over the course of time they would become the great nation that God had promised. All these millennia later, we are still being blessed through God's promise to the elderly Abraham and the once-barren Sarah. Our God is sovereign over all people, things, and circumstances. He is good beyond measure—and He always keeps His promises.

• THINK ABOUT IT •

God blessed Abraham and his family greatly. How has God blessed your family?

Prayer

Heavenly Father, Your promises give enduring hope. Just as You spoke promises to Abraham, I know You have also declared them to me. Help me to be watchful and wait on Your Word to be fulfilled, with joy and singing in my heart. In Jesus' name, amen.

A NEW SELF

You were taught, with regard to your former way of life, to put off your old self, which is being corrupted by its deceitful desires; to be made new in the attitude of your minds; and to put on the new self, created to be like God in true righteousness and holiness.

EPHESIANS 4:22-24

My parents taught me to value the things of God. I knew my parents before they were Christians. We went to church every week, but I remember the transformation that came in their lives when they made a commitment to follow Jesus. I was old enough to process that. The temperature in our home changed. The relationships in our home changed. The conversations in our home changed. Everything changed. Over the years I saw many changes in the focus of their hearts and lives—some they announced, and some I just observed. One of the changes was the rearrangement of their priorities as the things of the world became less important to them and the things of God became increasingly significant in their lives. I have learned many things from my parents over the years, but perhaps I am most grateful for them teaching me the value and wisdom of making God's priorities first in my life.

• THINK ABOUT IT •

Where do God's priorities fit into your life? Are they first, second, or somewhere further down the line?

Prayer

Heavenly Father, Jesus' sacrificial blood offers forgiveness for the ungodliness that separates me from You. Help me reorient my life to increasingly receive and walk in Your provision—forgiveness, acceptance, righteousness, healing, and abundance. In Jesus' name, amen.

CULTIVATE TRUST

Trust in the LORD and do good; Dwell in the land and cultivate faithfulness.

PSALM 37:3 • NASB®

Faith is not as complicated as some people would have you think it is. You don't have to read Greek or Hebrew or have a degree in theology. As a matter of fact, some people with those skills and degrees struggle mightily with their faith. You simply need to have confidence in Jesus and be willing to "cultivate faithfulness" in Him. Trusting Jesus is not a one-time choice. Just as a farmer cultivates a field—plow, sow, reap, plow, sow, reap—it's a choice we'll make over and over again as we struggle with life's questions: Where am I going to put my confidence when the people I trust are falling away? Whom will I trust to deliver me from a situation that I did not create or deserve? What will bring me comfort during this season of hardship? What will I stake my future on when the world seems to be shaking? We are learning to put our faith in Jesus, and it is a trust that increases as we witness His faithfulness time after time.

• THINK ABOUT IT •

The better we know Jesus the more we will want to trust Him. On a scale of one to ten, how much do you trust Him to comfort you, deliver you, sustain you?

Prayer

Heavenly Father, I have believed in Jesus Christ of Nazareth for my salvation. Over and over I have given You my requests in His name—never have You failed me. You are the Most High God, and in You, Lord, I will forever put my trust. In Jesus' name, amen.

NO NEUTRAL GROUND

"You belong to your father, the devil, and you want to carry out your father's desire. He was a murderer from the beginning, not holding to the truth, for there is no truth in him. When he lies, he speaks his native language, for he is a liar and the father of lies."

JOHN 8:44

Jesus is telling His listeners that without a relationship with Him we are not just enslaved, we are enslaved to a liar and murderer—the very personification of evil and the opposite of Jesus, who is Truth and gives life. Jesus wants us to know that this is life-and-death serious; the battlefield in our hearts and minds is not a playground where we are engaged in an innocent game. Evil by definition will take unfair advantage and exploit the most vulnerable places in our lives. It may promise pleasure for the moment, but it does not intend good for us. We don't have enough strength of will or force of character to overcome evil because it's more powerful than we are. That's why we must choose a godly perspective; because apart from a relationship with Jesus and the power of the Holy Spirit, evil will own us. Praise God for His gift of deliverance!

• THINK ABOUT IT •

Good and evil are our only two choices; there is no neutral ground. How do you maintain a godly perspective on your daily choices?

Prayer

Heavenly Father, thank You for delivering me from Your enemy and releasing me from bondage to my sinful nature and fear of death. I am now Your child and choose Your perspective in every aspect that I might be free to serve You all my days. In Jesus' name, amen.

AWE AND RESPECT

"The fear of the Lord—that is wisdom. . . ."

JOB 28:28

There are very few things in Scripture that have more promises attached to them than the fear of the Lord—not fear in the sense of shrinking away in terror or dread, but in terms of regarding Him with awe and respect. No matter what you accomplish or what resources you accumulate, if you don't hold God in awe and respect, you haven't yet acquired the seeds of wisdom. Likewise, no matter your education level, or your social and economic status, if you've cultivated a respect and fear of God, the Bible says you are a wise person. Indifference and disrespect toward God are increasing in our world, and I want to be careful to hold God in a place of awe. I want to be familiar enough with Him that I am comfortable in His presence, but I don't want to be so familiar that I lose my respect for Him.

• THINK ABOUT IT •

Is your first reaction to an issue trying to figure out what you think, or going to God's Word to see what He thinks?

Prayer

Heavenly Father, grant me godly fear and respect as I walk increasingly in the knowledge of You. Reverence of You fosters wisdom, and I need Your great wisdom to live well, walk humbly with You, and value those around me. In Jesus' name, amen.

SIMPLE TRUST

Jews demand miraculous signs and Greeks look for wisdom, but we preach Christ crucified: a stumbling block to Jews and foolishness to Gentiles, but to those whom God has called, both Jews and Greeks, Christ the power of God and the wisdom of God.

1 CORINTHIANS 1:22-24

The Jewish religious establishment was opposed to believing that Jesus was the Messiah, no matter how many miracles He performed. The Greeks of the day were on an intellectual quest for wisdom that would lead to a more meaningful earthly existence. Both groups tried to find ways to not have confidence in Jesus, in spite of all the evidence they had seen. They were proud of being skeptics. It's easy to reject Jesus as Lord by claiming we need more information. It's easy to ignore everything we know about Him and continue to try to disprove the facts. It's easy for religious people to put our confidence in our church attendance, the ways we've served, and the dollars we've given. Let's not do that. Let's put our confidence—proudly, unashamedly—in Jesus of Nazareth, the only begotten Son of God, the Savior of the world.

• THINK ABOUT IT •

Do you ever find yourself asking God for signs and searching for worldly wisdom rather than simply placing your trust in God to act on your behalf?

Prayer

Heavenly Father, I trust You and choose to say yes to You without reservation. Help me never sit in the seat of the skeptic and thereby miss opportunities to serve and care for Your people. All my confidence is in You, and I depend on Your wisdom to guide me. In Jesus' name, amen.

SHOW THEM

You shall follow the LORD your God and fear Him; and you shall keep His commandments, listen to His voice, serve Him, and cling to Him.

DEUTERONOMY 13:4 • NASB®

If you have a young child in your house, I would encourage you to cultivate the habit of from time to time putting a little oil on your hand, putting a cross on his or her forehead, and saying a word of blessing over them. Let them become accustomed to you anointing them and saying a sentence prayer specifically for them: "God, I thank You for my child. May he grow in the fear of the Lord. Amen." "May she follow the Lord and cling to Him." "May he listen to Your voice and serve You." Show them that you believe in the anointing power of God. Let them see that prayer matters to you. If they are grown and gone, but you didn't do that as well as you could have when they were living under your roof, you can do the same thing with a photograph. Pray that even now they will grow strong in the fear of the Lord. God can do things we can't do, so don't hesitate to open the doorway for God's possibilities in their lives.

· THINK ABOUT IT ·

Do you pray regularly and specifically for the young people in your life? Can they see that prayer is important to you?

Prayer

Heavenly Father, children perfectly model how to interact with You. May the little people around me know Your blessings as I do. Help me be an example to them of obedient trust and truth, dependent upon You in every respect. In Jesus' name, amen.

MADE PERFECT

But he said to me, "My grace is sufficient for you, for my power is made perfect in weakness." Therefore I will boast all the more gladly about my weaknesses, so that Christ's power may rest on me.

2 CORINTHIANS 12:9

Evil exists in the world. It's important for the Church to grasp that reality. I read a book by a psychiatrist who concluded after years of practice that evil exists on the earth and that it generally does not show itself through some horrific condition; it looks and sounds like us. He had concluded that you could not reason with evil; evil will only yield to a power greater than itself. Evil will negotiate when it is in a vulnerable position, but as soon as it has gained the upper hand it will influence in an evil way again. You and I are no match for Satan. In our strength, intellect, and power, we will lose every time. But we don't stand against him in our own power and authority. In this verse we see God assuring the Apostle Paul that his weakness is an opportunity for God to display His power in and through Paul's life. Don't fear or resent your weaknesses. Give them to God and watch to see His power at work in your life.

• THINK ABOUT IT •

Do you live as though evil exists? Do you recognize its power to strike in your vulnerable places? How do you counteract it?

Prayer

Heavenly Father, help me focus my heart: Though taking seriously the power of evil, my heart rejoices in the all-victorious power of an Almighty God. Your grace is sufficient—Your power is made perfect in my weakness. May Your peace guard me. In Jesus' name, amen.

GROWTH PLAN

They arrived at Ephesus, where Paul left Priscilla and Aquila. He himself went into the synagogue and reasoned with the Jews. When they asked him to spend more time with them, he declined. But as he left, he promised, "I will come back if it is God's will." Then he set sail from Ephesus.

ACTS 18:19-21

Some people think that church growth is a great mystery available to only a few congregations, but growth is less about mystery and more about intent. Paul had a strategic plan to take the gospel to the Roman world. He chose important centers of regional commerce, then went there to establish a church, knowing that the Jesus-story would radiate to the surrounding area. He first taught in the synagogues, explaining that Jesus was the Messiah they had been waiting for and supporting his teaching with the Hebrew Scriptures. When he left, helpers such as Priscilla and Aquila stayed behind to care for the new believers in the emerging church. A strategic plan is important in the spiritual realm. If we are to experience spiritual growth, both personally and in our congregations, we should ask the Holy Spirit for His direction, then follow through on the plans He shows us.

• THINK ABOUT IT •

What is your plan for your personal spiritual growth? What challenges might arise as you begin to follow your plan? How might you respond to those challenges?

Prayer

Heavenly Father, forgive me when I have either not had a plan in place for spiritual development or did not follow the plan provided. May Your Holy Spirit direct me into a strategy for spiritual growth and help me implement His plan. In Jesus' name, amen.

HEART CONDITION

The heart is deceitful above all things and beyond cure. Who can understand it?

JEREMIAH 17:9

One of the things that gives integrity to the Bible is that it tells us in the plainest of language the weaknesses that we all struggle with. Here God says plainly, "Your heart is deceitful." We can excuse and justify almost anything in our lives. All it would take is a quick Internet search to find someone who says we are right in our wrongness. We could easily find a group of people who want to be involved in the same ungodliness, and we would support and encourage one another. But the candor of Scripture also expresses the remarkable grace of God. For all of the weaknesses of the human condition, including our deceitful hearts, God has provided a solution so that we can be victorious and triumphant: the redemption we can find through a relationship with His Son and the empowering we can know through the presence of the Holy Spirit. Yes, we are weak; but through the grace and goodness of God, we are not left alone in our weakness.

• THINK ABOUT IT •

Do you find yourself struggling through temptation in your own strength, or do you ask the Holy Spirit to help you in your weakness?

Prayer

Heavenly Father, You know my heart and report it's condition with accuracy. You also provide the cure through the shed blood of Jesus Christ. Help me not trust in my own heart, strength, or wisdom, but trust in Your grace and power. In Jesus' name, amen.

GRATEFUL SERVICE

Therefore, since we receive a kingdom which cannot be shaken, let us show gratitude, by which we may offer to God an acceptable service with reverence and awe. . . .

HEBREWS 12:28 • NASB®

I would encourage you to purposefully make serving God through serving your local church a part of your life. Serving one another is not just a way that we sustain congregational life; serving is a big part of maturing as a Christ-follower. The more we recognize the magnitude of what God has done and continues to do for us, the more we will want to serve Him with gratitude. Scripture says that we are given various gifts and talents in order to build each other up. You use your gifts and talents to benefit others, and they use their gifts and talents to benefit you. As we build each other up, we build the Church of Jesus Christ and increase our witness to the world. Don't be a spiritual spectator. Show your gratitude to the Lord by serving His people.

• THINK ABOUT IT •

Are you serving your local congregation? Think about the gifts and talents God has given you and how you might use them to serve His people.

Prayer

Heavenly Father, Your loving provision through the cross has restored my life. Now, I want to express my thanks. Reveal how I can serve You and Your people. Help me see and humbly accept Your invitations to reflect Your character to others. In Jesus' name, amen.

SECOND AND THIRD CHANCES

Then the Philistine said, "This day I defy the ranks of Israel! Give me a man and let us fight each other." On hearing the Philistine's words, Saul and all the Israelites were dismayed and terrified.

1 SAMUEL 17:10-11

Goliath had bellowed the same challenge morning and evening for forty days without a single response from the Israelite soldiers. Can you imagine the state of the morale among those men? I promise you when they were sitting around the campfire, not one man was looking another in the eye. We're not being called out by a giant, but we all know what failure feels like. When you've lost your courage or made a poor choice, the enemy will tell you that you are a failure, that you will never succeed. His objective is to break your will so that you will never try again. Do not let Satan win this spiritual battle. Our God is a gracious God of second chances and third chances, and His power that formed the universe is available to you as you face life's challenges. When you see His power at work in your life, your faith will grow and you will trust Him to show Himself faithful again.

• THINK ABOUT IT •

Consider the times when God has shown His power in a situation that you thought was hopeless. Do you trust Him to help you again?

Prayer

Heavenly Father, You used life-circumstances to expand the faith of several biblical characters. Help me to likewise trust You to break through my barriers of disappointment, failure, and fear. Thank You for expanding my faith also. In Jesus' name, amen.

TOPIC

DAY

TOPIC

DAY

TOPIC   DAY

TOPIC

DAY

NOTES

NOTES

NOTES

NOTES

NOTES

NOTES

NOTES

NOTES

NOTES

NOTES

ONE-YEAR DAILY DEVOTIONAL

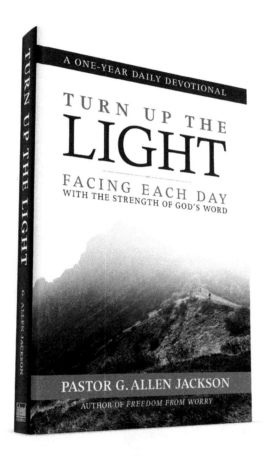

TURN UP THE LIGHT

This book is intended to add a little positive momentum to each day.
Few things bring strength like God's Word and a moment of prayer.
Your perspective on God's Word will shape the trajectory of your life.
Each day arrives with opportunities and challenges. We can be
hindered by the darkness, or we can turn up the light!

THREE-VOLUME SMALL GROUP VIDEO STUDY & GUIDE

THE WHITEBOARD BIBLE™

The Bible tells a story, and these small group studies will help you more fully understand it. The three volumes of *The Whiteboard Bible* develop a twelve-point timeline that serves as the framework for all the characters and events in the Bible, beginning with Creation and concluding with Jesus' return.

For more from Allen Jackson—including sermons, books, and small group materials—visit:

allenjackson.com

About The Author

Allen Jackson is passionate about helping people become more fully devoted followers of Jesus Christ who "respond to God's invitations for their life."

He has served World Outreach Church since 1981, becoming senior pastor in 1989. Under his leadership, WOC has grown to a congregation of over 15,000 through outreach activities, community events and worship services designed to share the Gospel.

Pastor Jackson's messages are available to watch on Nashville local television and TBN channels, and streamed over the Internet across the globe. He may also be heard over Moody Radio and Sirius XM. Jackson has spoken at pastors' conferences in the U.S. and abroad, and has been a featured speaker during Jerusalem's Feast of Tabernacles celebration for the Vision for Israel organization and the International Christian Embassy- Jerusalem. Allen Jackson Ministries coaches pastors around the world, writing and publishing small-group curriculum used in 34 states as well as Israel, Guatemala, the Philippines, Bermuda, Mexico, the United Kingdom, and South Africa.

With degrees from Oral Roberts University and Vanderbilt University, and additional studies at Gordon-Conwell Theological Seminary and Hebrew University of Jerusalem, Jackson is uniquely equipped to help people develop a love and understanding of God's Word.

Pastor Jackson's wife, Kathy, is an active participant in ministry at World Outreach Church.

CPSIA information can be obtained
at www.ICGtesting.com
Printed in the USA
LVHW050809271118
597808LV00001B/1/P